business management for the personal fitness trainer

business management for the personal fitness trainer

Charles M. Ware, MS, CHES, NSCA-CPT

Charles E. Bamford, Ph.D., MBA

Garry D. Bruton, Ph.D., MBA

Mc Graw Hill

Connect
Learn
Succeed™

BUSINESS MANAGEMENT FOR THE PERSONAL FITNESS TRAINER
Published by McGraw-Hill, a business unit of The McGraw-Hill Companies, Inc., 1221 Avenue of the Americas, New York, NY, 10020. Copyright © 2013 by The McGraw-Hill Companies, Inc. All rights reserved. No part of this publication may be reproduced or distributed in any form or by any means, or stored in a database or retrieval system, without the prior written consent of The McGraw-Hill Companies, Inc., including, but not limited to, in any network or other electronic storage or transmission, or broadcast for distance learning.

Some ancillaries, including electronic and print components, may not be available to customers outside the United States.

This book is printed on acid-free paper.

1 2 3 4 5 6 7 8 9 0 QDB/QDB 1 0 9 8 7 6 5 4 3 2

ISBN   978-0-07-337708-7
MHID   0-07-337708-2

Vice president/Editor in chief: *Michael Ledbetter*
Vice president/Director of marketing: *Alice Harra*
Senior sponsoring editor: *Natalie J. Ruffatto*
Director, digital products: *Crystal Szewczyk*
Development editor: *Raisa Priebe Kreek*
Executive marketing manager: *Roxan Kinsey*
Digital development editor: *Kevin White*
Director, Editing/Design/Production: *Jess Ann Kosic*
Project manager: *Jean R. Starr*
Buyer II: *Kara Kudronowicz*
Senior designer: *Srdjan Savanovic*
Senior photo research coordinator: *John C. Leland*
Photo researcher: *Agate Publishing, Inc.*
Manager, digital production: *Janean A. Utley*
Media project manager: *Brent dela Cruz*
Media project manager: *Cathy L. Tepper*
Outside development house: *Agate Publishing, Inc.*
Cover design: *Srdjan Savanovic*
Interior design: *Herman Adler Design*
Typeface: *11/13 Minion*
Compositor: *Agate Publishing, Inc.*
Printer: *Quad/Graphics*
Cover credit: *© Brian Hagiwara, Brand X images/Gettyimages (RF)*
Credits: *The credits section for this book begins on page 277 and is considered an extension of the copyright page.*

Library of Congress Cataloging-in-Publication Data
    Business management for the personal fitness trainer / Charles M. Ware, Charles E. Bamford, Garry D. Bruton.
        p. cm.
    Includes index.
    ISBN-13: 978-0-07-337708-7 (alk. paper)
    ISBN-10: 0-07-337708-2 (alk. paper)
    1. Personal trainers—Handbooks, manuals, etc. 2. Personal trainers—Vocational guidance. 3. Personal trainers—Finance, Personal. 4. Physical fitness centers—Management—Handbooks, manuals, etc. I. Ware, Charles M. II. Bamford, Charles E. III. Bruton, Garry D.
    GV428.7.B67 2013
613.7'1—dc22

2011006981

The Internet addresses listed in the text were accurate at the time of publication. The inclusion of a Web site does not indicate an endorsement by the authors or McGraw-Hill, and McGraw-Hill does not guarantee the accuracy of the information presented at these sites.

www.mhhe.com

brief table of contents

table of (contents)

Charles M. Ware Charles Ware is Executive Director of Professional Fitness Institute, a provider of personal-training curricula to the career-college sector. Charles came to PFI in 2005 with over twelve years of training with various populations, with an emphasis on corporate fitness and wellness and sport-specific training. In his tenure with PFI, Charles helped launch the Personal Training program for the brick-and-mortar campus, as well as the Online Division of Pinnacle Career Institute.

Charles is a graduate of the University of Central Missouri in Warrensburg, MO, where he received his Bachelor and Master of Science degrees in Exercise and Sport Science. In addition to those degrees, Charles is currently a doctorate student at A.T. Still University, pursuing a doctorate degree in Health Education.

Charles is a Certified Personal Trainer through the National Strength and Conditioning Association, as well as a Certified Health Education Specialist and a licensed Emergency Medical Technician. He also is a volunteer for the Medical Reserve Corps of Kansas City and Co-Chair of the Jump for Joy Foundation.

Dr. Charles E. Bamford Dr. Chuck Bamford is Professor of Strategy and Entrepreneurship and Dennis Thompson Chair of Entrepreneurial Studies at the McColl School of Business at Queens University of Charlotte. He earned his AS degree at Northern Virginia Community College, a BS degree at the University of Virginia, an MBA at Virginia Tech and a Ph.D. in Strategy & Entrepreneurship at the University of Tennessee. During a twelve-year span prior to pursuing his Ph.D., he held positions managing Business Analysis (Mergers & Acquisitions, Dispositions, and Small Business Consulting) for Dominion Bankshares Corporation (now Wells Fargo Corporation). Other positions during his business career included Director of Corporate Training, Systems Analyst, COBOL programmer, and full-time instructor in the early 1980s at Virginia Western Community College.

His research has been published in the *Strategic Management Journal, Journal of Business Venturing, Entrepreneurship Theory & Practice, Journal of Business Research, Journal of Business Strategies, Journal of Technology Transfer,* and *Journal of Small Business Management.*

Chuck has taught courses in Strategic Management and New Venture Management at the undergraduate, graduate and executive levels. His teaching experience includes courses at universities in Scotland, Hungary, and the Czech Republic. Prior to joining Queens University he held positions as an Associate Professor at Texas Christian University and at the University of Richmond. He has taught executive MBA courses at TCU,

The University of Notre Dame, Tulane University, and at Queens University of Charlotte.

Dr. Bamford is an active consultant whose clients have included numerous small business start-ups, as well as large regional and international businesses.

Chuck has won seventeen individual teaching excellence awards during his career, including eight Executive MBA Teacher of the Year Awards. He is a Noble Foundation Fellow in Teaching Excellence.

Dr. Garry D. Bruton Dr. Garry Bruton is a Professor of Entrepreneurship and Strategy at the M. J. Neeley School of Business at Texas Christian University in Fort Worth, Texas where he holds the Fehmi Zeko Faculty Fellowship. He received his Ph.D. in 1989 from Oklahoma State University. Prior to that time he had received his MBA from George Washington University, and his BA with Honors from the University of Oklahoma. He worked as a bank economist for one of the leading commercial banks in the Southwest United States prior to pursuing his doctorate.

Professor Bruton has published over 75 academic articles in some of the leading academic publications for small business and entrepreneurship, including the Academy of Management Journal, Strategic Management Journal, Journal of International Business, Journal of business Venturing, and Entrepreneurship Theory & Practice. Garry currently serves as editor of the Academy of Management Perspectives and is immediate past President of the Asia Academy of Management. He serves on six additional editorial boards. His research interests focus on entrepreneurship in emerging economies.

Dr. Bruton's publications have been used in some of the leading MBA programs around the world and writings have appeared in the Wall Street Journal. He was selected as the first holder of the Kathryn and Craig Hall Distinguished Chair in Entrepreneurship in 2005, sponsored by the Fulbright Program.

Professor Bruton has taught around the world including courses in Russia at the Moscow Institute of Electronics Technology; at Wirtschaftsuniversitat-Wein, Vienne, Austria; and at Chinese University of Hong Kong. The courses he has taught at the graduate and undergraduate levels have included small business management, entrepreneurship, venture capital, international strategy, strategy, and international management.

He has won a variety of teaching and research awards at each of the schools with which he has been associated. In addition, he has advised a number of MBA teams that have participated and placed in regional and national competitions for business plans and case analysis.

preface

The fitness industry is an ever-changing environment. Over the last decade, personal training and other fitness-related services have skyrocketed in interest and participation. As the industry changes, so do the participants and the need to stay ahead of the trend. What has not changed is the theory and practical application of sound business practices. This book is a tool to give you an introduction to these practices. It is meant to provide future fitness entrepreneurs with an understanding of how to start a business, generate income, and create growth and sustainability in the fitness industry.

What's new in this ever-changing industry? More people are taking their health more seriously. As the percentage of overweight and obese individuals in the United States continues to climb, the need for well-equipped, knowledgeable fitness professionals has become even more evident. According to the U.S. Bureau of Labor Statistics, employment of fitness workers is expected to increase 29 percent over the 2008–18 decade, which is much faster than the average for all occupations. These workers are expected to gain jobs because an increasing number of people are spending time and money on fitness, and more businesses are recognizing the benefits of health and fitness programs for their employees.

Personal training, a direction that many fitness professionals choose to take, is one of the fastest-growing professions in the health and fitness industry. In the last decade, personal training has gone mainstream. In 1999, four million Americans were using personal trainers. Since 2004, that number has hovered near the six million mark, according to an IHRSA study on personal trainer use. (*Source: IHRSA/ASD National Survey of Personal Training Usage*).

This text is written specifically for fitness professionals who have entertained the idea of going out on their own and starting their own business. You should view this text as a handbook or entrepreneurial tool to expand your knowledge, and to develop an understanding of the necessary elements in designing, starting, and managing a small business in the fitness industry. The book is full of valuable stories, new ideas, and creative concepts to start and grow your fitness business. Applying genuine business practices with real knowledge will provide you, the fitness professional, with business skills and experience that are fundamental to your success.

Chapter Outline

To develop the understanding necessary to design, start, and manage a small fitness business, this book consists of 13 chapters. These chapters are in turn organized into five major sections. The first section provides a history of personal fitness and, by introducing key business concepts, it sets the groundwork needed before you develop a new business idea.

Many individuals have considered starting a new business when an opportunity was presented to them or they were frustrated by their current positions. However, prior to this step there are several areas that demand examination. The potential entrepreneur(s) should carefully examine her own tendencies or willingness to take on risk. Chapter 1 describes the history of personal fitness and provides students with an understanding of the impact of small business in society. Chapter 2 develops the criteria necessary to evaluate individual needs and desires, as well as the group dynamics so common in the start-up of a new venture. Chapter 3 focuses on how to generate ideas for a small business.

The next section of the text is dedicated to making sure that your business gets off on the right foot. It coaches you on how to think as critically about your own business idea as you would about the purchase of another business. Chapter 4 shows you how to think competitively so you can translate your fitness expertise into a viable business in today's market. Chapter 5 expands on this idea by explaining how to decide on your business's mission and strategy. Chapter 6 provides tools to assess the financial fitness of your business idea. Taken as a whole, these chapters guide you in the research and analysis that are necessary before you jump into starting your own business.

Section 3 is designed to put all of this analysis into action. The difference between people with good ideas and those that are entrepreneurs is the action of establishing and running a business. Chapter 7 reviews the legal frameworks for a new small business, regulations that impact the operation of any business, and the basics of developing and executing contracts. Chapter 8 begins the examination of the actual business operations of your small business. Finally, establishing the accounting and financial framework crucial for a business is discussed in Chapter 9.

The fourth section examines operational issues as your business begins to expand. The topics included are the establishment of human resources (Chapter 10) and marketing (Chapter 11). Both of these topics are uniquely important in the early growth of a new small business.

The last section examines two other issues critical to a small business. Chapter 12 examines a wide variety of ways for exiting a business. Chapter 13 looks at two means to buy into a business rather than starting it from scratch. They are buying an existing business and franchising.

Key Text Features

Each chapter includes key features that help illuminate important ideas in interesting and applied ways.

Chapter Openers

Each chapter begins with a **case study** of a small personal-fitness business. These realistic portraits provide an overview of both the everyday successes and the failures associated with small business ownership. **Learning outcomes** identify the concepts students need to master.

Exercises

Throughout the chapter, **exercises** ask students to think critically about the topics being discussed. They help students apply what they are learning to the real-world challenges of starting a business.

Ethical Challenge Boxes

These dilemma-based questions look at ethical realities within the successful creation of a small fitness business, such as utilizing a client list when starting your own club. These features encourage students to examine the moral complexities of small businesses.

ethical *challenge*

Paula had recently started her business as an independent-contractor personal trainer and was looking forward to training individuals in their homes. Her first client, Joyce, had prepaid for 12 sessions, which were to take place three times a week. The sessions would be a challenge due to Joyce's physical infirmity, but Paula knew she was up to the challenge. At their first session, as Paula went over the standard paperwork with Joyce, Paula realized that she had failed to include an assumption of risk and liability waiver. After a short discussion, Paula and Joyce decided to proceed with the initial workout without having Joyce sign the waiver and assumption of risk form; she could sign the form before the next session.

For this first session, Paula decided to do a series of fitness assessments with Joyce, one of which was the three-minute step test. One minute into the step test, Joyce stepped awkwardly and rolled her ankle. After taking a break, Joyce said she felt fine, and they completed their session.

The next day, Paula called Joyce to confirm their next session for the following day. Joyce told Paula that her ankle had been bothering her all night and now it was swollen. Paula canceled the session and told Joyce to call her back when she was feeling better. Paula noted in her records that the client was too injured to participate.

Paula was very busy over the next few days with other clients and realized a week later that she hadn't heard from Joyce. After leaving several messages over several days, Paula decided to drive to Joyce's house to check on her. When Joyce opened the door, she seemed surprised to see Paula and asked that she remain at the door while she went and got something. She brought back a demand letter from an attorney stating that because of negligence, Joyce was requesting a refund of her prepaid fee. Is Joyce entitled to the return of any or all of the fee? If so, what is the determining factor?

key terms

ADA 119	LLC 114	sole proprietorship 108
contract 116	LLP 111	standard of care 120
draw 109	partnership 109	Subchapter C corporation 113
general partner 111	scope of practice 120	Subchapter S corporation 112
independent contractor 114		

End-of-Chapter Review

Key terms are bolded in the chapter text and defined in the margins, making it easy for students to keep track of the new concepts they refer to. These key words are listed at the end of the chapter for easy review. Like the exercises throughout the chapter, **review questions** at the end of the chapter ask students to consider specific questions and challenges of starting and running a small fitness business. **Individual exercises** help students think as small-business owners, examining and resolving the issues that can come up for any small business. **Group exercises** encourage students to work in teams to address larger questions, practicing the cooperation and creativity that are vital to the success of a small business.

review questions

1. What is a sole proprietorship? Name one advantage and one disadvantage to owning a sole proprietorship.
2. Define limited liability corporation.
3. Define tort.
4. Explain the benefits for club owners of hiring independent contractors.
5. Using the Internet, study local and state regulations and licensing requirements for fitness professionals or fitness facilities (your choice) in your area. Formulate a paragraph describing how you would implement these regulations and licensing requirements.
6. Would offering advice on diets for weight loss be within the scope of practice for a personal trainer? Why or why not?
7. Justify why it is imperative for a personal trainer to have professional liability insurance even if incorporated as a limited liability corporation.
8. Assess the phrase "reasonably prudent person." What makes a "reasonably prudent" fitness professional?

individual exercise

Compile a list of legal issues that you might have to deal with in your own fitness-related business. Consider the form of your business, contracts, leases, regulations, licenses, and insurance. Also consider costs. You may choose to make a table to organize this information.

group exercise

Break into groups of four or five. Together, design a waiver of liability for a local fitness club that offers both personal training and group instruction. Samples can be found online. Debate why you should or should not include certain features. Discuss why having clients sign such a waiver does not necessarily release the club from all liability, and determine what types of insurance will help to protect the club.

Supplementary Materials

Test Bank: Every chapter provides a series of test questions, available in our Test Bank. Questions are organized by Learning Outcome and Bloom's Taxonomy. The Test Bank is available both in EZ-Test Online and Word document formats.

Instructor's Manual: The IM outlines course materials, additional in-class activities, and support for classroom use of the text. It has been organized by Learning Outcome to both give instructors a basic outline of the chapter and assist in all facets of instruction. For every question posed in the text, the IM provides a viable answer. Ultimately, this will be to an instructor's greatest advantage in using all materials to reach all learners.

PowerPoints: PowerPoint slides include important chapter content and teaching notes tied directly to Learning Outcomes. They are designed to engage students in classroom discussions about the text.

Asset Map: We know that instructors' time is valuable. To help you prepare, we have created an Asset Map. The Asset Map identifies the chapter, Learning Outcome, page number, and exactly which supplements are available for you to use.

Acknowledgments

This book could not have been written without the efforts of several fitness professionals. Their diverse backgrounds and perspectives contributed to the readable, engaging approach of this book and ensured that students will come away with valuable knowledge of the industry and of small business.

Tommy Boyer-Kendrick, MS, CSCS, Rockwood Clinic

Michelle Hutton, BS, TwinFitness

Jason Parsons, MS, L.A. Boxing, ClubSport of Green Valley

Kristie Winter, BS, TwinFitness

James Wong, NASM-CPT, Studio 222

Special thanks are due to Carla T. Hardy, MS, NSCA CSCS, AFFA Certified Group Fitness Instructor, for her check of the page proofs to verify the book's accuracy.

Outcomes

Our ultimate goal is that students will leave this class not only with a much greater appreciation for what it takes to start a small fitness business, but with the foundations necessary to actually start that business. The small businesses that surround you every day—doctors' offices, law firms, construction companies, and gyms—did not come into operation or stay in operation by chance. Small businesses take tremendous effort to become and remain successful. We expect that some of you will be able to take what we present here as a foundation for your own business in the fitness industry.

business management for the personal fitness trainer

Laying the Groundwork for Small Business

Introduction

After studying this chapter, you will be able to:

1.1 Explain the rationale behind starting a small business.

1.2 Discuss the history of entrepreneurship in the United States.

1.3 Define small business.

1.4 Discuss the history of personal training and its evolution.

LO 1.1 Why Start a Business?

Small business is the growth engine of the U.S. economy. To illustrate this, consider the following statistics from the **United States Small Business Administration (SBA)**[1]:

1. There were approximately 22.9 million small businesses in the United States in 2002.

2. Approximately 75 percent of all net new jobs are added by small businesses.

3. Small businesses represent 99.7 percent of all employers.

4. They employ 50 percent of the private workforce.

5. They represent 97 percent of all U.S. exporters.

6. They pay 45 percent of all U.S. private payroll.

Beyond the statistics, there are countless stories of small business success in every community around the world. Some of these firms ultimately grow to be very large. For example, Google was formed in 1998 by two students, Sergey Brin and Larry Page. These two did not set out to establish the dominant search engine on the Internet; instead, they simply sought to establish a small business to meet their needs and those of their friends. In the years since its founding, Google has come to lead the industry, and the company has annual sales of more than $20 billion. While Google's growth was amazingly fast, this story is not unique. Recall from fitness-industry history that entrepreneurs such as Mark Mastov (24 Hour Fitness), Peter Taunton (Snap Fitness), Jeff Klinger and Chuck Runyon (Anytime Fitness), and Joe Gold (Gold's Gym) all started out as small business owners. Every

[United States Small Business Administration (SBA)]
The agency officially organized as a part of the Small Business Act of July 30, 1953, to "aid, counsel, assist and protect, insofar as is possible, the interests of small business concerns." It provides a wealth of information and assistance at all levels of organizational development and management. See www.sba.gov.

business that you can name today started out as a small business. Each one was the brainchild of a single individual or a small group of people. This does not mean that every small business will ultimately grow to dominate some aspect of world business. What it does mean is that small business is the foundation for all businesses. Some grow large; some do not. Regardless, they all initially go through a process much like the one you will study in this book, and that process of business development is quite different from those followed by established businesses. We suggest that the process of initiating, developing, and running a new business is its own unique area of study.

Contrast the success of small business in the United States with the facts that **Fortune 500** companies employ fewer total employees today than they did 10 years ago, and that 10 years ago, that figure was smaller than it was 20 years ago. There is a consistent pattern of decline in employment by large firms in this nation's economy. The decline in large firms has been offset by a growth in small business.

The success of small businesses is derived in part because they are simply more efficient in many ways than their large corporate counterparts. On average, small firms produce 13 to 14 more patents per employee than do large firms, and those patents (legal protection for an innovation) are historically among the 1 percent most utilized.[2] There is also evidence that the research impact of small businesses is increasing.[3]

Large firms have the ability to obtain **economies of scale** in some industries. In other words, large firms can do some things more efficiently due to their ability to operate on a large scale.[4] For example, advertising is typically much cheaper per unit if purchased in large volume. Thus, a large chain fitness facility like 24 Hour Fitness can buy its advertising much cheaper on a per unit basis than can a small retailer. Similarly, in manufacturing it is often much cheaper to produce large volumes of a product than to produce small volumes. This is the reason that small car manufacturers must charge an extraordinarily high price to cover their costs.

Years ago those apparent efficiencies led some economists to predict that small businesses would be largely replaced by a much smaller number of large businesses. Instead, the ability of small businesses to respond more quickly and to operate more effectively has led to a growth in the number of small businesses rather than a decline. Even in a mature, established industry like banking, each year there are almost 200 new, independent banks born in the United States.[5] So the growth of small business occurs not only in new, expanding industries but also in mature industries.

This text develops the methods, applications, and processes that lead to the idea generation, investigation, start-up, and successful management of a new small business. We firmly believe that the development and implementation of a new business is part art and part science. This text lays out a process for the "science" of

[Fortune 500]
The list published annually by *Fortune* magazine of the 500 largest corporations (by sales) in the United States.

[economies of scale]
A condition that allows the long-run average cost to continue downward as production increases. It leads (in its most extreme case) to a condition where a single firm making 100 percent of the product is the most efficient. In reality this condition is moderated by the ability of management to control the size.

Economies of scale allow companies that produce large quantities of goods to gain cost advantages over smaller manufacturers.

What is the goal of business? Milton Friedman (among others) argued that the only goal of business should be to make a profit. If the business owner pursues anything other than a singular focus on profit, then that person is diverting the money from the investors who rightfully own that money. On the other hand, a wide variety of people have argued that all businesses are part of a larger society and, as a result, should seek not only to make a profit, but also to try to better society by providing employment, making wise use of resources, giving back to the community, and supporting the efforts of the community to provide a better place to live for all people.

Does a business have an ethical obligation to do more than observe the laws of a society? While the absolute minimum requirement may be that a businessperson must observe the laws, ethical decision making is the conscious examination of a wide variety of issues, including the purpose of the business. All business owners need to examine these issues, and different ones will likely reach different answers.

DISCUSSION QUESTIONS

1. How do you weigh the importance in business of making a profit versus providing broader benefits to society?
2. Do you believe that obeying the laws is sufficient for making an ethical choice?

forming and managing a new small business in a clear, sequential manner that is both rich in its practical application and well grounded in research. The "art" is a matter of practice, example, and the skill of the founder or founders of the new business. The text encourages you as you go through the process of developing your ideas and work to develop your own business plan. While we will not be with you as you actually found your business, the goal of this text is to help you have everything as well developed as possible before you do. Generally, more than 50 percent of new businesses fail during their first four years, and in some industries that number tops 80 percent.[6] We believe that the principal way to be a part of the group that survives and thrives is to thoroughly plan and lay a solid basis for the business.

EXERCISE 1

1. Define economies of scale.
2. Visit the United States Small Business Administration (SBA) website (www.sba.gov). Identify some services that the SBA can provide to a small business owner.
3. Use the Internet to research what a "triple bottom line" is and summarize what you discover. Explain how it is similar to and also different from Milton Friedman's argument.

LO 1.2 A Brief History of Small Business in the United States

Before we start looking at the growth of businesses in the fitness industry, it is important to gain a perspective on the role that small business in general has played in the country's success. Alexis de Tocqueville was a Frenchman who toured the United States in the early 1830s and wrote a famous analysis of the country. One of his observations was that the United States was not so much a nation with ventures that were marvelous in their grandeur, but, instead, a nation of innumerable small ventures. Thus, the history of the United States has always been intimately tied to small business. In fact, until the mid-1880s, almost all businesses in the United States were small businesses.

The 1880s saw the initial development of the nation's large industrial base. It was from these beginnings that the robber barons developed. We associate their names today not only with great success but also with great abuses in business. They took advantage of the economies of scale that were suddenly possible with the industrial age and quickly came to dominate new sectors of the economy (as, for example, Andrew Carnegie's domination of the new steel industry). However, the robber barons were coming to dominate industrial sectors that had not existed historically, so they generally did not put small operations out of business. In fact, small business continued to thrive during these times as new businesses grew up to serve the needs of these new industrial sectors.[7]

The Great Depression of the 1930s was harder on small businesses than on large businesses, and it encouraged industrial concentration. The result was that following World War II, small business as a percentage of the economic output of the United States began to decline. It was during this time that Charles Wilson, secretary of defense for President Eisenhower, made the famous statement that "what is good for General Motors is good for the nation." The implication was that what was good for big business would be good for all of the people in the country.

In the late 1970s and early 1980s, the nation was in economic turmoil. Many of the large firms that had grown to dominate the U.S. economy were having difficulty. Entire industries, such as steel and automobile manufacturing, were in decline. It was during this time that President Jimmy Carter described the country as in a "malaise." The Japanese were in the dominant economic position in the world, and the widely discussed fear was that the United States was in decline much as the British had been 100 years earlier. However, the decline of the large multinational firms in the United States opened new opportunities that small businesses rose to fill. The economic growth and success that the nation experienced in the 1990s was due to small firms that grew very rapidly, such as Microsoft, and a vast number of small businesses that are still small and push innovation and efficiency to new levels today. According to the SBA, from 1979 to 2003, self-employment increased 33 percent among women, 37 percent among African Americans, 15 percent among Latinos, 10 percent among white Americans, and 2.5 percent among men. In 2005, *Entrepreneur* magazine identified niche health and fitness as a "hot market."

Therefore, as you begin your study of small fitness business, you should recognize that you are examining a domain that has historically been the backbone of the economic success of the nation. Small business today continues to play a dominant role in the ability of the nation to adapt quickly and to make economic progress. The timeline of business in the United States (Figure 1.1) highlights the central role of small business. Note that some firms have been in operation since before the signing of the Declaration of Independence.

EXERCISE 2

1. Name some successful small business entrepreneurs whom you know personally.
2. What types of businesses do they run?
3. Explain why you think they are successful.
4. Predict how they would define success.

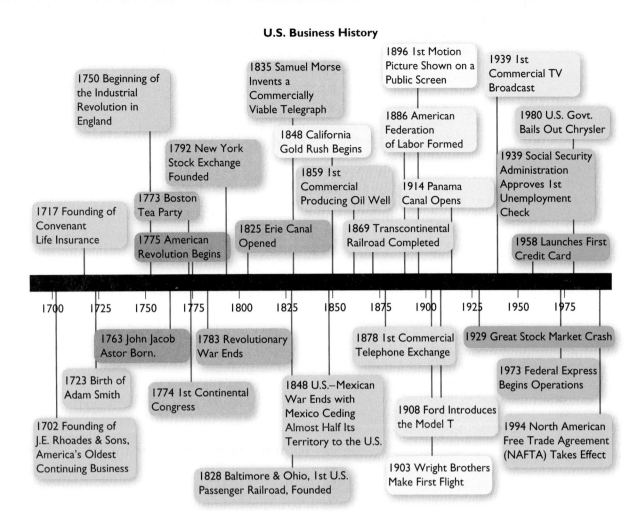

Figure 1.1
Business Timeline
The timeline of business provides both constants and natural evolution.

LO 1.3 What Is a Small Business?

It is clear that small business has benefits for individuals and society within the United States and around the world. But what do we mean when we say "small business"? For classification purposes, the U.S. government considers any business with fewer than 500 employees to be a small business. We would suggest that a business with almost 500 employees is actually a large firm requiring formal personnel policies, specialized groups, and an administrative structure that is in no way close to the reality of most small businesses. For the vast majority of students in this class, the businesses you will form will have far fewer than 500 employees.

We suggest that there is a further level of definition that will provide some insight into studying small business. You will hear these types of businesses referred to as entrepreneurial businesses, as small businesses, or sometimes as small-to-medium-sized businesses or enterprises (SMB or SME). These terms are roughly equivalent and do not specify the differences between the two main types of new business. Without an understanding of these two main types, it is difficult to discuss new ventures clearly. While all these types of businesses are founded by an entrepreneur or an entrepreneurial team, each type then takes a unique track. The two common types of new businesses are described below.

The first type is formed as a high-growth, often high-tech venture that has several unique characteristics and is generally referred to as an entrepreneurial firm:

1. The businesses are well-funded by venture capitalists or "**angel investors.**" In fact, without such capital it is virtually impossible to begin this particular type of venture.* Venture capitalists are a specialized type of investor; they typically do not invest less than $1 million, and they expect extraordinary returns.

2. The businesses are formed with a **harvest plan** in place; this is a plan to exit the business, allowing the founders to take advantage of growth. A harvest plan may include selling the business to another firm, selling it to a group of investors, or even participating in an IPO (a public offering of stock). Size is the deciding metric in a potential public offering or sale to a larger organization.

3. As a result of the harvest plan, these firms are organized to grow as quickly as possible and are generally heavily laden with debt.

4. They have a developed organizational structure.

5. They often hire an experienced president to grow the company.

6. They tend to start operations in multiple locations simultaneously.

7. They are inherently risky operations whose growth is dependent on the exploitation of unknowns in the market (a new invention, unique patents, etc.).

8. These businesses either start with or soon grow to employ a relatively large number of employees.

The second type of business is a more common type of business, most often referred to as a small business start-up, and is defined by these characteristics:

1. The start-up is self-funded or closely funded.

2. The development plan is oriented around positive cash flow.

3. The management structure is designed to take advantage of the skills of the founder or founders.

[angel investor]
Investors who provide funding to early-stage, start-up companies that have used up their initial financial support from other sources.

[harvest plan]
A plan to exit a small business. Typically, the owners plan to sell the business to another firm or take it to an initial public offering (IPO).

A harvest plan allows a business owner to exit her business at the appropriate time and reap the rewards of growth.

---

* The concepts of venture capital and angel investors will be dealt with in greater detail in later chapters. For reference here, both are investors who provide capital to the start-up firm in exchange for ownership in the new firm. This ownership level can be and often is over 50 percent of the firm.

4. The operation is designed in the image of the founder(s).

5. The business is oriented toward the personal goals of the founder(s).

6. The number of employees may be zero or as few as one, and typically would not be expected to grow to more than 50 to 100.

Although Curves and 24 Hour Fitness (formerly 24 Hour Nautilus and Family Fitness) were founded as small businesses, we would more accurately describe them as high-growth businesses, as each quickly required millions of dollars of investment from venture capitalists to grow. In contrast, the businesses of the majority of millionaires, who made their fortunes in areas such as lawn mowing, plumbing, and electrical work, were almost all founded in a manner consistent with the second type of small business. This text examines the issues and systems applicable to founding and developing this type of business. While some of the concepts are applicable to high-growth firms, the focus in this text is upon the systematic designing of a successful small business. Many of the legal structures in U.S. law begin to apply when a firm reaches milestones of 35 and 50 employees. As a result, firms that exceed that number of employees must develop new systems to operate and are more within the purview of established management practices. Thus, our focus here is on those firms that are truly small, those with fewer than 50 employees. It is important to remember that firms with fewer than 50 employees represent the majority of all firms in the United States, and also represent approximately 33 percent of all full-time employees in the United States.[8]

Business Plans—Another Difference in Types of Firms

Another critical difference between small businesses and entrepreneurial firms is in the length of and detail required in their business plans. A small business's resources are significantly more constrained than those of entrepreneurial firms. While the entrepreneurial firm generally develops a business plan as a promotional tool to be sent to venture capitalists and other potential investors, the small business develops a business plan as a guide for running the business. Many entrepreneurial ventures hire professional consultants to assist them in the development of their business plans; in contrast, we strongly advise all small business owners to develop their own plan as part of their process. A high-growth venture's business plan runs from 25 to 45 pages long. The business plan for a small business should be relatively short (on the order of 20 to 25 pages) and should be developed in a manner that helps the small businessperson understand the industry, the firm he wants to develop, and how he needs to go about being successful in that business. Thus, the business plan for a new small business is developed with three goals in mind:

1. To be a guide to managing the business in its early development.

2. To provide a self-evaluation: putting the information down in writing allows for evaluation and honest analysis.

3. To provide potential, closely held investors with the critical information necessary to evaluate the key criteria of the business: its cash flow, management team, and competitive advantage.

The business planning process that we develop in this text is a very practical and logical guide for the establishment and initial management of a new business. We do not develop the long, intricate business plans that are sometimes written to attract venture capital. Instead, you will develop a working document that is grounded in the needs of the new business. A well-thought-out business plan has heightened importance for the new small business as a tool to think through a wide range of issues, as most small businesses will not actually obtain financing from formal investors. This type of business will either be self-funded or obtain financing from friends and family. These individuals are not looking for a slick five-year formal plan; instead, they are looking for a document that explains the value of the business and how it will succeed.

Therefore, we will not use any of the cookie-cutter business plan programs that are available. If you search the term "business plan" on the Internet, you will find any number of programs that encourage you to plug in information and allow the program to "generate" a plan. We believe such programs really inhibit the process of designing a business. Each business plan, much like each business, should have its own voice, feel, and presentation. We suggest to you that a good business plan is best developed by the individual(s) contemplating the business, not by paid consultants who will have none of the enthusiasm of the founder(s). The fact that potential investors to a small business will be those closest to the founder makes it critical that the entrepreneur(s) seek to ensure the chances of success by doing thorough planning and thinking. It is one thing to lose money and close a business if the investment comes from investors you know casually. However, if the investors are your parents, in-laws, grandparents, or siblings and the business closes, it can be truly painful and may, in fact, cause ruptures in the relationships you hold most dear. A well-designed business plan will have already helped the founder(s) consider every aspect of the new business and allow everyone else involved to have a true "feel" for where this opportunity is heading.

We believe that if you do the planning and thinking described in each chapter of this text, the business plan for the new small business will develop naturally from the material. The final chapter of the book has a fully developed small business plan and a full discussion about each section of that plan. The plan in the appendix is one developed by students as a class project. Our hope is that you will be able to produce an equally detailed plan in this class. The business plan you produce should ultimately be a good solid start on a plan you could use to begin your business. You will want to refine the plan more after you complete the class, but the class will provide you with the tools to begin the process of forming your own business.

EXERCISE 3

1. Analyze the differences between a high-growth entrepreneurial firm and a small business start-up. If you could open either type, which one would you choose and why?

2. Which type of business do you actually expect to open? Why?

3. Suppose you are starting a small personal training studio. Hypothesize what would be the best way for you to approach working on a business plan. How many pages should your business plan be?

LO 1.4 The History of Personal Training

The personal training industry we know today dates back more than 70 years. Though it is hard to believe, there once was a time when doctors thought weightlifting would cause heart attacks and "make women look like men." Thanks to many pioneers in the field, along with scientific research and proven results, physical training is respected and revered as a vital component of health and wellness.

Known as "the godfather of fitness," Jack LaLanne opened the first modern health studio in 1936 at the age of 21. At the time, personal training really did not exist in this country. There were no certifying agencies, academic courses, or institutes of higher learning for physical exercise.

Many other people had a significant impact on the birth and development of personal training. Dr. Kenneth Cooper published his first best seller, *Aerobics,* in 1968—the first time the term had been used. Based on his preventative medicine research, Dr. Cooper founded the Cooper Institute in 1970 and motivated millions of people to start exercising. Even before

Jack LaLanne, who died in 2011, is shown here in 1986 at age 72.

that time, the American College of Sports Medicine, founded in 1954, was the first professional organization to lead research and education in the field of sports medicine and exercise science. It would pave the way for the first courses offering certification for exercise professionals and remains one of the most highly respected health and fitness agencies in the world today.

The 1980s saw an incredible growth in this industry, and with it came a greater diversity in organizations, philosophies, and exercise methods. ACE, IDEA, AFAA, NASM, and NSCA are just some of the organizations that have brought formal education and career opportunities to the personal training profession. Even within the profession there has been tremendous growth in the diversity of services and specialized training programs. Books, videos, and exercise equipment have helped to bring fitness practices to the general public for decades.

Fitness has grown to be such a large and dynamic profession today that many personal trainers focus on a specialty within the industry, such as strength and conditioning, yoga, and Pilates. A tremendous growth in athletic training, especially for youth athletes, led to the development of specialized certifications and organizations focused solely on this segment. Similarly, specialized licensing and professional opportunities now focus on other demographics, such as the elderly and people with physical disabilities. The incredible diversity will only continue to grow in the years to come. The fitness industry remains healthy and growing despite the recent economic downturn in America. Market analysts expect the growth of the fitness industry to continue its upward trend. Analysts recognize that with the continued maturation of the Baby Boomer generation and increased attention given to general health issues such as obesity, the American pubic will continue to seek services and solutions in personal fitness. In a 2008 survey by *Money* magazine, 48 percent of those who responded said they would not give up their gym memberships. A majority of respondents said they would rather give up an extra car, premium cable, and eating out than a gym membership. Industry analysts are noting that the American public has begun viewing fitness as a necessary expense rather than a luxury.

In this fertile growth environment, professional opportunities in fitness have grown and diversified, and so too have business opportunities for incipient entrepreneurs. Although it is clear that certain companies are large, the great majority of businesses in the profession are small and privately owned. Small personal training studios and health clubs can be

found in every region of the United States. The health club industry has proved hardy. Since 1992, the number of health clubs has increased by almost 40 percent, from 12,635 to 17,531 facilities. According to IHRSA.org, membership also grew by almost 60 percent, from 20.8 million to 32.8 million.

So how does one become a successful entrepreneur in this fertile industry? Many ideas and companies have been hatched out of necessity. Most personal trainers at some point in time look to be not an employee but the employer. Any trainer can go out and recruit and train clients, either at home or in a facility, and instantly become an entrepreneur. The main question to ask is, "Can they stay in business?" Personal training is the number one service in health and fitness clubs, and many trainers use that advantage to venture out on their own.

There are several business options for trainers who want to develop their businesses. Club training is one possibility. Trainers who choose this option work directly for the club as an hourly rate employee or pay the club a percentage of their hourly fee or pay monthly rent. Or there is the personal training studio, where training is the only service offered. Trainers normally pay a rental fee for use of the training establishment. Training in clients' homes is more aligned with being a true entrepreneur, as is training clients from your home. Both require you to establish yourself as a business entity. Many trainers are now joining forces and combining both space and time and offering services through their newly founded business.

No matter what kind of business venture you choose to pursue, every fitness entrepreneur needs to understand some of the basic practices, terminology, and standards of starting and running a small business. In this book, we will explore these areas and focus our examination on how small-business practices can be applied to fitness businesses.

EXERCISE 4

1. Assess the number of niche fitness services available in your area. How many fitness centers and/or individuals offer personal training? How many personal training studios are there? Do they specialize? How many yoga studios are there? Pilates? How many businesses offer other forms of physical activity training in your area (and what are these other forms)?

2. Given the information you assessed, do you think you will start out as an employee or as an employer? Justify your response.

3. What kind of niche fitness services interest you the most? If you were to open a business that offers one of these services, appraise how well you think it will perform in your area, based on other available services or attitudes of the population.

key terms

economies of scale 5
Fortune 500 5
harvest plan 9
United States Small Business Administration (SBA) 4

review questions

1. What percentage of new businesses close their doors within the first four years?
2. Name a major way to survive and even thrive as a new business.
3. Why was the Great Depression of the 1930s harder on small business than on large business?
4. A small business has fewer than _____ employees, according to the U.S. government.
5. This text focuses on businesses with fewer than _____ employees because firms with that number of employees represent the majority of all firms in the United States.
6. As you read, Charles Wilson, secretary of defense for President Eisenhower, made the famous statement, "What is good for General Motors is good for the nation." Identify a major American company in today's economy that is equally important to the general well-being of the nation.
7. Given the trends in the evolution of the fitness industry, and the projection by *Entrepreneur* magazine that you learned about in this chapter, what type of small fitness business do you think would do well in the current economic climate?
8. Who are some business pioneers other than those mentioned in this chapter? What makes them pioneers?

individual exercises

1. Create a brief report on the life of Jack LaLanne, explaining why he was the godfather of fitness.
2. Whom do you consider to be some of today's fitness heroes and heroines? Are they entrepreneurs? What makes each of them a leader or an authority, in your opinion?

group exercise

Break into groups of three or four. Together, select either a pioneer in fitness or a modern fitness entrepreneur; it may be someone local or not well-known. Prepare a three-minute presentation about this person. Explain the type of business or fitness service the person is involved in and how this person made an impact.

Individuals and Small Business Start-ups

After studying this chapter, you will be able to:

2.1 Discuss the importance of an entrepreneurial orientation.

2.2 List the triggers that encourage new business formation.

2.3 Compare and contrast various types of small business supports.

2.4 Recognize the expanding scope of specialization in fitness and discuss the various types of businesses that comprise the health and wellness industry.

2.5 Discuss and explain the qualifications of a personal trainer.

CASE STUDY # 1

Chris and Stephon had been personal trainers in the same suburban area for several years. They had worked in the same clubs more than once and had become friends as well as colleagues. They both had ambitions of one day owning and operating their own private training facilities. After talking about their aspirations with each other, they gradually decided that they should open a facility as partners in business. They realized that on their own, they would never amass the savings needed to launch a club without going into deep debt. But if they pooled their savings they could make a start with only about $25,000 of investment cash. One of the keys to their potential partnership was that they each brought different skills and experiences to the partnership. Stephon had worked for his father on a start-up marketing company and had a lot of computer experience—he even designed his father's website. Stephon's father was also willing to provide marketing support at no cost. Chris had been a finance major in college and had worked his way through school as an accounting temp, so he had a solid understanding of finance.

The two friends discussed their business plans over many coffees and lunches for nearly a year, but they never felt comfortable taking the leap of quitting their jobs and starting the business. But then one day Chris told Stephon some great news: his wife, who was in software sales, had just completed a stellar year and received a huge bonus. Chris and his wife had discussed it, and she was willing to become the investor they needed to start their company.

CASE STUDY # 2

Ryan and Jovita both felt as if they had reached a plateau in their earnings because they each had a full list of clients at their respective clubs. It didn't leave either of them with much of a way to increase their income or advance his career without trying this on their own. They also both had several years of experience and had confidence in their skill and knowledge of the industry and how to deliver their services for a good fee. Neither of them had children, but both wanted to have a family someday and be able to provide for them. They were both motivated to put in the long hours to make the business work, and as equal partners had a vested interest in making it successful. They understood there were risks in owning a business, including the possibility of failure and with it financial responsibilities. They were willing to take those risks, and it eventually paid off.

In large, well-established companies, no one person is crucial to the survival of the business, even the president of the company. This is due partially to the strong structures, such as written procedures, in place at most large organizations. Large organizations also have wide dispersion of knowledge throughout the business; in other words, there are multiple people who know about any given aspect of the business. As a result, if any single person leaves the organization, it has the ability to continue with minimal interruption. Finally, large organizations have greater excess resources, including financial resources, that allow them to hire outside experts to fill any critical needs that arise. These excess resources are referred to as **organizational slack;** they allow large organizations flexibility that is not available to start-up and small business ventures.

[organizational slack]
Excess resources in an organization, typical of large organizations but not of small businesses.

A small business is started as the brainchild of a single person or a small group of people, each of whom has an ownership stake in the business. The small business has few formal procedures, a concentration of knowledge in one or a few individuals, and limited slack resources.[1] The absence of slack financial resources means the small firm does not have flexibility in responding to issues such as the need to hire replacements if the company loses key individuals. As a result, the founders of a small business play a far more critical role in the business's success than does the senior leadership of the typical large organization. The importance of the individual entrepreneur in the founding and managing of a small business leads to the focus in this chapter on the individual entrepreneur who starts a small business.

This chapter will include a discussion of why individuals are so important to the success of a small business. It will also provide ways for you to understand your own entrepreneurial orientation. The examination of your orientation will include an examination of your risk tolerance and boundaries that may exist in your perception of events in the environment. It will also include an exercise to test your own entrepreneurial orientation.

Every individual brings a unique set of supports she can call on to help her in the founding process, and these supports are critical in the success of a new business. Therefore, we will examine those supports, the most critical of which is the family. In some businesses the family will play an even more important role; these businesses are referred to as "family businesses." Family businesses have unique issues that extend beyond those of the normal new small business. We will address family businesses more at the end of this chapter.

The founders of small businesses usually play critical roles in all phases of the business.

LO 2.1 Evaluating Your Entrepreneurial Orientation

There are a number of issues that potential entrepreneurs need to consider about themselves as they look at starting a new business. Examined with some depth, these issues will shape the small businessperson's analysis of the potential of any business idea. These include (1) risk tolerance, (2) prior experience, and (3) personality orientation of the individual.

Risk Tolerance

The potential small business owner must determine her own individual level of tolerance to risk. You are probably familiar with the concept from dealing with your own financial investing. The typical advice provided to most individuals is to build an investment portfolio in a manner consistent with your risk tolerance.[2] We use a similar concept here, but we use it more broadly, asking you to consider your tolerance to a wide range of potential risks that extend far beyond just financial considerations. Initially, an individual needs to evaluate whether she has the risk tolerance to actually start a small business. She then needs to evaluate what level of risk she will accept in a given small business situation.

Any individual entrepreneur must make a frank analysis of his or her risk tolerance. A failed small business can lead to severe personal financial hardship.

To illustrate, a potential small business owner needs to first determine if she has the risk tolerance to open a small business. If you work for a large corporation, there is relatively low individual financial risk. In a normal economic environment, even if a large corporation has a poor year and loses money, it will still meet payroll, pay the workers' benefits, and not close its doors on short notice. On the other hand, the small business owner is faced with a substantially different situation. When starting a business, it takes time for the business to reach a level at which revenue coming into the firm is sufficient to cover expenses. (We examine this in significant detail in Chapter 6; this point is referred to as a **break-even point**.) However, the small business may quickly reach a point where its funds have run out and it needs to close its doors quickly. If the business does close, then the small business owner(s) may find that he has to pay the debts of the firm that are left, since he had to sign personal guarantees for the loans of the business. Thus, the financial risk for the small business owner can be quite high. As a potential small business owner, you will need to consider how much debt you are willing to take on. In general, the greater the debt you are willing to take on to start your business, the higher your risk tolerance.

[break-even point]

The time when a new business has reached a level at which revenue coming into the firm is sufficient to cover expenses.

To determine her tolerance for risk, a potential small business owner would ask herself:

1. How much debt am I willing to undertake to provide a footing for my business idea?

2. How much of my personal savings would I be willing to risk on my business idea?

3. At what point would I close the business?

4. If I were the recipient of a $100,000 inheritance, what portion would I be willing to invest in my business?

As a potential new business owner, you need to determine the risk level you are willing to accept in a new business and let that information help you decide which business to pursue.[3] There is not a correct answer as to what level of risk tolerance you should be willing to take on. Instead, the key is that you must be aware of your own tolerance of risk and establish a business in a manner that is consistent with that tolerance. You must be sure that the level of risk is consistent with your background, values, and family situation. Evaluation of the risk profile for a particular type of business is more art than science.

Fran Jabara, a well-known entrepreneur from Wichita, Kansas, provides valuable advice on risk tolerance.* His argument suggests that one never do anything that does not allow one to sleep at night. This rule of thumb can help a small business owner to determine the risks with which he will be most comfortable. In future chapters we will return to the evaluation of risk as we look at specific risks, such as financial risks, strategic risks, and market retaliation risks.

Prior Experience

The second element of entrepreneurial orientation is prior experience. Every individual brings to a new business her own view of the world. This view of the world places boundaries on what a decision maker will consider as she makes decisions. These boundaries are set by experiences, history, culture, and family values, among other things. Boundaries help each of us make sense of the world. For example, in the United States, when you see a red octagonal sign at a corner, you typically assume it is a stop sign. You automatically assume that it is a stop sign because of your history and experience.

However, if you were in another country, such an octagonal sign may not be a stop sign; it might be a warning to slow down before a curve. Our experiences, history, culture, and values not only help us interpret the world, but they also place boundaries on how we see that world. Thus, our experiences, history, culture, and values also establish what we consider to be both possible and practical. This is referred to as the individual's **bounded rationality**. It is the presence of bounded rationality that often leads young people to be pioneers in an area, as they are not limited by the restrictions of the past.

Bounded rationality is the reason individuals from outside an industry are able to establish a new business in a manner not previously considered. To illustrate, consider the airline industry maverick Southwest Airlines. Today it is a major employer, but it started as a small business with a few rented planes. At the time everyone felt that air travel had to be done with what is referred to as a hub and spoke system. That is, the planes would fly into a major center such as Chicago or Atlanta from all the airports in that region. Then, people from all of these feeder airports would be placed on the same flight to a given location. Southwest wanted to go back to the way air travel used to be. Among many other things, this meant lots of short-haul flights of less than an hour between airports. Herb Kelleher (one of the founders of Southwest) was trained as a lawyer and brought fresh insight on how to compete in the industry. His innovation was not bounded by the current state of the airline industry.

Or, in the fitness industry, consider 24 Hour Nautilus and Family Fitness Centers. These organizations started out small and became one of the largest fitness conglomerates. 24 Hour Fitness brought accessibility and affordability to the fitness market, which had previously been marked by many clubs' aura of exclusivity. Recognizing the need to combine local areas' chains and then expand to other areas across the United States is what helped then 24 Hour Nautilus and Family Fitness Centers combine to become what is now know as 24 Hour Fitness.

[bounded rationality]

Rational decision making that is constrained by the background and history of the person making the decision.

---

*Fran is head of Jabara Ventures Group, a large and very successful merchant banking firm. He was also founder of the entrepreneurship program at Wichita State University. His students went on to found such ventures as Pizza Hut.

It is important for individuals to understand how their decision making is bounded by their own version of rationality. It is important to know your potential partners' backgrounds and how their decision making is impacted by their history. These issues will impact how you and your partners act. It will also impact a wide range of issues, from how you set up the business to how you run the business.

Personality Orientation of the Individual

The third element of entrepreneurial orientation is an examination of your own personality. There is a wide variety of personality tests available to assist individuals in an analysis of their traits and tendencies. These tests should not be used to judge whether you are right to start a small business. There will be successful businesspeople in all personality categories. Additionally, in general, you as an individual will probably score differently on the same test if you take it on different occasions.

Therefore, you can use these tests to help better understand yourself and your strengths, but you should not use them as a guide for your career. In this section, we review some of the major personality tests that are available. If you enter the names of these tests into a search engine, you will find that there are numerous versions of the tests available on the Internet, often for free.

Myers-Briggs. This is one of the most widely used tests for personality evaluations. It was developed in the 1940s by Katherine Briggs and her daughter Isabel Myers. The rationale for the test is drawn from Carl Jung, a Swiss psychoanalyst who broke from Freud and sought to incorporate broader issues into his analysis. The test focuses on four pairs of variables: extroversion-introversion (focus on outward world or internal), sensing-intuiting (how people gather information), thinking-feeling (how they make decisions), and judgment-perception (order vs. flexibility). The different potential arrangements of variables are believed to indicate the different ways that individuals deal with other people and their environments.

Enneagram. The underlying philosophy of this test is that a person is the result of all the experiences in his life. Thus, the factors in childhood are central in developing who we are today. As a result of this foundation it is also believed that as adults we will not change this personality over time. The test is based on the belief that there are nine different types of personalities. Through a series of questions, the test assigns you to one of these primary types. These nine types and a few of the characteristics of each type of individual are as follows: reformer (idealist/perfectionist), helper (caring/good interpersonal skills), achiever (competent/driven), individualist (sensitive/dramatic), investigator

Personality tests can help identify many different types of traits and inclinations, which can inform our strengths and weaknesses as business owners.

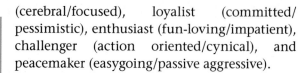

1. What are the three main issues that potential entrepreneurs need to consider about themselves as they look at starting a new business?

2. Define bounded rationality, and explain how it can be a source of innovation in industry.

3. Match each personality test with its description.

A. Enneagram
B. Myers-Briggs
C. Big Five

1. _____ Components of an individual's personality include open-mindedness, conscientiousness, agreeableness, emotional stability, and extroversion.

2. _____ Components of an individual's personality include reformer, helper, achiever, individualist, investigator, loyalist, enthusiast, challenger, and peacemaker.

3. _____ Components of an individual's personality include extroversion-introversion, sensing-intuiting, thinking-feeling, and judgment-perception.

(cerebral/focused), loyalist (committed/pessimistic), enthusiast (fun-loving/impatient), challenger (action oriented/cynical), and peacemaker (easygoing/passive aggressive).

Big Five. The Big Five is a popular personality test in universities. It is composed of five factors: open-mindedness, conscientiousness, agreeableness, emotional stability, and extroversion (the factor names vary a little among authors). These are considered by many researchers to be the five key components of an individual's personality. The Big Five test was developed by two independent research teams. These researchers asked thousands of people hundreds of questions and then analyzed the data statistically. The researchers did not set out to identify the five factors; instead, the factors emerged from their analyses of the data.

LO 2.2 Triggers for Starting a Business

Starting a new business is often the result of some particular event or condition within an individual's environment. These triggers tend to encourage the forming of new small businesses, as they encourage individuals to think creatively. Individuals get comfortable with their lives, and it takes a trigger to force them to think in new ways. You may not be faced with such triggers as motivations, and still decide to start a small business. However, many people do start their businesses when one of these triggers is present, and therefore it is useful for you to understand them. The triggers in the formation of a new small business can come from

a positive or negative stimulus that occurs in an individual's life. Some typical triggers include the following:

1. Being laid off from established employment.

2. Being approached by one or more people with a new business idea.

3. Reaching a point financially where the risk/return level is tolerable.

4. Having very little to lose financially by a failure.

5. Developing a concrete idea to improve a given situation.

6. Being spurred to action by attending a seminar, reading a book, or talking with successful entrepreneurs.

7. Experiencing a midlife (or early-life, or even late-life) crisis.

8. Observing the establishment of an incubator or business development effort within the community.

9. Experiencing the inability to climb the corporate ladder due to circumstances beyond one's control. These might include not having graduated from the "correct" school, being female in a male-dominated business, having a marketing background in a manufacturing business, etc.

Often, more than one of these triggers may be present at the same time. For discussion purposes, we segment these triggers into two categories: personal motivations and circumstance motivations. While the exact dividing line between these two categories is somewhat fuzzy, this categorization will allow for the examination of the various issues involved in starting a business.

Personal motivations are driven internally by the individuals themselves, and as such are the strongest motivations available. Personal motivations drive people to make career and life-altering moves irrespective of "practical" advice. Small business founders driven by personal motivators will tend to be more proactive and drive relentlessly toward their goals.

Circumstance motivators tend to result in more of a defensive positioning. The environment and environmental changes make opportunities available to potential business owners, but the motivation is substantially different. This is an opportunistic start-up whose staying power is more determined by other competing opportunities.

To illustrate personal triggers, consider that today one of the fastest-growing groups of small business owners is women. In large part, women are starting new businesses when their career opportunities are blocked at larger corporations. The barrier is often referred to as the "glass ceiling." It involves not formal rules, but the practical reality that in some organizations there are limits to the level in the corporate hierarchy to which women are allowed to progress. If you question the presence of such ceilings, simply note how many women are in senior management positions at most major corporations. A particularly fast-growing segment of small business owners are minority women owners. Minority women–owned firms are expanding at an estimated rate of 31.5 percent per year.[4]

There is a circumstance motivator, for example, when individuals are laid off by their prior employer. Human nature is such that most people get comfortable with their current status and financial position. When individuals are laid off, are demoted, are forced to take reduced pay, or even survive a layoff, they are forced to think about new opportunities that they never would have considered previously. For example, research has found that when a factory or military base closes, there is a blossoming of new small businesses in that area.[5]

Our opening story of Chris and Stephon illustrates how personal and circumstance motivations merge. The two individuals who considered establishing their new small business might have felt that they had little chance for significant career advancement in their current jobs. Based on this fear, they started looking for new areas that would allow them to build a business that would provide significant opportunities for themselves and their families. These individuals all had small children, and they wanted to provide a better standard of living for them. In this

EXERCISE 2

1. Identify at least five triggers that often motivate an entrepreneur to start a business.

2. Which, if any, of the triggers discussed in this section is motivating to you with regard to starting a business?

3. Report on how your motivations for starting a business are personal, circumstantial, or perhaps a little of both.

One of the important choices that every person has to deal with is what she may take with her when she leaves a business. This becomes more critical when the person leaving is starting her own new business. Whether it is voluntary or involuntary, leaving a job can be frustrating, and sometimes individuals are frustrated enough to wish to do harm to the business they are leaving. Beyond that, there is a question as to where the line between personal and business information exists. If the person leaving does something that harms the prior business, then the prior employer can sue the former employee. The impact on a fledgling business can be substantial.

To illustrate, consider an employee who has worked for a large fitness club. In her former position, she had access to the club's client list. The employee might realize that it is unethical to take the entire list and use it to generate her own customer base. Not only is this unethical, the former employer could sue her over the lost business. However, the employee believes that the handful of clients with whom she worked while employed by the club were as much "her" clients as they were the club's clients. She feels she has the right to notify these clients that she is starting her own business because she is certain that many of them would follow her.

QUESTIONS

1. What are some ways you can build a client base when you leave a firm without crossing ethical boundaries?
2. Beyond the customer list, what would be other things you could take from a former employer that would present an ethical problem?

case, the two potential business founders not only had one of the strongest personal motivators available to individuals—that of providing for their children—they also had a strong desire to change their overall circumstances.

LO 2.3 Supports

This chapter focuses on the individual entrepreneur who starts the small business. It has been stressed in the chapter that this individual is central to its success. Generally, she is far more important than a single individual in a large firm.

This does not mean that an individual, or team of individuals, creates a successful small business without help. There are supports and resources available to the entrepreneur. No one of these supports or resources assures success, but the small businessperson should evaluate which resources and supports she has access to in an effort to increase her chances of success.

The supports and resources available are typically unique to the entrepreneur and where he lives. Not all individuals come to the process of founding the business with equal endowments or supports. The entrepreneur should avail himself of all the supports possible to make his entrepreneurial efforts successful. The support and resource areas the small businessperson should examine include (1) family, (2) social networks, (3) community, and (4) financial resources.

Like all structures, your small business needs supports to operate.

Family

Few people know you—including your abilities and shortcomings—like your family does. These individuals are a resource for support, guidance, suggestions, and potential funding for a small business. A spouse who is willing to handle the financial burden while you begin a new venture, a parent who will contribute time and money, an uncle who has been in the industry and is willing to review your plan and advise you so that you might avoid basic pitfalls—all are immensely valuable to the new small business owner. We advise potential new entrepreneurs to work with their family members not only for their advice and potential funding, but also as a reality check and support structure. Family members are in a unique position to provide you with key insights when you may be pursuing the wrong approach to an issue. Too many other individuals will not be willing to tell you when you may be wrong. Most individuals will tell you only positive things. In addition, you will need your family's support to push forward to success, as there will be times when you will have to deal with significant discouragements.

To fully utilize your family resources, we suggest you list those family members with whom you have regular contact, and also list the capabilities those individuals possess that might provide support to the new business. The benefit of such an activity is that it will allow a small business founder to think systematically through the items that need to be discussed with various family members. The small business owner needs to make sure she obtains the resources desired from family members without wasting the time and effort of these individuals simply because they are very familiar to her.

The role of family is so critical to the success of a new business that many small businesses in fact end up being what are referred to as family businesses. In such firms, the principal staff members of the business are family members. There may be other employees in the firm, but typically, family members hold the key managerial decision-making positions.

The long-term management of family businesses is unique when compared to that of nonfamily-owned small businesses. In the initial stages of formation, the support of the family can help the small businessperson overcome many difficulties that might cause the failure of non-family-supported small businesses. For example, when family members are the principal staff, a month in which payroll cannot fully be met by the company is more acceptable. These individuals' level of commitment to the founder may be high enough that they are willing to take only a partial or no salary that month. These individuals also are often willing to work at times and in conditions that other employees would not accept. For example, Christmas season is critical to all retailers, but paid staff may not be willing to work the extra hours needed at this time, while family may be more willing to do so. It is this level of commitment that has produced such success for many immigrant families that open a restaurant or a service business, such as a grocery

store or a dry cleaners. In these settings, the reliance on family is a key reason the firms are able to survive and prosper.

However, there are also potential negative long-term issues that accompany a family business. While family members have a greater commitment to you as an entrepreneur because of your close relationships, those close relationships make issues such as firing family members difficult. If a family member is not a good employee, how will you fire him, or even reprimand him, without rupturing the close relationships in the family? Similarly, because family members know each other so well, they are willing to say negative things to a small business owner that a regular employee would never say. These negative things may have no connection to work but might be issues that are simmering in the family. These negative comments can be particularly caustic in the firm, since the owner may be hesitant to fire the family member, and can finally rupture all relationships with the individual and other extended family members. Finally, the presence of family in the business can cause difficulties with other employees that are not family members. As will be discussed in Chapter 10, human resource management is one of the most important and contentious issues in a company. Unfortunately, if it appears there are different expectations and rewards for workers depending on whether they are related to you, it can cause turmoil among employees.

Family is usually an important resource for a new business. The new entrepreneur needs to consider the balance of benefits and drawbacks to building a family-based business.

Social Networks

Beyond your family, another key support is the network of individuals in your life. These networks may have formed from former employers, individuals you know from a fraternal organization like the Rotary Club, friends at school, or individuals you know from another organization such as a church or synagogue. Individuals in your network can be particularly helpful in providing some legitimacy to your business, in addition to providing feedback and advice to you.

To illustrate, a small start-up company may experience difficulties in establishing relationships with suppliers. For instance, a new company may not be able to obtain credit from a supplier for some time. Only after a history of prompt payment is built up might the supplier allow the new business to carry credit. A network can help overcome some of these debilitating issues early in the life of the business by providing a level of legitimacy. Support from companies in your network cannot only provide revenue, but can also help to indicate to others your seriousness and staying power.

Alumni organizations are just one type of social network that can be a support in starting a small business.

Community

There are also more formal community supports that can lower the overall risk for a new small business in the community.[6] In most communities there are **Small Business Assistance Centers**. These centers are funded by the Small Business Administration and advise individuals wishing to start new businesses. The supports vary widely, but usually include research aids such as information on funding sources in the area for small business. There are other services available, such as counseling provided by the Service Corps of Retired Executives (SCORE). These retired executives work with small businesses as advisers on a wide range of issues. Still other supports are available at centers tailored to aid women or minority entrepreneurs. One specialized program is the Minority Enterprise Development Program. There are also programs targeted to veterans or those firms that are geared to export. Fitness businesses can look to local rehabilitative health facilities as potential support sources. These facilities have several critical businesses under one roof, such as chiropractic service, massage therapy, physical therapy, athletic training, and a fitness facility for cardiac rehabilitation.

[Small Business Assistance Centers]
Centers funded by the Small Business Administration that advise individuals wishing to start new businesses.

Each community has its own unique set of resources. The federal government provides some of the funds, but it encourages the local administrators and government entities to tailor the services to what is needed locally. Therefore, each potential small businessperson needs to survey what services she has available. A quick review of the Blue Pages (those focused on government) in the telephone book under titles like Economic Development will provide an entry into these services. The potential entrepreneur would be well served to take an hour or two to visit the offices identified and obtain information on their services. The potential entrepreneur should also ask these entities for leads on other agencies that have services for the start-up business. Almost all such agencies work with each other and want entrepreneurs to take advantage of all resources available, whether from them or from other agencies.

Financial Support

Another key element for a new business is the financial support it develops. The detailed evaluation of financial resources will follow in the text. Specifically, in Chapter 9 we will examine the financing issues related to starting a firm. However, a few points need to be made briefly here. Potential small business owners need to have a full understanding of the cost/benefit of the small business.[7] In particular, the entrepreneur needs to account for the financial resources that may be required by a small business. It is simply good business practice to ensure that sufficient financial resources are available prior to the start of that business. It may be a waste of effort to go forward if the goals of an individual are widely divergent from the financial resources that are available. The development of the small business is not "blue sky" thinking. The processes detailed in this book are a practical and applied effort to make the small business a reality.

Using a Support Analysis chart (Figure 2.1) a potential business owner can analyze the resources he might be able to call on.

From an individual evaluation of capability, nothing more is required at this point than a realistic vision of what resources are needed and available. If, for instance, a potential entrepreneur is considering starting a training studio, he needs to recognize that the equipment and setup for even a very small, modest studio may exceed $150,000. This cost increases dramatically unless the potential small business owner leases or buys used equipment. Regardless of the type of business contemplated, it is critical that the entrepreneur be able to fund that business or obtain the necessary funding.

Figure 2.1
Support Analysis

CATEGORY	SOURCE	DESCRIPTION
Family		
Social Networks		
Community		
Financial Support		

1. Relate the pros and cons of enlisting your family members in your business start-up.
2. Examine the formal community supports in your area. What organizations are available? Record the contact information for those community supports you plan to visit or call for information.
3. Assemble a tentative cost analysis for your business start-up costs.

Therefore, the potential small business owner needs to have a broad understanding of what financial resources he possesses and a realistic idea of what he will need to expend. Chapter 6, "Your Financial Fitness," devotes an entire section to this exact issue. Here, we stress that even at this early stage, the potential small business owner needs to have in mind how much money he and others starting the business may be able to generate.

LO 2.4 Specialization

The fitness industry has an ever-expanding network of specialized niche businesses, each with many opportunities.

Community-Based Wellness Specialties

Many opportunities revolve around community-based wellness centers. These are centers devoted to providing the community with health courses and health activities to improve individual and community health. They sometimes have community-based health education, promotion, and screening programs. These centers include:

- **Residential Wellness Centers** These facilities are specific to a residential area and are common within a homeowners association. They typically contain spa services and feature golf and/or tennis as a mainline sport.

- **Senior Fitness Centers** As the name implies, these types of facilities are geared toward older adults but may also cater to younger adults with specific diseases or disabilities. Exercises and activities are geared toward the older adult population to improve physical and mental health.

- **Athletic Performance Centers** These centers typically specialize in providing amateur, semiprofessional, and professional athletes with athletic training, injury prevention, rehabilitation, and performance training in an effort to achieve each individual's highest level of performance in life or athletics.

Group Exercise Specialties

Group exercise includes many disciplines, but these are the most popular specialty classes:

- Aqua aerobics
- Pilates
- Cardiokickboxing
- Yoga
- Step aerobics
- Muscle conditioning and toning

The addition of these specialty offerings to an existing fitness business allows the business to expand outside its core setup. Yoga and Pilates are sometimes separated into their own classification under the holistic programs of study, but ultimately they are, in fact, group exercise.

Other Specialties

Other opportunities for fitness specialization may focus on special populations of clients. A special population is classified as anything outside the general population. This could include children, older adults, or those with disease and disability. Other specialization areas include wellness coaching, corporate or worksite wellness, and gender-specific facilities.

EXERCISE 4

1. Imagine you are starting a community-based wellness center in your area. Is there much competition already existing in the region? Which type would you start, or would you decide not to start one? Why? Consider your personality and the support and resources available to you.

2. Predict whether or not you have the personality type to start a facility that focuses on group exercise. Explain why or why not.

LO 2.5 Personal Training as a Business

The unique nature of the personal training industry presents both challenges and opportunities to a potential small business owner. Entrepreneurs should remember that just being a top-level personal trainer is not the only skill needed to be a fitness business owner. There are several sides to personal training and components of a personal training business, including marketing, business structures, psychology, communication, legal responsibilities, management ethics and professional duties, certification, program design, and safety. All areas are crucial to a small businessperson's success. It is important to remember to have and hire employees who are well-versed in all of these areas.

There is no single, correct way to begin a personal training business. Many fitness professionals make the leap from being an employee to business ownership by becoming an independent contractor. While independent contractors are often seen as employees in many respects, an independent contractor is, in fact, the sole proprietor of a small business. This status allows the individual to work in multiple clubs and lends the sense of being one's own boss. Independent contractors working in clubs are paid hourly or per client/class. Some clubs also allow independent contractors to work out at the club for free or at a reduced rate.

This is by no means the only way of starting up a small business in the fitness industry. Many entrepreneurs have followed other paths. In-home personal trainers, online virtual trainers, fitness consultants, and other models are all possible ways of setting up a fitness business.

For those entrepreneurs who want to establish a studio-based business, one immediate choice the entrepreneur will make is whether he is going into business on his own or with a partner or partners. (In Chapter 7 we discuss the technical aspects of different forms of businesses, such as sole proprietorships and partnerships.) A single owner benefits from the satisfaction of building something by oneself, as well as the financial rewards that can come with success. However, a single owner may not possess all the required skills or the time to launch and operate a business solo. The owner can become overwhelmed with the administrative responsibilities of running a personal training business and have little time to do personal training. She may find it necessary to hire more trainers than she initially envisioned.

A partnership allows multiple skill sets, backgrounds, and other inputs to strengthen the foundation of the business. Consider our example of Chris and Stephon. Chris is better with administrative duties and organizational details, while Stephon has sales and marketing experience. In a partnership, the owners have more flexibility to be active employees as trainers while dividing administrative and management duties. Of course, the risks of a partnership are somewhat different from those of sole ownership. Partners must be able to trust each other entirely, and one partner cannot necessarily overcome the errors or shortcomings of another partner. Frustrations can arise when the financial investment of one partner is placed in peril by the actions of another partner.

Whether establishing a business on your own or with partners, it is essential that any new entrepreneur seek legal advice before making any decisions about the structure of a business. There are numerous state and local rules and regulations for forming a business. In addition to working with an attorney who specializes in small business, it is important to hire a qualified accountant and bookkeeper. Unless you have substantial experience in finance, any business plan should be examined by an accountant who works with small businesses, and once a business is up and running, any owner who feels uncomfortable with keeping accounts may benefit from hiring a part-time bookkeeper.

Some people buy a franchise in the fitness industry, but these can require a large initial investment, sometimes upward of $250,000. If you are able to marshal such financial resources, there are many advantages of a franchise: mainly, you are purchasing an entire turn-key business, from the facility to the marketing to the operational procedures. This does not imply that a franchise is any easier than starting a business from scratch—franchise owners have to work just as hard as independent business owners due to the larger scale of the franchise operation. The potential downsides of a franchise include the obvious financial risk, as well as the lack of creating an entity from scratch. For many entrepreneurs, it is the act of creation and the excitement of conceiving a brand-new business concept that supplies an irreplaceable thrill and sense of satisfaction.

EXERCISE 5

1. Assess and describe your skills in each of the following areas: personal training, marketing, business structures, psychology, communication, legal responsibilities, management ethics and professional duties, certification, program design, and safety. You may choose to use a rating system (1 being poor skills and 5 being excellent skills) or verbal descriptions (low, medium, high).

2. Based on the assessment of your skills, would opening a personal training business suit you? Why or why not?

3. A personal trainer who is a successful independent contractor decides to start hiring employees so he does not have to turn away business. What are some of the considerations the trainer will have to make?

key terms

bounded rationality 18
break-even point 17

organizational slack 16
Small Business Assistance Centers 25

review questions

1. Define organizational slack, and explain why there is more of it in a large business.
2. Define break-even point, and explain how it is related to risk for a small start-up business.
3. Paraphrase the four questions a new business owner must ask and answer to determine his or her risk tolerance.
4. Answer the four questions you just paraphrased to determine your risk tolerance.
5. Research online where you can take, for free, one of the personality tests covered in this chapter. Take the test. What personality type are you according to the Myers-Briggs, Enneagram, or Big Five test?
6. Study the triggers that often act as motivators to starting a business. Which of these or other triggers apply to you? Record the results of your analysis of personal and circumstance motivators.
7. At a high level, analyze how much money you would need to generate to start the kind of business you have in mind and cover your expenses until your break-even point.

Consider space, equipment, and administrative tools or supplies. Do you think you can generate this amount? Why or why not? If not, what resources and support might you consider to assist you in obtaining funding?
8. What are the areas of specialization to which you think you are most suited (residential wellness center, senior fitness center, athletic performance center, group exercise such as aqua aerobics, or muscle conditioning)? Why?
9. To what type of personal training business do you think you are most suited (independent contracting, partnership, franchise)? Why?
10. Prioritize the following skill areas needed for successfully running a personal training business: personal training, marketing, business structures, psychology, communication, legal responsibilities, management ethics and professional duties, certification, program design, and safety. What makes one skill area more important than another, in your opinion?

individual exercise

Construct a support analysis chart (see Figure 2.1). Consider the individuals or organizations in your family, social networks, business community, or financial community who can offer support and resources for a business you start. Show how each might provide the beneficial support and resources needed.

group exercise

Break into groups of four or five. Imagine you are a family of siblings going into business together. You decide to start a senior citizen fitness center because your parents and friends of their age have expressed an interest. Discuss what skills you bring to the family business. Decide who will be responsible for what area of the business. How will you make business decisions? Will you hire nonfamily employees? What are some issues or concerns that you face in this situation? Will your parents and their friends bring additional issues and concerns? How will you resolve these?

After studying this chapter, you will be able to:

3.1 Describe a systematic means for examining skills in order to generate ideas for opening a small business in the fitness industry.

3.2 Discuss the elements of opportunity analysis.

3.3 Analyze how to choose a business.

Business Idea Generation and Initial Evaluation

CASE STUDY

Sometimes businesses are born when personal experience comes face to face with market demand. Such was the case for Troy Wells. Troy, a former gym rat turned bodybuilder, loved everything about the gym. Working out five to six days a week sometimes wasn't enough for him, and he never tired of making the 20-minute drive to Universal Fitness. There were other gyms closer to Troy. In fact, one was actually within walking distance of his home. But Troy loved the ambiance and amenities at Universal. The only drawback about Universal was that the club was poorly managed.

Although the gym's advertised opening time was 6:00 A.M., on several occasions Troy arrived at 6:30 A.M. to find the building locked and no staff person on the job. Troy spoke to the gym's owner, Wes, who said that the employee who was supposed to open the gym often couldn't make it because her husband could not always drive her to work on time. So Troy asked, "Why don't you do it?" Wes laughed and said, "Because I'm the owner!"

One day, Troy found the locker room at Universal was a mess, with dirty towels and trash strewn about on the floor. But what bothered him most was that this was the very same mess he had seen the previous day! Troy spoke to April, the general manager, who explained, "Our cleaning crew didn't come in last night." Troy asked, "Why didn't you do it?" April walked away with a look of disgust and said, "Are you kidding me? That's nasty!" Troy was so put off that he muttered aloud, "I should just own the gym because I *can* do it myself!"

Troy did not realize it, but Wes overheard this exchange and decided to approach Troy about gym ownership. Wes had already been meeting with lawyers and financial advisors about exiting the fitness club business, and Troy seemed like an ideal owner to replace him. Within a few weeks Wes and Troy met to discuss the possibility of transferring ownership of the gym. Troy was ecstatic. He felt confident that with his attention to detail and work ethic, he could bring significant improvements to Universal.

Troy met with his financial advisors and proceeded to acquire the funds he needed to buy the gym. Soon enough, Troy was the proud, new owner of Universal Fitness. The first few months went well. He did, indeed, come in at 6:00 A.M. to make sure the gym opened on time. And some days he worked until 11:00 P.M. His work routine was becoming tiring, yet he was barely breaking even. Despite these challenges, Troy remains upbeat and faithful to his business, and he remains positive about launching his new career as a small-business owner.

Individuals come to the decision to begin a small business from many different perspectives and backgrounds. From a diverse group of individuals come many successful business ideas. Research shows that successful new business ideas are not determined by who your parents are, your race, your gender, or your religion. Instead, quality ideas are a function of the creativity and thoughtfulness of the person creating the business.

So how does someone come up with an idea for a new business? Many times the idea for a new business comes from the entrepreneur's professional background or hobbies. These are domains that the individual knows very well, allowing him to see shortcomings in the current offerings in these areas. Great insight can also be gained from individuals whom the entrepreneur respects or those who have been successful in founding a business themselves. Thus, there are a wide variety of sources that can be called upon for ideas about potential businesses. In this chapter we identify a systematic way in which to generate a list of potential businesses. The initial steps in evaluating the viability of these ideas will also be presented as a key element in this process.

LO 3.1 Generating Business Ideas

While individuals may determine that they want to open a small business or take over an existing one, the exact type of business to launch is much more difficult to determine. We encourage everyone, even individuals who feel confident that they know which type of business they wish to pursue, to examine all options through the processes detailed in this chapter. We have found that both new and existing business owners often feel strongly about the type of business they wish to pursue, and yet, upon a more systematic examination, they move to an alternative idea. Frequently, they do find an opportunity in the market, but it may not be the exact business concept that they initially conceived. Alternatively, they may conclude after their analysis that the business they conceptualized would not be successful. Therefore, rather than reacting in a knee-jerk manner to what appears to be an opportunity—or even worse, quickly dismissing a promising idea—an individual needs to make a rational evaluation of a business opportunity and its potential.[1]

As discussed in Chapter 2, the desire to own/operate a fitness business is a first step, but what business might that be—individual trainer, small club owner, large-chain fitness club owner, training studio owner, for-profit commercial facility, not-for-profit community facility, corporate-based fitness organization? The generation of business ideas is not something that occurs automatically. Rather, it is a process of identifying the skills of the potential small business owners, identifying opportunities in the market, matching the initial financial funding available, and then marrying these together into a business idea that interests the potential founders. As noted in Chapter 1, the establishment of a successful small business is challenging. The high demands placed upon everyone involved in the process necessitate that the founders truly enjoy what they are doing. The process presented below is intended to be an open one that considers passion and enjoyment as important elements to success.

While not a sequential formula, we would suggest the following approach to the development of a quality business idea. First, the founders should list and evaluate their personal skill set. These skills may arise from hobbies, current work, past work experience, and/or family history. The next step is to carefully analyze the market and look for a gap, or some need that is not being met effectively. Finally, the potential founders need to compare their ability to fill those gaps with the opportunity that seems to be available. We suggest the means to do this is the development of a chart that allows for an open, systematic examination. We will now look at each of these steps in turn in more detail.

Skills Analysis

Why do we start with the skill set of the entrepreneur rather than an opportunity in the market? There are literally millions of "opportunities" in a wide variety of fields, but without the requisite skill set, pursuing these opportunities would be a frustrating exercise of wasted money and time. There may be tremendous opportunities in the spa services business. However, if a potential business owner had no skills in this area, then those opportunities would not be easily available to him; nor could any initial advantage be held for long when faced with competitors who did have the necessary training in the area. The small businessperson must have not only the necessary skills, but also a depth of understanding, so that he can build a long-term advantage in his domain. Perhaps as important as the small business owner's skills in a particular area is the need for the potential owner to have interest in or passion for starting a business in that domain. Without a passion for the business the entrepreneur will not be willing to devote the time and energy necessary for the business to be successful.

Your hobbies can influence your business career. Do you have any hobbies that might lead to solid business ventures?

As we mentioned previously, skills come from a variety of areas and are relatively idiosyncratic to the individual. In general, our skills are derived from our history, experience, and interests. Several specific areas that potential business owners might examine include hobbies, education, work experience, and family history. Each of these will be examined in turn.

Hobbies

Hobbies are those pursuits that an individual does as an avocation. The individual does these things because they are enjoyable, so there is typically great passion associated with them, which can help encourage the success of the small business. A rule of thumb in the founding of businesses has always been that the owner whose business is both her vocation and her avocation is difficult to beat. The potential business owner should probably ask herself these questions:

- What hobbies do you pursue on an active basis?
- What hobbies have you pursued in any manner over your lifetime (whether or not you were serious about them)?
- What is it about your hobbies that really excites you?
- What were the specific skills that these hobbies required?
- What have your experiences in the hobby taught you that could help others?
- What products and services did you use in these hobbies?

Education and Certifications

The second set of skills is education, either formal or informal. Although a general education is important, it is the type of education and the nature of the information you receive in that education that will provide guidance toward your end goal. As the health and wellness industry grows, there will be more demand for educated individuals who have a comprehensive knowledge of the industry. Those who want to enter the field should become well-versed in the profession by attending industry conventions, reading professional journals, and exploring other educational opportunities. As part of your professional makeup, education stands not alongside but next to your personal conduct—you must set a high professional standard. A college degree and certification are requirements for fitness club or gym ownership. Any person who hopes to become a viable business owner in the industry must acquire a personal training certification from an NCCA accredited institution. You should be certified in your focus discipline, and you must maintain that certification continuously. You should also seek additional education or certification in certain aspects of business management. For instance, learning Microsoft Office applications is helpful, but *mastering* them will enable you to operate on a professional level when creating financial reports in Excel or producing promotional flyers in Word.

To further your skills analysis, answer the following questions:

- What courses did you take that were particularly enjoyable?
- What courses did you take where the material came to you very easily?
- Have you attended any unusual education programs?
- Have you taken specialized training in any specific area?
- If you had to do it all over again, what areas would you pursue now?

Work Experience

Another set of skills comes from work experience. Such skills typically have direct applicability to the pursuit of a new business. In each job, individuals build up skills that they take with them when they start a new business.

- What businesses have you worked in?
- What skills were critical to the jobs you performed?
- What positions have you held in business?
- In what areas would you be considered an expert on some level?
- What did you *really* enjoy about the positions that you have held?
- What frustrated you about the positions that you have held?
- When were you the most excited about your work?

Family History

Your family history is an often overlooked source of skills. As we all know, every family is unique. There are often things that you do with your family in which you develop expertise. Many times potential entrepreneurs overlook this area of developed knowledge. If your family is vegetarian or follows another type of strict diet, perhaps a business related to the nutrition industry could be a great use of your skill set.

- What is your family history with new business ventures?
- What types of travel/vacations does your family enjoy?
- What skill sets exist within your nuclear family?
- What are the financial resources of your extended family?
- Are there unique things your family does that others seem very interested in?

Your family can be a great help in developing a business. What are some of the risks and rewards that you associate with the idea of working with your family?

Additional Skills

Beyond these categories, we suggest that you also ask yourself the following questions:

1. What are your top three personal skills?
2. What things do you like doing best each day, each week?
3. When you look back over the past year, what one or two things did you enjoy more than any others?
4. What are the magazines and books you read?
5. What are your three greatest accomplishments in life? What skills were involved in these accomplishments?
6. Do you enjoy working with people? Or would you prefer to be left alone to concentrate your efforts in a particular area?
7. What industry (commercial fitness, independent training, corporate wellness, residential fitness) would you prefer to work in?

Clearly, the goal of all these questions is to explore the range of potential skills and abilities that each of us possesses. A few more questions can help you tailor your business to your unique skills and personality.

1. Do you prefer to work extensively with people or not? If you thrive on interacting with people and have the corresponding skills, then a small training studio may be ideal.
2. Do you have an intense detail orientation? If you are very detail oriented, then a commercial facility that is procedurally complex and involves managing a wide variety of services (spa, group exercise classes) may be appropriate. Remember that there are many people and companies out there that will pay handsomely for someone to manage the details of life. Alternatively, an individual who finds this level of detail frustrating should pursue a business with a simpler business model similar to Anytime Fitness or Fitness Together.
3. Are you trained in the area in which you want to work? Your experience and educational skills will have a critical impact on the direction of the business. Someone may believe that there is a need for a personal training studio in your part of the city. However, if the individual does not have the education, training, or skills to manage such a facility, it is futile to consider such a business.

EXERCISE 1

1. What are the three steps in your approach to developing a quality business idea?
2. What are the four main sources of information that can help you determine your skill set?
3. What are some additional sources?
4. How would you describe your skill set, based on this system for examining skills?

What is clear from the above is that the founder(s) of a small business need to be intimately involved in the design, funding, and running of the new business. Often you will hear individuals quickly claim that they are "idea" people and plan to simply hire everyone needed to run the business, design the procedures, etc. These folks are not founders; they are bankers with vision. They are simply providing funding and the concept. Such a model might work for businesses that enjoy high profit margins, but for small businesses with fewer than 50 employees, this model is difficult to pursue successfully. Therefore, in this text in general, and this chapter in particular, we utilize the basic assumption that the founder will be intimately involved in the new business.

LO 3.2 Opportunity Identification

Once you have developed a list of your skills, abilities, and interests, the next step is to examine the marketplace for opportunities to utilize these in a business. The method that we use and recommend is a form of **gap analysis.** In such an analysis, individuals identify a gap that exists between the demand by customers and the supply provided by firms in the market. The new business owner must then determine if she has the skills and abilities to fill that gap.

[gap analysis]
A relatively simple process of systematically examining the difference, or gap, between what is expected and what occurs. One type of gap analysis, called *opportunity analysis*, examines opportunities in the marketplace side-by-side with the individual's ability to address those gaps.

Potential Businesses

There are a variety of ways to identify gaps, or business opportunities, in the marketplace. These include the following:

1. Examine trends around the region/nation/world that may not have reached your particular geographic location. Trends do not start uniformly. Notice that a number of smaller fitness centers or clubs have developed significant businesses in smaller cities throughout the United States. These opportunities evolved when their founders examined how clubs such as Anytime Fitness, Fitness Together, and Snap Fitness were achieving success in major cities. These businesses achieved a strong local position because the national clubs, such as 24 Hour Fitness, Gold's Gym, and Bally's, couldn't reach the same markets.

2. Interview and talk about opportunities with key successful entrepreneurs in the area. Most successful entrepreneurs are great sources of ideas that have the potential to be successful given the right set of circumstances and people. From their own experiences, these individuals have a keen eye for what businesses are needed in an area. Since these individuals are often so busy with their own businesses that they don't have time to pursue new ventures

themselves, they may be willing to advise new entrepreneurs. They may even help identify and fund such opportunities. In effect, they become mentors to new entrepreneurs.

3. Discuss potential businesses with family members. Your family members know your abilities and disposition. Furthermore, they are uniquely positioned to provide a much-needed honest perspective on your efforts—in other words, a reality check. If any of these individuals have small businesses of their own, they might be useful in the process of helping you decide which businesses work best with your particular set of skills.

In thinking about business trends, consider trends that you can tap into but that a large, national chain such as Gold's Gym might not be able to address.

4. **Brainstorming** with key entrepreneurs and family members can also be useful to the potential small business owner. Brainstorming is a creative process in which a group of individuals is brought together and asked to generate ideas related to a specific topic or problem, with little effort given to evaluating the true potential for those ideas. In this case, a group may be provided information on the skill set of the entrepreneur and be asked to generate a list of businesses that might be appropriate for that person. The interaction within the group leads to a dynamic that can lead to new, innovative ideas. Such brainstorming sessions work well in informal groups. Think of friends or family gathering over a meal and talking in depth about the options that are available; this is brainstorming. An important rule of brainstorming is that no idea is a bad idea.

[brainstorming]

A creative process in which a group of individuals is brought together and asked to generate ideas with little or no effort made to evaluate the potential for each idea.

5. Take a look at the things that frustrate you and your family. Daily frustrations are an incredible source of ideas, as you saw with Troy and Universal Fitness. How would you solve his frustration? What is it about the frustration that needs to be solved? You will find that you might have as many as a dozen aspects that could be solved, but only a few that truly fit with your capabilities and interests. Most (if not all) needs in society are currently being met. However, the degree, level, detail, efficiency, effectiveness, politeness, or access all provide means for improving the satisfaction of a particular need.

EXERCISE 2

1. In your own words, summarize the five ways by which you can identify business opportunities in the marketplace.

2. Characterize the fitness businesses you are aware of in your community. Compare those businesses to other businesses you are aware of outside of your community. What regional, national, or global fitness trends can you identify that have not yet reached your area?

LO 3.3 Choosing a Business

The process of generating ideas is not something that is done in a single sitting. Instead, it is a process that takes time, interaction, consideration, evaluation, and iteration. These steps do not occur in a linear fashion, but should occur in an interactive manner. For example, if a successful entrepreneur suggests a new business that seems to fit well with your skills,

The process of generating a new idea for providing services is fraught with many obstacles, and as we have seen, it is vital that you seek input from friends, family members, and other professionals. But to what extent do you "own" all the ideas generated in this process? For example, you invite three friends to sit down and brainstorm with you about ideas for new services for your fitness facility. In the course of the meeting, many ideas are generated. One intriguing idea is to add a new up-and-coming training technique that has only been talked about in theory but has not been formally introduced to the fitness industry. Walking into the brainstorming session, you had never considered this idea and it seems there is a need for this kind of training in your area. Also, you have a different friend who is familiar with this training technique and is looking for a business opportunity as well. Do you have the right to use this new idea on your own, or should you ask for permission from your brainstorming group beforehand? Does another member of your brainstorming group also have the right to use this unique idea?

then an investigation into the opportunity may be warranted. In discussions with trusted friends and family, the idea will morph and be refined. New skill sets may need to be brought to bear by the inclusion of others on the founding team. As a result, the generation of ideas is truly a process that takes time and interaction. However, done well, this effort should lead to a list of three to five businesses for which the founders have the appropriate skills and there appears (at least on the surface level) to be an opportunity.

To illustrate, consider this entrepreneur who had strong retail experience and an interest in opening a fitness club. This individual enjoyed working with people and had great orientation to detail. Three opportunities were initially identified by the individual. First, several large-scale fitness corporations were encouraging the individual to pursue a business similar to theirs in his city. These individuals thought the potential entrepreneur had the skills for that business and they could coach him in the business. Second, some experienced businesspeople in the area whom he knew identified a gap in personal training services that were available. There was a chain fitness studio in the small "downtown" area in the town, but it did not provide any really high-quality personal training, despite the relatively large number of potential clients in the area. The focus of the chain store was on groups, self-service, and high-volume/low-quality results. Third, this individual had noted a trend on the West Coast of the United States (not his area of the country): the growth of corporate wellness facilities, which fell between upscale fitness facilities and small-scale gyms. These corporate wellness facilities typically focused on a customer-service-based atmosphere. They featured an upscale decor and focused on meeting individual club members' needs, first and foremost. Thus, it was a different format than large-scale gyms he had noticed in his area.

Each of these businesses had a relatively high level of detail involved in the operation of the business, and the processes to operate the businesses were relatively well known. Additionally, each of the businesses required high levels of interaction with customers, and customer service seemed to be a critical element of the business model. The background and skills of the potential entrepreneur appeared to fit with all of these businesses. Now he would have to pick one business idea.

Initial Analysis

Any potential businessperson, as in the example above, will likely have several viable ideas but will need to identify one business on which to perform a due diligence analysis. Chapters 4, 5, and 6 identify the process for performing in-depth analysis on that single business idea. It is possible that after doing that in-depth analysis, the potential businessperson will decide not to pursue the business and therefore begin the analysis of business ideas all over again. However, the nature of the effort required to truly perform an effective due diligence study necessitates a focus upon a single business concept. The analysis and thought processes require focus, time, and some financial investment. If the potential businessperson is to be successful, she will need to move from the three to five ideas initially generated to a single idea on which to focus. Thus, the would-be entrepreneur in the prior example had to determine whether to focus further analysis on the large-scale fitness center, the personal training studio, or the corporate wellness facility. One means to identify which business to pursue is through a gap analysis.

Gap Analysis

How do you decide that a sufficient business opportunity exists and that you have the resources necessary to take advantage of that opportunity? Starting with the list of three to five potential business ideas that you have generated, you can now develop a chart that examines the issues that impact the potential success of the new business. The business ideas are listed in the first column, with a brief explanation of what each idea entails. (Later, each of these descriptions will be put into a short paragraph explaining the business and its opportunity for economic success. You should be able to tell anyone succinctly—in less than two minutes—what your idea is and how it will bring substantial success. Taking more time simply indicates that you have not clearly identified the opportunity or how it will work.) We refer to this as gap analysis, and it should look roughly like the one in Table 3.1. We have filled in the three business ideas generated by the small business founder discussed in the previous section (large-scale fitness center, personal training studio, and corporate wellness facility). However, you would use this form for your own business ideas.

In the second column, next to a given idea (and this may take several spreadsheet pages), list one category you will use to analyze the idea. We urge you to consider, one at a time, at least these five categories, which are crucial to the founding and successful running of a business: finances, time, nonfinancial resources, risk, and competitors. Each of these categories will be discussed in greater detail once we illustrate why this is a gap analysis.

Table 3.1
Sample Gap Analysis
Chart

Business Idea	Category	Our Resources	Resources Required	Deficit
Large-Scale Fitness Center High-quality commercial gym				
Personal Training Studio Family support				
Corporate Wellness Facility Positioned between upscale fitness facilities and small gyms				

In the third column, the potential businessperson should provide a realistic estimation of his resources in that category. In the fourth column, he should list his estimates of what resources are required for success. For the last column, the potential businessperson then qualitatively compares his resources with the perceived requirements of that particular business and records the perceived deficit, or gap. Then he can answer an important question: Is that deficit surmountable, or does it kill the idea?

This qualitative chart can be completed with minimal or no research. At this stage of investigation we are looking for a gut-level, reasonably quick analysis to see if the business passes an initial test. The gap analysis is intended to be completed by the entrepreneur or entrepreneurial team in a very short time period (about 1-2 days).

The second column lists "categories." These are categories that will be used for analysis. There are a number of categories the small businessperson needs to consider as he conducts a gap analysis. Following are the five important categories we have listed briefly. The list below is not meant to be exhaustive, as every type of new business will have its own unique categories.

1. *Finances.* You must examine the finances required to start and operate the business. A principal cause of small business failure is insufficient financial resources at founding. A new businessperson may have a good idea but run out of funds long before a sufficient client base can be built. This will be discussed further as we examine cash flow in Chapter 6. However, we feel that at this stage of analysis, the small businessperson needs to have a basic understanding of the financial demands of the business.

   a. Your resources—What financial resources do you have that you can realistically commit to the new venture? This should include estimates of savings, retirement accounts that may be closed, your spouse's salary, etc. Do you have family resources that could be committed to the effort? How much money could you realistically raise on short notice? Will this be a full-time venture for you, and can you afford to leave other employment to take it on?

   b. Business need—Estimating at a very high level, how much money do you expect to need in order to start and to stay in business for one year? Without a lot of investigation, consider the following:

rent, furniture, utilities, advertising, renovation, equipment, supplies, an employee or two, your salary, taxes, and fees. Take whatever number you develop and increase it by 50 percent. New start-ups take twice the money than was initially forecasted to achieve a sustainable level of operation. Is this number within the range that you would be willing to commit?

2. *Time.* It takes time to start a business. You will hear many successful small businesspeople say that they estimate the time it will take to do something from scratch and then triple it. Again, you need to assure that you have the time necessary to start the business. Each type of business started will require different time frames. This is an area that many small businesspeople grossly underestimate.

   a. Your resources—If you are currently employed, how much time can you dedicate to starting this new venture? Will you quit your current job to work in the new business? How much time on a weekly basis are you willing to commit to the business once it is up and running? What other time commitments have you made? Does your family support your efforts?

   b. Business need—What will the hours of operation require? How many additional hours will be required to manage the operation? Do you need staff early in the life of the business? When do you eat, sleep, etc.?

3. *Nonfinancial Resources.* There are other resources the new small business will need beyond financing. This list can be long and may include such things as special contacts with suppliers, connections to potential clients, and the physical location of the business. This is a category where the small businessperson should exercise some creativity as she analyzes her situation and the needs of the business.

   a. Your resources—What do you bring to the business beyond the financial? What unique capabilities/experiences/knowledge provide you with a competitive advantage? Are these visible to the rest of the world? Are there others, such as family members, who can provide other critical needs of the new firm?

   b. Business need—What unique skills will be required to run the business? Can you contract with individuals for the areas that you are missing? Can you obtain the resources in short order? (For example, to open a printing business, a potential entrepreneur might first gain a lot of experience and training working on various types of printing presses by working for different printing companies.) What unique resources are necessary to develop a competitive advantage in your business?

4. *Risk.* All small businesses have an inherent amount of risk associated with the starting and operation of the business. While it is determined by the entrepreneur, the level of risk needs to be commensurate with the rewards and within the tolerance level of the individual involved in the business founding. To determine your own risk tolerance, you should look at your own life over the past few years. When the economy is not in a recession, do you invest primarily in high-risk stocks or in safer places like savings accounts? If you invest

in savings accounts, then you are probably somewhat risk adverse. There are two types of specific risk you should consider: personal and business.

a. Personal risk—Risk at a personal level has many definitions and potential means of examination. It is certainly well beyond just the financial. What level of personal reputation risk are you willing to live with? If the business fails, what will you do? There is a strategic risk to starting a business when you are not ready, not committed, or not sufficiently funded. A failed business idea may lead to others imitating your idea and doing it better, or may affect your ability to pursue that or a similar type of business in the future.

b. Business risk—How aggressively does the business need to grow? Is there a competitive advantage that is fleeting? What level of product or geographic breadth is necessary to not only be a player, but be a success in the industry? What are the limiting factors in the growth of this business?

You can also characterize and examine business risk by considering three threats to business success: (1) threats to the profit margin, (2) threats to sales generation schemes, and (3) threats to operational financing.[2] Each of these areas represents a systematic examination of business risk.

a. **Threats to Profit Margin.** A significant threat to the success of a new venture is the challenge of establishing and maintaining a high-margin product or service. That is, can the firm make a high level of profit on each unit of product or service sold? What might inhibit your pricing or cost structure? Who are your significant competitors? Why do people buy services from your competitors? How will you attract people to bypass your competitors?

b. **Threats to Sales Generation Schemes.** A new venture must have the opportunity to sell to many customers and to obtain repeat business. The ability to develop a sales scheme that is broad enough to appeal to a wide variety of customers is critical to the development of a successful business.[3] Can your competitors meet or exceed your quality? Undercut your price? Position themselves better physically? Appropriate your clients?

c. **Threats to Operational Financing.** There are a number of specific threats to the new venture in obtaining the necessary financing for its growth. Some such threats are high development costs, rapid expansion plans, high equipment needs, and/or an entrepreneurial team with a low asset base. As will be discussed in Chapter 6, one of the greatest risks to a new business is fast growth. Typically, you will be selling things on credit but having to pay cash for your inputs as a new firm. Thus, rapid expansion can quickly overextend your financial resources. Research has shown that firms with higher initial capitalization have the opportunity to grow faster.[4]

5. *Competitors.* The small business also must be realistic about its competitors. If the new business is going to have to compete directly with Walmart, then the level of difficulty will rise substantially.

A firm like Walmart obtains the products it sells cheaper than any other firm because it buys in such volume. It also has some of the cheapest retail space available, as it develops all of its properties itself. Combine this with the fact that Walmart is so wealthy that it could lose money for years without going out of business. As a result, a new low-price retail entrepreneur who tries to compete directly against Walmart would likely end up as the loser. We would generally suggest that the small business look for a fragmented market with relatively weaker or more dispersed competitors.

There are many reasons why a small business owner would not want to compete directly with a large-scale retailer like Walmart.

To illustrate how critical the accurate evaluation of these issues is to the success of a new firm, consider a business we worked with at the onset of the Internet boom. This firm proposed to use the Internet to automate (and make remarkably more efficient) a process that previously had been done only through extensive use of the telephone—one call at a time. The former process involved making 30 or more phone calls to various individuals and then trying to coordinate their activities in a stepwise fashion while waiting for each to return the call (which usually came in while the initial caller was on the phone with another individual—these were the days before call waiting). The small business developed a Web-based product that would perform this function. The initial response was immediate and positive. The software behind the product was modestly complex; nonetheless, once it was available and visible, it could be imitated by a well-heeled competitor in just a couple of months. The real key to the business was to obtain commitments from the principal customers, of which there were less than 300. Once these customers (who were widely dispersed across the United States) were exclusively tied to the system, there would be an effective barrier to entry by a competitor.

The founders really believed that the Web-based approach, not the early commitment of customers, was the key to their success, and that the rollout could be incremental. They wanted to limit their risk and use cash flow to fund their expansion with a systematic plan to expand the business slowly. We pointed out that the critical limiting factor was obtaining exclusive commitments from as many of the 300 core customers as soon as possible, before the competition realized what our owners were doing. This examination of the importance of the customers changed the whole approach for the new business. The owners decided that rather than rolling the business out incrementally, they would seek to sign up the core customers as quickly as possible. The solution chosen by the entrepreneurs was to hire a sales company that put 35 contract salespeople on the project for 90 days. The cost and risk of this approach were significantly higher for the founders. However, the result was that before competitors even realized that there was a new company in the field, the founders had locked up over 210 of the 300 customers. The first competitor showed up 70 days after they started their operation and was able to sign up only 14 customers after a year in business.

For this new business, there was a significant strategic risk of misreading the critical factor(s) in the business, and a great idea could have simply

Table 3.2
Completed Gap Analysis
Chart

Business Idea	Category	Our Resources	Resources Required	Deficit
Large Scale Fitness Center High-quality commercial gym	Finances	Savings and some ability to get loans	Equipment, staff	Medium
Personal Training Studio Family support		Savings, loans, family money	Basic equipment, small rental space	Low
Corporate Wellness Facility Positioned between upscale fitness facility and small gym		Savings, loans	Significant equipment, expensive location	High
Large Scale Fitness Center High-quality commercial gym	Time	Full time	6–10 and high-volume work	Low
Personal Training Studio Family support		Full time, plus family time and experience	6–9, need support for customer traffic, delivery	Medium
Corporate Wellness Facility Positioned between upscale fitness facility and small gym		Full time	8–5, need lots of support, service, cleaning	High
Large Scale Fitness Center High-quality commercial gym	Resources	Little knowledge	Club management expertise and experience	High
Personal Training Studio Family support		Significant knowledge in family	Arrangements, design, stocking	Low
Corporate Wellness Facility Positioned between upscale fitness facility and small gym		Little knowledge	Facility preparation, legal requirements, system for efficient delivery and payment, insurance reimbursements	High

limped along because of a poor implementation decision. If the business founders had not recognized the risk of their business idea being copied, they might have implemented the wrong approach and would likely have been replaced in the market by a larger, richer firm. You can see that a business founder needs to develop an in-depth understanding of his deficit analysis on each business idea before moving forward.

Now let's go back and take a look at our entrepreneur who was debating between a large-scale fitness center, a personal training studio, and a corporate wellness facility. The entrepreneur contemplated the situation and developed the following insights.

1. *Space.* The large-scale fitness center would not have to be in prime retail space, since it was not going to focus on customers like the large chains in neighboring locations, but instead was to focus on business customers. The personal training studio needed to be in prime retail space for visibility and ease of access. The size of the space needed and the need for excellent access to customers would make the personal training studio's location the most challenging of all three.

2. *Competition and Profit Margins.* The personal training studio's competition would be the strongest, and the profit margins in that industry were lower than in the other two industries. The large-scale fitness center had good profit margins, but the investment in the equipment necessary was relatively high. Based on geographic location and population there may be more than one commercial or large-scale facility that could pose as competition. The corporate wellness facility seemed to have the highest risk. The nature of corporate wellness was eclectic and faddish. Individuals might want to work out before work or during their lunch break for a while. But many people would put off their workouts until after work, when they commonly want to go home or visit a gym near their home.

3. *Time.* The time needed to start up the large-scale fitness center and the corporate wellness facility would be longest. The time needed to set up and start a personal training studio can be quite short due to the nature of the space required for the studio itself. The large-scale fitness center would have a developed character and must be decorated, while the studio might just have white walls. Additionally, there is a far bigger staff in the large-scale fitness facility, so the need for extensive hiring and training is an inherent and integral part of the business.

4. *Finances.* The entrepreneur had financial support from his family as well as some personal savings. He had been laid off from his job, so he had a lot of time to dedicate to the business. He was single, so family responsibilities would not compete for his time. He was also dedicated to starting a business. The deficit analysis for three of these factors is provided in Table 3.2.

As a result of this analysis, the potential small business owner decided to focus his due diligence on the personal training studio. The due diligence proved that there was a need for the business (this concept will be discussed more in Chapter 4); that a successful and sustainable strategy had the potential to be developed (this concept will be discussed more in Chapter 5); and that the potential business had the opportunity for positive cash flows (this concept will be discussed more in Chapter 6). As a result of this due diligence process, the small businessperson established the business and has made it a success.

EXERCISE 3

1. Create a list of resources you think are essential in starting a fitness business. Next, organize the list in order of importance. Then organize the list in order of difficulty of obtaining the resources. Compare the lists and decide whether there is a correlation between the importance of and difficulty in obtaining certain resources.

2. Create a list of potential competitors to your fitness business in your community. Based on what you know of these competitors, evaluate each competitor's strengths and weaknesses. Rank the competitors in order of strength.

key terms

review questions

1. Define *brainstorming*.
2. Name as many sources as you can recall for generating a list of one's skills.
3. Identify at least two ways of identifying gaps in a market.
4. Explain the difference between a gap analysis and an opportunity analysis.
5. What are the pros and cons of high, medium, and low deficits?
6. Summarize how an analysis of all categories of resources available relates to an analysis of all categories of resources required.
7. What are the features of an opportunity analysis, and how are they best illustrated?
8. Distinguish threats to the success of a business.
9. As the owner of a small fitness studio, how would you plan to solve or minimize the following potential competitive hazard? On the same day two of your four personal trainers give you two weeks' notice; they say they have found higher-paying positions with a large-scale facility.
10. Based on what you have learned in this chapter, choose the most important characteristics and skills of a fitness entrepreneur.

individual exercises

1. Create a list of about six potential fitness business ideas, and then choose the three ideas that seem most interesting to you from your list.
2. Construct a chart with the same column headings as the ones shown in Table 3.2. Choose three categories with which to analyze your business ideas and write these categories in the second column.
3. Now fill in the next two columns, listing your resources and the resources required.
4. Then fill in the resources deficit in each category for each business in the last column.
5. Analyze the results of your chart and decide which business idea is best for you.

group exercise

Break into teams of three or four. You are going to be brainstorming partners. Following the rules of brainstorming as described in this chapter, your group should spend about 15–20 minutes and create a list of fitness business ideas. Remember that brainstorming does not involve evaluation, just creation of ideas.

Due Diligence on the Business Idea

Thinking Competitively

learning outcomes

After studying this chapter, you will be able to:

4.1 Describe how to examine the industry that the new business plans to enter.

4.2 Discuss how to create a profile of the target customers for a new business.

4.3 Explain how to categorize competitors of the new business using external analysis.

4.4 Explain how to construct competitive maps.

4.5 Ensure that the entrepreneur has considered a full set of concerns in his or her external analysis.

4.6 Differentiate between those elements of the business that provide a competitive advantage and those that do not.

CASE STUDY

In college Leslie Powers changed her major from economics to exercise physiology. Now that she had graduated, she wanted to do something productive with her diploma. Leslie had worked as a personal trainer at the Maple Grove Health Club while she was finishing her degree and had developed a clientele of about a dozen people. She was thinking of opening her own small studio gym for personal training, but she wasn't sure if she could make the business run profitably.

Leslie felt like a middle-of-the-road trainer at Maple Grove—she just couldn't seem to increase her number of clients and move into the top echelon. As she spoke to the other personal trainers about a path to success, she found a wide array of answers. This made it difficult for her to piece together a contiguous plan to grow her own personal training business and then transfer the same success routine to a new facility of her own. Determined to find more insight as to how other trainers find consistent success, Leslie began to go to other fitness clubs as a client. She hired other trainers to experience first-hand what these trainers were doing differently. Soon enough, Leslie began to compile some common themes from these interactions. And as an interesting bonus, she developed relationships with some great personal trainers that she thought might turn out to be a great addition to her own gym in the future.

Starting a small business should be based on the observance of an opportunity.[1] The recognition of an opportunity may come from a frustration with the way that existing businesses operate (poor service, lack of selection); a new technology that makes an idea that was previously impractical become available (i.e., an Internet-based service, computer animation); a hobby that provides you unique skills and insight; or a new vacancy at the perfect location for a business. However, while there are many ways to identify an opportunity, the new businessperson must be sure that what she is observing is truly an opportunity. What may appear to be a great opportunity to you may in fact not be viable as a business. The key to opportunity recognition is a detailed understanding of the external environment.

There are a number of critical steps in examining the nature of the external environment. These include the following:

1. Define the industry in which you are competing.

2. Define your customers.

3. Research the industry yourself.

4. Identify competitors within that industry.

5. Research those competitors and analyze their strengths and weaknesses.

6. Draw a competitive map.

7. Examine and develop insights about additional economic aspects of the industry, including substitutes, elasticity of demand, ease of entry/exit, benchmarking, and industry trends.

8. Determine your competitive advantage.

We shall look at each of these steps in turn in analyzing the external environment.

LO 4.1 Redefining Your Industry

The first part of an external analysis is to determine the industry within which the new business will compete, as well as the general makeup of the industry.[2] In doing so the small businessperson should seek to be as specific as possible. For example, one might ask, in what industry does a new smoothie shake store compete? Clearly, the industry will include other smoothie stores. However, if the smoothie store will make a significant part of its revenues from selling smoothie shakes, then the industry might be best viewed as including a broader group of shake providers that sell competing products, such as ice cream shops. If the smoothie store sells both handmade smoothies and prepackaged smoothie mixes, perhaps the industry includes natural-food stores and grocery stores that also sell ready-made smoothies. Defining the firm's industry is not something that should be taken lightly.

Basic information on the industry chosen can be obtained from the Internet, at the library, or via a magazine or journal that covers a broad category of firms to which you believe your new business will belong. While there are many ways to obtain this categorization, there are two relatively simple means available. At an aggregated national level, the data gathered on a firm's industry have some value; however, it is the rare new business that intends to draw customers from across the United States at its founding. Most of the data available will be on a national basis, which provides the new businessperson some information on national trends but provides little understanding of the local competitive environment. The national industry may be doing very poorly, while your immediate area might contain virtually no competitors and have the potential to do very well. For example, in the recent recession, housing construction businesses in California, Florida, and Nevada were severely hurt, while at the same time the housing construction industry in Texas and Missouri experienced limited economic slowdown.

The new businessperson should define the industry in which he will compete broadly enough to be inclusive of all potential competitors, but not so broadly as to be overwhelming. If you were starting a new jewelry store, it is most likely that not even all the jewelry stores in your area are likely competitors. If your store were in a shopping mall, clearly, other stores in similar malls will be competitors. However, if there is a Tiffany's in the same city, it might or might not be a direct competitor, depending upon the specific customer market that you are seeking to serve. Someone who buys jewelry at Tiffany's is not likely to purchase items in a small, shopping-mall store, and vice versa.

Even more important, the small business must be clear about the practical level of actual competition. For example, what is a reasonable geographic customer draw for a new small business? Opening up a sandwich shop in the downtown area of a city means that the shop most likely competes with other sandwich or fast-food shops within a one- to two-mile radius—and perhaps less, if walking is the primary means of transportation for downtown lunching workers. There are limits to how far someone will travel for a sandwich. Drawing a practical radius around your potential new business location will also help target the customers who are most likely to patronize your business.

Specifically for a small business, the **industry** is defined as those companies within a specified geographic radius that will be in direct competition with the new business.

EXERCISE 1

1. Define *industry*.
2. Name four ways in which a potential small business owner can start to analyze her external business environment.

[industry]

Those direct competitors selling similar products/ services within a specified geographic radius that is consistent with a customer's willingness to travel to purchase those products/ services.

LO 4.2 Defining Your Customers

Once the industry is broadly defined, then the exact nature of the customer should be developed. It is important to define a narrower group of individuals whom you believe will constitute your most likely customers. Where are they located? Where do they currently obtain the product/service? A new personal training gym that opens near a university is not competing against all gyms in the country, so overall industry figures for the nation, state, or even city are of little assistance. Instead, the potential clients are going to be the students, faculty, and staff of the university, along with the immediate residents of the university area.

In defining the customer, the new business owner should be diligent in the effort to be as accurate as possible. We will discuss promotional activities such as advertising in Chapter 11 ("Marketing"), but here we note that defining the customer to which your company caters is important for the effective use of your marketing dollars, as well as the satisfaction of core, repeat customers.

For instance, a potential fitness facility owner might view his target customer market as those individuals from ages 18 to 60, from all income ranges, anywhere within a 50-mile radius. However, we suggest such a view is unreasonable. What would this type of definition mean to the operation of the business? He would have to have services that appealed to athletes, teenagers, adults, and senior citizens in all price ranges. His original concept for the fitness facility might be an upscale

center with some "flash" oriented around the architecture of the facility. The broad range of customers he is targeting will demand to be satisfied, and all of these customers must be equally valued. This egalitarian approach is probably appropriate for a political movement but is a poor approach to business success.[3]

If the owner realizes the expansive—and expensive—scope of his plan, he may decide to narrow his true target to adults aged 30 to 50 with a median income of $60,000 who live within about 20 minutes' drive from the facility. This is not to suggest that he will, or would want to, turn away anyone who wishes to sign up. It does, however, suggest that the only clients that he specifically targets are those in his demographic. An outcome of this approach is that if a college-aged couple comes in and complains about the music played on the sound system not being contemporary enough, the owner no longer has to feel the need to appeal to them and change his music selection. They are not his target customers.

This approach helps the small business clearly focus on its core customer. It also helps the new business maintain a strategic distance between itself and its competitors, since the business is not trying to do what everyone else may do. Finally, a clear understanding of the business's customers assists the owners in controlling expenses, as the business does not try to be everything to everybody.

EXERCISE 2

1. Identify at least three demographic pieces of information that would help a potential business owner define target customers.
2. Name two reasons why it is important to be as accurate as possible in defining the customer to which a business caters.

LO 4.3 Developing the Information for the External Analysis of Competitors

It takes a lot of legwork, networking, and the use of publicly available information to gather data on competitors. Next we discuss a number of ways to conduct such research.

Research Your Industry Yourself

At this point in your efforts to start a new business, you should have defined the fitness-industry niche that interests you, determined who your potential customers might be and why they might want to use your services, and gathered some information on these domains. The next issue is to identify your exact competitors. These competitors are those firms that directly compete for the same set of ideal customers as your proposed business. If the new business owners are very clear regarding their customers' needs, then the ability to identify direct competitors becomes significantly easier. As obvious and mundane as it sounds, the places to look for these competitors can be as simple as the local telephone book and the front seat of your car.

While it is certainly possible to hire a consulting company to perform the type of customer research service discussed above, the entrepreneur will gain invaluable insight by handling this process personally. Let us provide an illustration. A small group of golf professionals had the idea of developing an affordable, nonmember 18-hole golf course in the Dallas–Fort Worth (DFW) metroplex. Their idea was to offer a country club–level course without the membership commitment and expense involved with playing on some of the area's quality courses. The group had a tract of land that had been in the family of one of the potential founders and had been given to him upon the death of his father. While this was substantially larger than the ordinary small business idea, we believe the concepts point out the critical issues that any potential entrepreneur must address.

At the first meeting, the golf professionals were clear that they knew the market and what the market needed. However, basic market questions kept coming up that they were unable to answer. These are some of the questions raised for which they had no answers:

1. How many 18-hole courses are there in the DFW metroplex?

2. How many of these courses are not tied to a country club?

3. How many rounds of golf are played on a typical weekend at these courses?

4. How far does the average golfer drive to play a round?

5. Are there capacity problems at some of the more popular courses?

6. How much does the average golfer spend in food/drink while playing 18 holes?

7. What is charged to play at various times of the day/week at each of the open courses?

8. Where is the population growth area for golfers?

9. What is the profile of a typical golfer?

It was clear that these individuals who wanted to start the business loved golf and thought they had a great understanding of the local industry, but they had not done a true in-depth study of the market. These individuals were frustrated when they realized that they did not have a detailed understanding of the potential customer. In response, they were ready to hire a company to collect this information, despite the high cost of pursuing that option. Instead, we encouraged them to collect this information themselves. Doing so would make them the experts in the area and enable them to develop a plan for a business that would give them a competitive advantage. The benefits of planning and analysis are the insights they provide to the individuals performing the activities. Hiring a company to gather information not only is expensive, but also limits the insights that can be obtained.

Therefore, the founders prepared a list of questions about a golf course that would help differentiate their business. After doing some quick research to find every 18-hole course in the metroplex, they divided up the courses and visited each one. The questionnaires that they developed were completed after each visit and an overall analysis describing the entire market was completed.

Defining Competitors

An effective industry analysis starts by identifying every potential competitor within that previously defined reasonable distance from your planned establishment location. What a reasonable distance consists of is a matter of interpretation, and the interpreter is the new businessperson. While someone could argue with any individual's assessment of that distance, it must be established, and this is much more a matter of art than a matter of science. In any case, the first step is to define a radius from which you believe you will draw a majority of your customers. Make this distance reasonable, not just a wish.[4]

For example, you are planning to start a small-group boot camp business in a medium-sized city. For the purposes of this example, we'll use Reno, Nevada. You need to define a reasonable radius from which to draw your desired clients. Your first inclination may be to draw clients from the entire metropolitan Reno area because you don't want to lose out on any business. We certainly don't suggest that you forgo business unnecessarily, but an assessment that a business draws from an entire metropolitan region the size of Reno is unreasonable for many reasons. Just one is that if you were to try to cater to everyone in Reno, you will distort your advertising efforts and dramatically increase your costs.

So instead, you decide to focus on clients within a reasonable commuting distance from where the boot camps will be held. You eventually narrow that distance to 20 minutes of driving in traffic. While you may indeed draw clients from outside this area, those outside the area are not your primary group at the outset. If you need to rethink this distance as your operations mature, then you can. The core information is already in hand and will still be relevant if you expand or contract the market radius later.

Once you have identified the area you want to serve, you begin driving the area to see what competitors there might be in the area. You also use the phone book. The end result is that with relatively little expense, you are able to identify those boot camps and other types of group fitness businesses that would be your direct and indirect competitors.

Once you have established a reasonable radius from which you will draw your primary customer, the next step is to examine each of your potential competitors. It is easy to discuss practices in the industry in general terms. For example, you might hear that all the area fitness clubs have poor customer service and long waiting lists for personal time with the good personal trainers. These general feelings about the industry may help an entrepreneur see an opportunity, but actually running a business requires more specific knowledge about your competitors.

[fragmented markets]

Markets in which no one competitor has a substantial share of the market and the means of competition varies widely within the same market space.

Small businesses typically compete in what are referred to as **fragmented markets.**[5] These are markets that have no clear dominant competitor and are instead made up of a large number of similar-sized small firms. If the small business is competing directly with large firms, this virtually guarantees that, at a minimum, the small business will be operating at a cost disadvantage and will have to compete on some other basis. In any case, the number and size of all competitors need to be detailed. Additionally, the differences in how the various businesses compete and their competitive advantages also need to be understood.

In the Reno boot camp example above, the ability to drive by and visit the various other boot camp locations as well as other group fitness entities allows you to understand the situations with each of those establishments, and which might be the strongest competitors. Straightforward observations made by a small business owner who understands the competitive issues of the industry can provide valuable insight. However, there is another tool available to the small businessperson that can provide additional information. Specifically, an analytical tool that has the ability to digest information and display this information to others is a **competitive map**.

EXERCISE 3

1. How is determining a radius around a business an art?
2. What is a possible consequence of interpreting a radius incorrectly?

[competitive map]
An analytical tool used to organize information about direct competitors on all points of competition.

LO 4.4 Developing a Competitive Map

At this point in the process, the amount of detail that needs to be organized raises the need for a systematic means to categorize that information. Thus, the next step in your external analysis is to develop a competitive map in order to better understand competitors and their capabilities.[6] While there are many companies available who are in business to examine competitors, as we have stated previously, we recommend that the entrepreneur develop this map personally, for the following reasons:

1. It is less expensive.
2. Knowledge of what is right and wrong with each of the competitors allows the entrepreneur to better position the new business.
3. Insights will be developed regarding positioning, pricing, and facility layout.
4. A competitive map, once developed, can be updated easily, providing a constant track on the industry.
5. Obtaining financing needed by the firm will be greatly enhanced by a detailed knowledge of the industry.

Developing a competitive map requires that the entrepreneur visit ALL of the potential competitors. Furthermore, we recommend that you be a customer at these competitors' places of business. There is nothing quite like the customer perspective from a series of such visits; the comparisons to your potential competitors become easier with this type of insight. With this in mind, the entrepreneur must develop a list of criteria that she wishes to take away from each visit and record that information after each visit. While this list might change depending upon the type of establishment, we suggest this list of potential items to consider:

1. Parking availability (how many spots and what quality?)
2. Access from road
3. Nearby services for customers

4. Size of facility

5. Décor

6. Pricing

7. Breadth of services

8. Depth of services

9. Staffing (number and quality)

10. Capacity

11. Brochures/advertising material

12. Customer traffic at several different times of day

13. Average sale

14. Friendliness/helpfulness

15. Unique features

16. Suppliers of retail items, if any (what company is delivering to their business?)

An example of a competitive map is shown in Table 4.1. This competitive map (for the Dallas–Fort Worth golf course discussed earlier) encompasses a number of criteria that could be used in the evaluations of the business. The eight-mile radius employed in this map is based on the distance the partners determined from their research that someone would drive to play golf.

Some of these items (and there will be other ones for your venture) can be easily categorized and analyzed. Others are more descriptive and give you a rich sense of what is available to customers right now. We have included a description of some of the findings from the group seeking to establish the golf course.

At this time the DFW area has 74 golf courses. However, it was determined from surveys with potential customers that, on average, individuals will drive no more than 30 minutes one way to the golf course. Therefore, rather than examine all 74 courses, we chose to examine only those courses in Fort Worth and those no farther than 30 minutes from downtown. This resulted in our visiting 24 golf courses, 25 percent of which were private. The private courses in this particular area are very difficult to join. The membership/initiation fees at these clubs are quite expensive, several are at capacity, the current members appear to be very particular about who is a member, and the benefits of belonging to the club are more oriented to social/business connections than to golf. Therefore, the focus shifted to the remaining 18 nonclub courses.

Of the 18 public courses, 5 appeared to be poorly maintained. However, the other 13 were in good shape, with at least 6 of those in excellent shape. In visiting with golfers at the courses and playing the courses themselves, the potential founders discovered that there was no difficulty in getting on the courses. Both the access and the nature of the courses were generally excellent. The fact that they were public courses was a result of city government subsidies.

EXERCISE 4

1. Study the sample competitive map in this section. Based on this information and your own understanding, determine the items (points of competition) that you would place in the far left column of a competitive map for your potential fitness business.

2. Examine the benefits of creating your own competitive map given in this section. What benefits would justify hiring a consulting company to answer questions and gather information about your competition?

After completing their map, the potential founders concluded that the competitive landscape was not at all what they had initially thought. They

Table 4.1
Competitive Map: Golf Course (Eight-Mile Radius)

	COMPETITOR #1	COMPETITOR #2	COMPETITOR #3	COMPETITOR #4	COMPETITOR #5
Population in area					
# of households in area					
Household income					
Average age in area					
# of driving ranges					
# of golf shops in area					
# of customers—weekday					
# of customers—weekend					
Average # of customers/hour					
Peak flow of customers					
Average charge/transaction					
Tee charge—peak/off-peak					
Clubhouse feel					
Course feel					
Variety of menu offerings— clubhouse					
Variety of menu offerings— course					

concluded that the DFW area was overbuilt and that the presence of public subsidies for many courses distorted competition. They decided that the market was not as attractive as they originally had thought.

LO 4.5 Additional Issues for External Analysis

There are a number of other economic issues that founders of a new business will want to consider as they develop their external analysis. These include substitutes, elasticity of demand, ease of entry/exit, benchmarking, and industry trends. Each will be discussed briefly.

Substitutes

The potential new businessperson should keep in mind potential substitutes for the activities of their business. A **substitute** exists if the service or product performs a similar function or achieves the same result as the planned business but is not a precise imitation.[7] In the case of golf, a substitute might be tennis or boating. Any other sport that the customer can pursue in place of golf could be a substitute.

In developing a competitive map, the small businessperson needs to be aware of such substitutes and the potential impact they can have. However, it is also important that the new businessperson not overwhelm himself

[substitute]

A product that performs a similar function or achieves the same result but is not a precise imitation.

with so many potential substitutes that it appears that there is no way to compete in the industry. Each new businessperson must judge the potential impact of a substitute, but the important issue is the recognition that at some price trade-off point, customers will switch to substitutes. While the substitute is not the desired activity or product, it will be chosen under some circumstances. For example, if you charge $500 for a single round of golf, individuals will eventually seek out other means of entertainment. Thus, substitutes can help form a ceiling on the price that can be charged for the product/service.

Elasticity of Demand

Elasticity of demand refers to how easy it is for a customer to switch to substitutes or not use a product as the price of the product rises.[8] A product/service for which customers are willing to pay virtually any price is said to have a very inelastic demand. In other words, for your cancer medicine, the price is irrelevant; you will still seek out the medicine and buy it. In this case, substitutes have very little impact. However, for a product that has elastic demand, such as rounds of golf, a price increase of $25 for a round may create a significant substitute impact. Chapter 11 will deal in more detail with the marketing and pricing of goods; it is sufficient here to say that the presence and power of substitutes need to be considered by the new businessperson. When developing your competitive map, you will need to include those companies that are close substitutes for your product/service and determine how to evaluate a trade-off value.

Ease of Entry or Exit

Another issue that needs to be considered is the ease of entry to and exit from the industry. Once a business is in operation, then expenses are being incurred. If those expenses are such that a small businessperson cannot easily recoup the investment, then the level of competition will be more intense. This is considered an **exit barrier**[9]—that is, a barrier that keeps an entrepreneur from leaving a business she has invested in. For example, the principal investments for a clothing store are the clothes in the store. Clothes tend to be very seasonal. If a piece of clothing is not sold in season, then it likely has limited value in the near future. Think about the value of white polyester suits if you need to be convinced. To close a clothing store is easy, but to recover the initial investment is not. The owner will need to sharply discount the price of the goods, often to the detriment of the store and its direct competitors, just to bring in some money before she has to close the store.

In our golf example, the initial investment for the golf course is very high, but the ease of exiting the business is also very high, since the real estate could be converted to another use, such as a housing tract. If a business owner cannot easily exit an industry, then that owner is more likely to use predatory pricing in an effort to generate cash flow and survive. The ability to exit the industry must be taken into consideration when evaluating the competitive threat posed by existing businesses. A clothing store would have very high competition, while a golf course would have somewhat less. In contrast to the clothing store, a liquor store's principal investment is alcohol. If a liquor store is not doing well and needs to close, there is always a secondary market for its goods. There is little need to have deep price discounts to seek to recover the investment. Thus, exit is relatively easy, and competition would be expected to be a bit lower. The ability to exit a business relatively easily tends to limit the intensity of competition in the industry and reduces the threat posed by a new entry.

Benchmarking

There may be specific areas in your business that you have identified as potentially providing you a competitive advantage. To strengthen those areas, you may consider **benchmarking** a business that is very successful in that particular arena but that does not compete in your industry.[10] The ability to provide a top-notch performance training center for your business could be dramatically improved by looking to companies in other industries that have excellent performance training operations. Most companies are more than willing to share their knowledge as long as you are not a potential competitor.

[benchmarking]
Working with and learning from a company outside of your industry that has a particular skill that is potentially critical to your operation.

Industry Trends

An overarching part of any analysis of competitors is an understanding of the trends in the industry. These trends shape the long-term perspective of the industry. For example, U.S. society is moving toward a more self-service economy, and companies that can move that process forward or take advantage of this movement appear to have an opportunity for success. Another example might be restaurant patronage. While the number of people eating at restaurants has not changed dramatically over the past few years, what they eat has been changing in a consistently predictable manner. Healthy, mid-price-range restaurant sales have been increasing dramatically. Thus, the percentage of individuals who are willing to pay a little more than fast-food prices for different fare is steadily increasing, while there has been little change in those willing to pay for very high-end restaurants. As a result, a restaurant that enters an emerging market (utilizing the Atkins Diet or another diet craze as a menu theme, for example) may be able to be among the first to enter that niche, and gain an advantage over other firms.

> ### EXERCISE 5
>
> 1. Detect and name some substitutes in a chosen area (i.e., radius around your potential business).
> 2. Propose a specific fitness service that could create a demand that is mostly inelastic.
> 3. In one sentence, compare the ease of exit of a small personal training studio and a large fitness facility. Include at least one reason why one business would have more of an exit barrier than the other.

LO 4.6 Competitive Advantage

Once the industry, customer, and competitor issues have been clearly identified, the new business must develop a deep understanding of its competitive advantages. A **competitive advantage** is made up of those things that your business does uniquely well, or better than anyone else in your industry (remember, the industry is defined by you, and consists of those businesses in direct competition with you in your area). This is the last step in your external analysis. We will discuss competitive advantage in greater detail in Chapter 5; it is important at this point to understand that these advantages (we hope there will be several) will ultimately be the reason that individuals come to your business and not to that of one of your competitors. Those areas that provide you with competitive advantages are the ones that

[competitive advantage]
The edge a business has over competing businesses, made up of those things that the business does better than anyone else in the industry.

are valuable, allowing the business to charge a price that exceeds that of its direct competitors while maintaining costs at an equivalent level.

A competitive advantage must provide the new business with the opportunity to make money in excess of the competition. Few new businesses perform better than their competitors in all areas, nor should they be concerned about doing so. Instead, there are many functions that a business must perform (and perform well) simply to be a player in the industry. In most industries the new business is similar to its competitors, but there is one (or, hopefully, several) fundamental characteristic(s) by which the firm exceeds the performance of the industry. These characteristics constitute the business's competitive advantage. In order to be able to define the potential areas for this advantage, it is imperative that you have completed the competitive map and are able to discuss the strengths by which each of your competitors stands out.

The source of the competitive advantage can be an activity of the firm, such as service or product selection. It can also be something structural, such as a high-quality location. The new business must be clear about what its own competitive advantages will be, as well as about those of its competitors. One of the causes of failure for new businesses is a lack of focus on their competitive advantages. Individuals might believe they have a great idea and work hard to implement it, but they may not clearly understand why someone chooses their business over that of their competitors. Your customers will have reasons to consciously choose your business, and you must know what those reasons are to maintain your advantage. In thinking about competitive advantage, it is helpful to examine the business as consisting of performance within two areas. The **orthodox** (normal) parts of the business must be done and done well, but there is little reason to do any of these things any better than the average in the industry. The **unorthodox** (unusual) parts of the business should be the focus of the energy, money, and time of the business, as they are the means by which a business can differentiate itself from its competitors. What is orthodox and unorthodox varies by industry, and it varies with time in an industry. The standard practices in an industry move, and they inexorably move to greater and greater heights. For example, when the frequent flyer program was initiated, it was unorthodox and allowed the pioneering airline to stand out, gaining customers and profit at the expense of its competitors. However, today virtually every airline has a frequent flyer program, and, indeed, many have shared programs. What starts out as unorthodox will (if it is effective) lead to imitation, and thus become orthodox in the industry.

[orthodox]

Describing those areas of a business that are simply standard practice in the industry and are necessary for the business to be a player.

[unorthodox]

Describing those areas of a business that are unique or unusual when compared to the standard practices of the industry, and that provide the opportunity for the business to gain value over and above the ordinary returns in the industry.

ethical *challenge*

How far can or should you go to collect information about your competitors? Most competitors will be private companies, and their financial information will not be part of the public record. Is it appropriate to be a customer of your competitor in order to collect competitive information? Can you hire a private investigator to find out information that is not in the public domain? What if the existing firm is owned by a friend? At what stage can you copy ideas from your friends and maintain your ethical standards?

That said, we suggest that the new businessperson examine his competitive map carefully. What is orthodox in the industry—that is, what does virtually everyone do just to be a player in the industry? These are the standard things you will have to provide just to be a business in this arena. What is unorthodox in your industry? What are competitors doing that varies from one to another? What can you do that is unorthodox and might form a competitive advantage?

The need to be complete in this area is critical. Table 4.2 explores the competitive advantage of a new restaurant. Although not complete, it provides a bit of insight into this process.

While this chart may appear to be a bit excessive, it is not nearly complete. It would be difficult for us to overemphasize the importance of

Table 4.2
Company Evaluation of Resources & Capabilities

NORMAL BUSINESS RESOURCES & CAPABILITIES (ORTHODOX)	UNUSUAL BUSINESS RESOURCES & CAPABILITIES (UNORTHODOX)
A storefront	A small, intimate facility
Tables	Fixed tile tables
Chairs	Roller, cushioned chairs
Floor covering	Tile floors
Lights	Mood lighting throughout
Cash register	Card swipe machines at each table
Signs	Custom neon signs
Menu	Touch screen at each table
Kitchen equipment:	
Freezers	
Refrigerators	
Sinks	
Stoves/ovens	
Cookware	
Safety equipment	
Fryers	
Plates, cups, silverware, napkins, salt & pepper shakers, sauce dispensers	
Shelving	
Tables & chairs	
Desk/work area	
Time sheets	
Staff:	
Cook staff	Trained chefs
Wait staff	Unique outfits; experienced, highly training staff requirements, formal
Bartenders	
Cleaning crew (tables, etc.)	
Host crew	
Management	
Trash cans (internal and external)	
Utilities	

developing this chart prior to beginning operations, so that entrepreneurs are clear as to what might form a competitive advantage for them. We have found few tools more helpful in defining the uniqueness of the potential start-up, as well as defining the potential start-up expenses.

Resource-Based View

To understand the unorthodox (unusual) resources and capabilities of a business and develop a competitive advantage, the new business owner should utilize a technique known as **resource-based analysis.** This tool helps the entrepreneur delve deeper into what creates that unorthodox ability. In the prior list of unorthodox actions for a restaurant, it was noted that tiles on the table could be an orthodox item. However, upon further consideration, the tiles are really just part of a larger resource that relates to the ambiance of the restaurant. The tiles themselves are good, but they need to be part of something more significant to have an impact. Resource-based analysis has been developed over the past 50 years by a variety of researchers;[11] it has become one of the most effective tools in defining a business's competitive advantages and in differentiating these from their competitors'. While we will cover this topic in depth in the next chapter, we feel that some introduction to this topic is warranted in the discussion of positioning relative to your competitors. The focus of this application is solely upon the unorthodox (unusual) products/services that you will offer in your business.

To develop into a competitive advantage, the unorthodox products/services need to meet all of the following criteria: they must be rare, durable, valuable, and relatively nonsubstitutable. "Rare" describes a quality that competitors will find difficult to obtain. For example, a particular fitness instructor's credentials or reputation might be unique, or a location may be particularly valued. "Durability" has to do with the length of time that you might be able to gain and hold a competitive advantage. How long would it take for a competitor to imitate you or to wash away your advantage? "Valuable" refers to your ability to gain extraordinary returns from your product/ service. A product/service might be rare and durable, but if you cannot obtain returns in excess of your competition from its sale, then it will not provide you with a resource-based advantage. Finally, the new businessperson must determine whether the product/service may be easily substituted by something else that a competitor could provide.

EXERCISE 6

1. Create a table showing orthodox and unorthodox business resources and capabilities for your potential business. Refer to Table 4.2 for an example, but complete your table as thoroughly as possible.

2. Assess the rarity, durability, value, and nonsubstitutability of the items you have listed in your table by using this scale: 1—high, 2—medium, 3—low. Those with the highest assessments are competitive advantages.

As you examine your list of unusual products/services for the new business, consider each one of these four dimensions. Those items that meet all four criteria are your primary points of competitive advantage. These are the points on which you should concentrate your resources, time, and effort. These are the areas that will provide you with a competitive advantage relative to your competitors, and will be the reasons that customers choose you over the competition. We will discuss this in much more depth in the next chapter.

key terms

benchmarking 61

competitive advantage 61

competitive map 57

elasticity of demand 60

exit barrier 60

fragmented markets 56

industry 53

orthodox 62

resource-based analysis 64

substitute 59

unorthodox 62

review questions

1. Name seven critical steps for examining the nature of an external business environment.
2. Give an accurate description of a target customer for a small fitness business.
3. Complete this sentence: Small businesses typically compete in _____ _____, where no one business has a substantial share of the market and _____.
4. Identify some questions that you might have regarding your market. For an example, refer to Section 4.3 to review the questions that the golf professionals had before they created a competitive map.
5. When you complete a competitive map, is it necessary to visit your competitors? Why or why not?

6. Predict an industry trend in the fitness business by benchmarking other businesses.
7. A certain market contains a hospital-related fitness facility with popular group classes, a corporate training facility, two personal training studios, and a large fitness facility with popular group classes. List the main competitive advantage for each of these businesses.
8. Are unorthodox business resources and capabilities the best competitive advantages to have? Why or why not? Consider the four criteria that make an unorthodox resource/capability a competitive advantage. What else could be a competitive advantage besides unorthodox resources/ capabilities?

individual exercises

1. Using the points of competition you outlined in Exercise 4, develop a competitive map for your potential business. It is not necessary at this point to visit your competitors as a customer, but do visit their websites or search for customer feedback about them on the Internet.

2. After you have completed your competitive map, describe the competitive advantages of each competitor. Include orthodox and unorthodox resources and capabilities.
3. List the competitive advantages of your own business. Does your competitive advantage really set you apart from the industry, and is it sustainable?

group exercise

Perform a resource-based analysis of a local fitness facility with which most of the people in the class are familiar. First, create a list of potential facilities. Then determine which one is the facility that most people in the group know. Next, discuss some of the orthodox and unorthodox business resources and capabilities of the facility. Discuss which of these are rare, which are durable, which are valuable, and which are nonsubstitutable. Debate why or why not, and argue using your knowledge of the competitive advantages of other facilities in the market.

Business Mission and Strategy

After studying this chapter, you will be able to:

5.1 Recognize how mission statements guide a new business.

5.2 Explain what constitutes a sustainable competitive advantage.

5.3 Identify a new business's assets and capabilities.

5.4 Distinguish which of those assets and capabilities are standard and which are extraordinary.

5.5 Apply a resource-based analysis approach to arrive at a list of true competitive advantages.

5.6 Determine a strategy to match the new business mission.

CASE STUDY

When she was first planning her personal fitness studio, Shawna knew there were already other established studios in her small metropolitan market. Shawna had a friend who was a graphic designer and had offered to design her studio's logo. They planned to meet to discuss her business idea, but a few days before the meeting, the designer e-mailed and asked Shawna to send her a copy of the mission statement for the business so she could start pulling together some design ideas. Shawna had not written a mission statement and used this as an opportunity to do so. The main reason she wanted to open her studio was so that she could be her own boss and bring her own style of training to the growing client base she had been developing as an independent contractor for several area clubs.

At their meeting, Shawna's designer friend didn't seem too excited about Shawna's mission statement. She asked several times what would be unique about Shawna's business—what special services would she offer that no other studios had. The designer said, "I could put your name in the logo, but that won't say a whole lot to people who don't know you." Shawna came away from the meeting deeply troubled. For several days, she worried that her business would fail because her name could only carry her so far. She was confident that most of her present clients would stay with her, but how would she get new clients to make the business grow? Other than word of mouth, how would she convince the general public that her studio was a good choice?

One day, Shawna was watching television and stumbled over a female bodybuilding competition. Suddenly, a new idea came to her. Shawna had been involved in bikini/fitness competitions when she was in college, and she realized that women who were involved in these competitions could use a one-stop-shopping club that would provide fitness training as well as know-how about the competition world. She knew that with her past experience she had the expertise to provide all the services these women would need. She wrote out a list of services she could offer, such as suit rental, airbrush tanning, online training, stage prep classes, seminars, posing classes, and more. By the time she finished the list, Shawna knew she had hit on a terrific idea. She opened her mission statement document on her computer and immediately began revising it.

[mission statement]

A brief statement that summarizes the goals of a business, and how and where it will compete.

[strategy]

The broad approaches a small business will use to accomplish its mission.

Defining the new business's mission and then formulating a consistent strategy for the business are two of the most difficult and critical elements in the success of any business. A **mission statement** is a brief statement that summarizes how and where the company will compete.* From the mission statement, the business then develops its **strategy**, which specifies the broad approaches the new business will use to accomplish that mission.

LO 5.1 Mission Statements

It is crucial to establish both the mission and the strategy of the new business prior to its inception. The mission and strategy guide the business development at its most crucial stage. As the business grows, it gets progressively more difficult to change its direction. Imagine establishing a new business oriented toward high levels of customer service with experts in each area of the business. The customers appreciate this extensive expertise, and as a result the business grows. However, the model that the founders have developed is expensive, and they wish to increase their profits. Therefore, despite the company's success, they decide to use cheaper labor without the expertise. The reaction from their established customer base will likely take place over time. It will not be a dramatic drop in one month, but over time customers will cease doing business with the firm.

Consider the example of Circuit City. Started in 1949 (originally as Wards in Richmond, Virginia) as an entrepreneurial venture based on a well-defined strategy, the company grew to be one of the largest electronic goods providers in the United States.[1] A dramatic change over time in the expertise the company offered its customers led to a loss of its traditional customer base and, more important, a loss in its unique positioning in the market. The result is that the entire business closed in 2009—one of the largest retail store closures in U.S. history. Sometimes firms find that they have to change their mission and strategy. However, any business seeking to radically change its fundamental way of doing business will find the road ahead difficult. The firm's mission and strategy are central to the new business's maintaining a clear vision about what it wants to be and how it will accomplish that plan.

We use the term "mission statement" here, but there are many terms used in creating the overarching goals of an organization. It is quite easy for a businessperson to become consumed in the proper labeling of the action rather than focusing upon the goals of the organization. As a result, you will likely see terms as varied as "company mission," "vision," "overall strategy," "goals," "simple rules,"

A mission statement is sometimes also called a "vision statement."

---

* Larger firms typically have a vision statement that is a very broad statement of the firm's direction, while the mission statement is more specific. For a small business we believe that mission alone is appropriate. The goal is to help direct the firm in its actions and not create unnecessary work. For a small business to try to differentiate between vision and mission would be splitting hairs. Thus, the student should recognize their differences in theory, but also recognize that here they are treated as the same item.

and "statement of purpose" to describe what we call "mission." The important point for the new businessperson is to be concise and well understood by everyone she works with as to what the company does and does not do.[2] We choose to use the term "mission," but we do recognize that others may use another term.

A company's mission helps the venture by targeting its efforts in specific arenas and on specific opportunities. No company generally, nor any new company specifically, can serve up all things to all people. Instead, the new business needs to focus on performing those activities where it has competitive advantage, or doing some set of activities better than everyone else. The company's mission helps the new business specify what the business does best in its industry (keeping in mind that the industry consists of those businesses you believe are your direct competitors). However, the mission statement also helps the small business stay away from things that opportunistically sound promising, but that take the business away from its principal focus. Realize that if you start wandering off to another area of competition, you will lose focus in your core area of business. If that occurs, there are always single-focused companies in any market that are ready to capitalize on your judgment errors.[3]

To illustrate the benefit of a mission statement in targeting a company's activities, let's take a look at a mission statement we have written that could apply to Shawna's business in the Case Study at the beginning of this chapter:

The mission of Shawna's Competitive Fitness is to provide top-level preparation for bodybuilding, fitness, and figure competitors, focusing on physical training, appearance, and show preparation.

Do you think this mission statement is an effective expression of Shawna's business? There are books galore regarding the development of mission statements, and the opinions seem to be as diverse as the individuals who hold them. There is, in fact, little empirical evidence regarding the most effective type of mission statement. We suggest that an effective mission statement and sustainable competitive advantage are inseparable. It should be recalled from Chapter 4 that a company's resources are generally constrained.[4] As a result, it is particularly critical that the new business conserve its resources and focus them upon those areas that have the potential to maximize the firm's success. A key aspect to that success is the firm's **capabilities,** or those resources that combine to allow the firm to perform better than its competitors.[5]

[capabilities]
Resources that combine to allow a firm to do things better than its competitors.

Designing a Mission Statement

In developing the mission statement, there are several key characteristics that should drive the new business founder(s).

1. Keep it short—Does it fit on a coffee mug?

2. Keep it simple—It has to be something that everyone in the company can learn and understand.

3. Make it universal—It should be able to guide every individual in the company each and every day.

4. Be specific—Tell everyone exactly what you do, and, by definition, you will tell them what you do not do.

5. Establish **measurable goals**—Develop a metric for every part of the statement.

[measurable goal]
An objective standard or measurement by which success or failure can be judged.

Keep It Short. We cannot overemphasize this fundamental aspect of a mission statement. The statement must be understandable and memorable for all those who come in contact with it. While it principally is written to guide the employees of the company, it must also speak to customers, suppliers, etc. It is not a tome that describes everything that you have done and might do, and how you will do it, so that the organization can impress external parties! It is a short, direct statement that is designed to guide the organization each and every day.

The mission of a firm is not "to make money"; that is a by-product of a good direction, and it is significantly more likely that the organization will indeed make money if the mission statement is clear, succinct, memorable, and known. We offer some past mission statements from established businesses as wonderful examples of effective and ineffective mission statements (Table 5.1). The poor statements typically are too long and too vague to be of use for employees of the company.

Keep It Simple. A mission statement that is not shared has little, if any, value to the organization. We have watched people spend countless hours crafting a statement only to have it poorly communicated and/or not reinforced by the senior management of the company. The new business owner must ensure that every employee can understand the statement and how it can be applied to day-to-day decision making. The key to the ability to communicate a mission easily is that the statement be simple, direct, and appropriate.

As the firm is developed, the founder needs to ensure that the mission statement is at the center of the various activities that are developed. Whether the firm is a new high-technology firm with Ph.D.s on the staff or a quick-order restaurant where many employees have no high school education, the workers will come closer to having an understanding of the mission of the organization if the statement is simple. The firm needs to ensure that the words and concepts employed in the statement are straightforward and have a clear meaning to all that hear or read them. A great line in the 2003 Disney movie *Pirates of the Caribbean* illustrates this concept wonderfully. The captain of the ship, somewhat taken aback by the demands and high-brow, patronizing language of his recent captive, tells her, "I'm disinclined to acquiesce to your request," pauses for a moment, and turns back to her and says, "Means NO." Avoid the use of lots of adjectives or descriptive language about how the company will accomplish its mission.

Make It Universal. It takes extraordinary care to develop a mission that guides the entire organization, and yet, for the mission to be effectively utilized by every member of the company, it must have direct applicability to even the most entry-level employee. Imagine the employee assigned to handle the customer service lines who is faced daily with customers calling in with concerns and complaints. If the mission of the organization is a long tome that fundamentally says "do good," or if it is like so many and simply exhorts the employees to "act like owners and maximize shareholder value," then what is the customer service employee to do? She will try to follow procedures and not get in trouble. Hiring people to follow procedures, rather than to use their skills and creative abilities, limits the employees and eliminates one of the differentiators of a new venture.

Table 5.1
Mission Statements

EFFECTIVE MISSION STATEMENTS	INEFFECTIVE MISSION STATEMENTS
Positive News Network	General Intelligence Corporation
The vision of the Positive News Network is to create, produce, and promote an alternative news service that will focus on positive people, stories, and solutions.	We view the Internet as just another medium similar to television. And, just as television programming comes to you via the networks at no cost to you, so too does our Webhosting service. But make no mistake, it's not FREE. It's just that YOU are not the one to pay us. Our service to you is advertising sponsored. In exchange for a cost-free basic website design and hosting we reserve the right to place one or more advertising banners on your webpages, just as ad pages are placed in a magazine. We then help you to succeed because, the more "hits" your site gets, the more attractive will be our server to our advertising sponsors. We see this as a win-win situation. Can you live with that?
American Red Cross	University Career Services
The American Red Cross is a humanitarian service organization, led by volunteers, that provides relief to victims of disasters and helps people prevent, prepare for, and respond to emergencies.	University Career Services, an integral part of the educational process, assists students and alumni in assessing their career possibilities, setting their personal goals, and achieving their objectives toward becoming productive citizens in the global community. While assisting its clients in identifying professional employment opportunities, University Career Services also provides the university community with insights into the ever-changing world of work to help develop realistic ways to better educate tomorrow's leaders.
Division of Geriatrics at UNTHSC	AmeriCredit
The Division of Geriatrics will promote health and quality of life for older adults and caregivers in the communities we serve through education, research, and clinical care.	To create value for our stakeholders by constantly improving our services, investing in innovative solutions and information-based strategies, and promoting a culture of teamwork, excellence, and integrity.

The mission of the business needs to be actionable. That is, it needs to help the employees to make active decisions in the moment, without having to refer everything up the chain of command. An advantage to a well-developed mission statement is that it is able to guide everyone in the organization toward the goals that the owners have set. A well-developed mission statement helps ensure that everyone in the organization is heading in the same relative direction, so that, although there will be some variance, there will not be decisions made that are counter to what the founder of the new business would choose.

Be Specific. In order to accomplish the three keys thus far listed, it is necessary that the mission be so specific that it clearly tells everyone what you do *not* do. Employees are constantly faced with decisions that appear to be of little importance, whereas they do have both individual and cumulative impact. A strong focus on a single mission statement keeps everyone in the organization constantly striving to achieve the goals of the owners.

[metric]
A measure to evaluate whether a person or firm is meeting stated goals.

Establish Measurable Goals. A **metric** is a measure used to evaluate whether a person or company is meeting its goals. From the mission statement, a new business owner should be able to develop a set of metrics that enable the owner to judge whether the mission is being accomplished.

Greater specifics on metrics and developing them will be presented in Chapters 9 and 12; however, a few brief comments are appropriate here. We typically recommend that each organization develop between five and eight measures of success for its venture. These are broken up into two categories: (1) quantitative measures—those that are tied to the financial or strategic goals of the organization and are easily measured; and (2) qualitative measures—those that are tied to the strategic goals of the organization but have more to do with the "feel" of the organization.

Metrics are best established at the founding of the business and are evaluated on a recurring basis. The baseline position is not nearly as important as the vector (direction and level of change) that the metrics are taking. We want to see positive movement on each of the metrics. They are the direct measure of the business's mission, and the more the business improves on each metric, the closer it is getting to its fundamental mission.

A mission statement is only as good as your ability to measure your progress in achieving the mission.

Mission Statement Impact

To illustrate the range of decisions that are impacted by the mission of the organization, consider three domains (advertising, location of the business, and staffing) for Shawna's fitness business example in this chapter and how they are impacted by market choice:

1. **Advertising.** If Shawna were to attract business from young women interested in bikini/fitness competition training, where would she place print advertisements? At which conferences or events would she set up a promotional booth? What kinds of endorsements would she seek from civic organizations or local professionals? What types of local organizations might *she* support (such as amateur/ professional sports organizations or youth organizations)?

2. **Location.** Given the single focus of the business, where should Shawna locate the business? Given that the potential clientele is mostly young women and teenagers, what type of location will provide her with optimal visibility and accessibility to that audience?

A mission statement has been called the guiding principle of a business, and yet many companies take the approach that the mission statement simply sounds good and that it should be carefully worded so as not to upset any potential constituency of the business. From this perspective, the real mission of the business is to make money. In fact, the real mission might be to make as much money as possible.

Customers, employees, suppliers, and the community at large all recognize that companies are in business to make money; however, no one buys from a business because it needs to make money. You don't use a dry cleaner because it really needs your money. You don't go to a convenience store simply because the store really needs you to shop there. Are businesses justified in not being vague or very general in their mission statements?

3. **Staffing.** Since Shawna's focus is on competition training and styling, how might her staffing decisions be affected? Is there room in her business for generalist fitness instructors, or should all her trainers have competition experience?

As you can see, Shawna's decision to focus the mission of her business on competition training necessarily impacted many fundamental areas of business planning and strategy. If these strategic decisions were made before the mission was fully formed, Shawna could easily have made key errors in the advertising, location, and staffing of her business.

Before founders can begin to build the new business, they must be clear about where and how they will compete. Almost all new ventures have a wide variety of activities that can be pursued. The mission statement should help by clearly specifying in which market the firm will compete, how broad a geographic range the firm will serve, and the major ways in which it will compete. If these activities are not precisely defined, the new owners will find themselves building an entity that in some ways is targeted to one business, and in other ways targeted to another related, but inconsistent business. Having everyone in the business moving in the same direction, toward the same group of customers, will provide immense benefits to the new firm.[6]

EXERCISE 1

1. Name the five key characteristics of a mission statement.
2. Provide a few key words that describe each of these characteristics.
3. Define the two categories of metrics.

LO 5.2 Sustainable Competitive Advantage

It was noted in Chapter 4 that a business needs to ensure that it has a set of *competitive advantages,* or areas of separation where the firm performs better than anyone else in the market that it serves. Here we will go into more depth on this critical topic and discuss how it impacts the implementation of the mission statement. In particular, we will examine competitive advantages in terms of a **sustainable competitive advantage**—that is, a set of advantages that provides you with the opportunity to make money where other businesses cannot easily copy your advantages.[7]

All competitive advantages eventually disappear as the industry generally trends toward those areas that are providing some companies extraordinary returns. However, all businesses should seek to maintain an advantage for as

[sustainable competitive advantage]
An advantage that others cannot immediately copy.

long as possible by continually refining their business model. A key part of building a competitive advantage is having a deep understanding of your customers' needs.[8] For example, a fitness club owner may identify the value of an onsite childcare center to watch after children while their parents work out. This may be a great idea that will attract customers if the client base includes parents of young children who are not yet in school. But for a club that is, for instance, situated in a downtown area and draws most of its clients from professionals on their way to and from work, the daycare center may be useless.

Traditionally, new businesses find that their greatest source of sustainable advantage is the personal relationships with their customers.[9] The development of a compelling personal relationship is something that large organizations find quite difficult. For the small company, building the relationship with the customer may be as simple as acknowledging the customer when you see him, or as complex as knowing what services he uses and suggesting new trends or variations in these services. The long-term difficulty for the small business owner comes from setting expectations now that you will need to maintain in the future.

EXERCISE 2

1. What are the three steps to identifying a new business's sustainable competitive advantage?

2. As you read, if a product/service has rarity, durability, nonsubstitutability, and value, it may hold a competitive advantage. Which two of these criteria are best reflected in the definition of a sustainable competitive advantage?

Prior to developing an effective mission statement, the small business must first develop a detailed list of what might constitute or what will constitute its competitive advantages. There are three steps to the process of identifying a new business's sustainable competitive advantage. While it is quite tempting to skip ahead, we suggest that the process itself leads to unique insights and will help the founder craft a business that has an opportunity for long-term success.

Identifying a Sustainable Competitive Advantage

Step 1: Develop a list of your business's assets and capabilities.

Step 2: Break that list into two groups: standard and extraordinary.

Step 3: Evaluate the extraordinary resources/capabilities.

LO 5.3 Step 1: Develop a List of Your Business's Assets and Capabilities

[tangible assets]
Hard assets such as equipment or a location.

[intangible assets]
Things that are not physical but are just as critical to success, such as a relationship with a key supplier.

The owner, or founding team, needs to develop a complete list of all the physical and intangible assets that the company will have at its founding. **Tangible assets** are those hard assets such as equipment or a location. The intangible assets are those things that are not physical but are just as critical to success, such as relationships and reputation. A key part of the **intangible assets** are the capabilities and skills of the founders or employees.[10]

Many start-up fitness businesses can be built primarily on intangible assets, depending on the focus of the services offered; however, tangible assets cannot be discounted.

Table 5.2
Tangible & Intangible
Assets

TANGIBLE ASSETS	INTANGIBLE ASSETS
Building location	Industry experience
Equipment (list)	Contacts
Initial financing (equity or debt)	Previous start-up experience
Inventory	Education
Patents or patents pending	Unique knowledge of the industry
Software and systems for business	(usually from previous research)
Build out of facility (list detail)—walls,	Skill set of founders (presentation,
fixtures, built-ins, etc.	innovation, etc.)
	Name branding

While this inventory process may seem a bit mundane, it is absolutely critical to the later steps and the development of an effective and focused mission for the organization. In evaluating the intangible assets and capabilities, the small business founders need to develop a clear and precise list that encompasses the breadth of knowledge within the founding team. This list will tend to be a bit long and should include absolutely *everything* that the company has now or will have at the point that it opens for business. See Table 5.2 for an example.

EXERCISE 3

1. Construct a list of possible tangible assets for a small personal training studio specializing in wellness for clients with diabetes.
2. Construct a list of possible intangible assets for this studio.

LO 5.4 Step 2: Split the List into Standard and Extraordinary Assets

The tangible and intangible assets can be further separated into standard and extraordinary, much in the same way we categorized actions of the entrepreneur and firm earlier as either orthodox or unorthodox. Most of the assets listed by a company are standard to be a player in the industry. For a gym assets might include a wide range of items, such as a building, weight and cardio equipment, locker room supplies, computers, etc. These assets allow the gym to operate. They are not things that necessarily provide a competitive advantage to the firm.

Some of the assets/capabilities that the entrepreneur or entrepreneurial team has, and perhaps some of the tangible assets, such as location, are potentially extraordinary. These are resources and/or capabilities that are unique, allow the business some period of time without a matching competitor, and cannot easily be matched by anyone else. There is a reason that individuals, or other firms, do business with a particular firm. The nature of individuals is that they are driven by inertia. Thus, individuals or businesses are not willing to make a change unless forced to for some reason. Your extraordinary capability will be the source of that motivation to do business with your new business. For instance, if you offer complimentary body fat measurements every time a client comes in to work out, this could be an advantage over your competitors.

The new business must have something that will motivate potential customers to select your business; these are your extraordinary resources and capabilities. It will be these extraordinary assets (or resources, if we consider the term more broadly) and capabilities that form a competitive advantage for the new business.

There is a wide range of potential resources and capabilities that can be the source of the competitive advantage. For example, customer loyalty can be obtained if customers are driven principally by something other than cost and the firm is the first to market. This is referred to as a **first mover advantage,** and those firms that come later are referred to as **followers.**[11] Such firms can benefit by learning from the mistakes of the first movers, but may not be able to obtain the loyalty of customers if there is any to be had. For the new business, this does not mean that you have to be the first to the market with the broad concept as long as you bring some unique resource/capability to the idea. A new business could never be the first to market with a general concept such as that of a mid-priced restaurant. However, you may recall from Chapter 4 that new businesses do not compete against the entire industry. Instead, there are limits to how far someone will drive for a restaurant. Therefore, a new business only needs to be the first in the industry that is relevant to a market. For instance, in a fast-growing suburban area, a new restaurant may be the first tapas restaurant in the area; it may therefore be positioned to gain a first mover advantage in that area. Note that in the Case Study in this chapter, Shawna built her mission counting on a first mover advantage.

There are other ways that a small business can build a competitive advantage. For example, a fitness studio that offers yoga classes could choose to specialize in a certain type of yoga that creates an advantage over other yoga providers in the area. A new model of fitness equipment can provide a competitive advantage. And physical location can be another source of advantage; those studios with prime locations that have easy automobile access might have an advantage over those businesses that are hard to access.

The range of potential sources of a new business's competitive advantage is as wide as there are activities in the business. But a small business's competitive advantage also needs to be defensible. That is, the advantage must be something that is not easily substituted away or matched by established competitors.

[first mover advantage]

The benefit of gaining customer loyalty by being the first firm to the market.

[followers]

Firms that enter a market after the first mover.

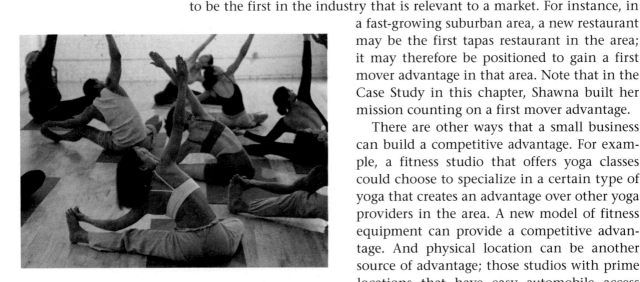

EXERCISE 4

1. Using the lists you created in Exercise 3 for the studio specializing in diabetes wellness, categorize the tangible and intangible assets into standard or extraordinary assets.

2. Would such a facility have the first mover advantage in your region?

LO 5.5 Step 3: Evaluate Competitiveness of Extraordinary Resources/Capabilities

Once you know what resources/capabilities your new business might have that appear to be extraordinary, you will need to examine each before you can claim any of these as a source of competitive advantage. Successful businesses generally have several sources of their competitive advantage. The new business may have a capability or resource that is extraordinary, but as noted before, that may or may not be the best resource on which to center a new business. The new business needs to focus its efforts on those areas that have the potential to provide the greatest competitive advantage to the business in its market. We refer to the financial gains garnered from an asset or capability that are in excess of the ordinary returns in that particular industry as **economic rents.** Ordinary returns in an industry suggest that you are doing no more nor less than the average of the industry. This should be accomplishable by simply matching the industry average for behavior, location, etc. Economic rents imply that the new business not only matches the norms for the industry, but in several areas, far exceeds the industry in a manner that allows it to charge well in excess of its additional costs.[12]

There are several means with which to analyze these resources and develop a small list of resources/capabilities that truly provide the new small business with the potential to obtain a sustainable competitive advantage. We have found the resource-based perspective to be the most effective method. For new businesses, there are four elements that seem to be most effective within this evaluation system—how rare, easily substituted, durable, and valuable a resource is.

Workout equipment is a tangible asset for a health club, but is it an extraordinary asset?

Each and every resource/capability that is listed as unorthodox in the previous step must be subjected to the following four questions. As mentioned at the end of Chapter 4, those unorthodox resources/capabilities that meet all four criteria are truly the keys to the new business's strategy.

[economic rents]
Financial gains garnered from an asset or capability that are in excess of the ordinary returns in that particular industry.

Is It Rare?

You must evaluate the uniqueness of each resource/capability relative to the competitors in your market. Is the resource/capability relatively unique for your industry? Can a competitor easily copy it? If it can be copied, how perfectly can it be imitated and how long would it take? These are qualitative judgments based upon the research and experience of the founder.

Is It Easily Substituted?

For every resource/capability that you determine to be indeed rare, you will evaluate the market for a close substitute. A substitute is not provided by a direct competitor but is something that satisfies the same basic need that is satisfied by your product/service. For instance, a Pilates instructor's direct competitors are other Pilates instructors or studios. Substitutes would be instructional DVDs or podcasts that individuals might choose to use on their own for instruction and guidance. As you can probably attest, any sort of fitness training is vastly more effective in person than on video. A video is not a particularly good substitute, and that is the question every entrepreneur needs to ask: How close are the substitutes for your extraordinary resource/capability, and are they good substitutes?

Is It Durable?

If you have determined that an unorthodox resource/capability is both rare and not substitutable, then the next step is to determine how long you might be able to hold onto those advantages. As noted before, no advantage lasts forever, but the new businessperson wants her advantage to last as long as possible. The time lag between the development of the competitive advantage and the point at which competitors can match your advantage is the window in which the small business can earn extraordinary returns. In some industries a competitive advantage will last only a few months, while in other industries it might last for years. This evaluation is done by estimating both the amount of time you believe it would take for competitors to match you in a particular area and whether you believe they would actually try to match you. Many companies have the resources to match the offering of any new business, and yet they don't. The entrepreneur's estimation of the time frame in which she will be able to enjoy the benefits of an unorthodox advantage is a critical element in this evaluation.

Is It Valuable?

The customer must be willing to pay extra for these extraordinary resources and/or capabilities. A key decision, then, is which resource/capability the customer will pay the most for. It is not uncommon to have a resource/capability meet all three criteria above, and yet be unable to attain value in one or more of the three means for doing so: (1) charging more, (2) obtaining more customers, or (3) reducing costs relative to the competition.

Table 5.3 summarizes these concepts.

Table 5.3
Components of
Resource-Based Analysis

CRITERION	MEANING	ILLUSTRATION
Rare	Few businesses have it.	There are only four corners at an intersection. Once they are used, no other businesses can locate there.
Nonsubstitutable	It cannot be replaced by something else easily.	After training several clients for years, you have developed a special rapport with them and understand their training history and their individual physical needs.
Durable	The advantages will last only so long before competitors match the offering.	Can a studio match the services you have in days, months, or years?
Valuable	Customers want it.	What you do is something that customers value and so they will pay more than what is charged by your competitors.

1. Produce a table that evaluates the competitiveness of each extraordinary asset you listed in Exercise 4.

Extraordinary Asset	Is It Rare?	Is It Easily Substituted?	Is It Durable?	Is It Valuable?

2. Interpret your responses: Identify the assets that will be key to the entrepreneur's strategy. Identify other assets that will be important, but not necessarily key assets.

LO 5.6 Strategy

While we have presented the content thus far in a sequential manner, the reality is that much of this is and should be done concurrently. An entrepreneur needs to build on his mission and develop an effective strategy for the new business. This building process, in which the mission is the firm's foundation, explains why such extensive attention is given to the development of a mission statement. The firm's strategy is how the firm plans to accomplish its mission. Thus, the mission is the foundation that the firm's strategy is built on. Strategy is a complex field of study, and we do not presume to cover the entire subject in this text. Our goal is to present the concepts we believe will be most valuable to a new small business start-up.

Michael Porter argues that there are fundamentally two broad means to view a business's strategy: low cost or differentiation. With a low-cost strategy, the firm seeks to be the lowest-cost competitor in the industry. A differentiation approach is one in which the firm finds a unique position in the market through product, service, location, etc. He goes on to argue that firms can narrow these two approaches to focus on smaller niches within those broad markets. He refers to this concentration on smaller niches as low-cost focus or differentiation focus.[13]

As a practical matter, most new businesses pursue a combination of these two broad categories. A small business is only rarely the absolute lowest-cost competitor in an industry (especially in an industry that is well established). There are actually several reasons for this, but one clear reason is that large businesses can typically obtain what are referred to as economies of scale.[14] There are simply many logistic/process areas that operate much more efficiently and cheaply on a large scale. The ability to gain those efficiencies from a large operation is called economies of scale. For example, a large firm (Kellogg's) owns Keebler Cookies. A start-up entrepreneur may make wonderful cookies that she wants to get into stores, but Keebler will obtain its inputs much cheaper than the start-up because of its systems and size. Similarly, its shipping will be cheaper and it will be able to rent store space much cheaper, putting the new small business in a position where it would be virtually impossible to be a lower-cost competitor than Keebler. As a result, the entrepreneur will need to utilize a differentiation strategy of some type if she is to succeed.

The new business will also find it difficult to be differentiated along all dimensions of a product or service (and actually may not really wish to be). Thus, the new business commonly will have what would be called a differentiation focus strategy. In choosing the elements where they may effectively differentiate, new business owners should reexamine the prior discussion in this chapter on competitive advantage. The resources/capabilities upon which the new business differentiates itself will constitute the key elements on which the firm builds its competitive advantage. To illustrate, the firm may believe that customer service will be one of its competitive advantages, so that should also be where it builds its differentiation and value strategy.

There are four logical steps in developing the firm's strategy.

Step 1: The firm's mission statement is employed to specify where the firm is to compete and how.

Step 2: A detailed strategic plan is laid out specifying a series of items that will be used to meet each part of the mission/strategy. This plan should include the area of the mission that is being addressed, the strategy employed, the specific action, the result desired, the person responsible, and the status of the action. This can be developed in a spreadsheet format for ease of analysis. Table 5.4 is a brief example based on Shawna's bikini/figure competition business.

Step 3: Following the approach outlined earlier, the strategy needs to meet the criterion of being defendable for some length of time (depending upon the industry, the length of time that would be considered sufficient may vary). The strategy should also provide the founder's (founders') economic returns above the industry average. If these two criteria cannot be satisfied, then the firm's strategy needs to be reexamined. However, if these two criteria can be met, then the firm should move forward with a focus on those activities that are defendable and have the potential to provide economic rents. The firm does not have to be excellent in all areas. Instead, it needs to have only those two to three competitive advantages that are its means of value differentiation.

Step 4: The firm's strategy needs to be constantly reevaluated. As noted, no competitive advantage or means of differentiation lasts forever. The small business must constantly evaluate its performance and its means of competitive advantage relative to its direct competitors to ensure that they are still relevant. For instance, using the example of Shawna's business, if a regional bikini/fitness competition goes bankrupt, then it is likely that the market need for Shawna's business will erode. She must continually reevaluate the market conditions that affect her strategy. This control function will be discussed in greater detail as we discuss analysis techniques in Chapter 12.

Table 5.4
Sample
Strategic Plan

MISSION	STRATEGY	ACTION	RESULT DESIRED	RESPONSIBLE PARTY	STATUS
Train clients for figure/ bikini competitions	Offer comprehensive services: fitness training combined with competition coaching and supplies	Require clients to train in studio three times per week	Place 85% of clients in competitions and gain notoriety in the fitness community	Founder	

Applying the Strategy

Implementing a strategy is about fit and alignment within the business. The key is that the firm seeks out a consistent set of activities around what typically will be a focus differentiation strategy. Chapters 10 and 11 will provide more details on how to build a consistent set of activities around the strategy of the firm. However, to illustrate the key role that strategy can play for the new business, consider another illustration from the fitness industry.

Darrell's fitness studio had been open for six months in a suburban strip mall location when one of his clients approached him with a business proposition. The client, Amalia, was a sales rep for a trendy fitness clothing company. It was a national brand, and Darrell had noticed the clothing appearing in department stores and fitness boutiques in the last few months. Amalia pointed out to Darrell that he had some vacant space at the front of his studio—a 10-foot wall near the check-in desk where there were a few seats and a large display board listing the week's schedule of classes and trainers. Amalia said that he could easily install a small retail area displaying her company's clothes. And, since the space was located next to the receptionist's desk, the receptionist could easily ring up the sales. Darrell liked the idea because he thought it would help his club's image as a trendy workout spot. Darrell agreed to the commission rate that Amalia offered, and the deal was made.

Within a month, Amalia had helped Darrell install the display. Amalia had been correct—he installed some simple racks on the wall and two spinning racks on the floor. The clothes were a good, attractive addition to the space. He moved the board listing the week's activities to a wall at the back of the studio.

As Darrell did his books after the first two weeks, he was surprised by how well the clothes were selling, and although he wasn't making a huge amount of money, the commission was a nice, small stream of extra revenue. The only problem so far was that he didn't really have adequate storage for the inventory, so he had four large crates of clothing stacked in his office, which was now cramped. He had also had to spend time tracking the retail sales in his books, dealing with sales tax, and keeping an eye on inventory levels.

A month after he started selling the clothing, the receptionist paged Darrell and asked him to come to the front desk. A client wanted to return a workout top she had bought because it had faded unevenly when she washed it the first time. Darrell realized immediately that he had not set up a return policy for his customers and he only vaguely remembered that there was a return policy in his agreement with Amalia. Not wanting to annoy his customer, Darrell took back the top and issued a refund. He later found that his contract with the clothing company did not allow for returns of clothing that had been worn or washed, even if they were defective. Darrell put up a sign stating there were no returns accepted on any merchandise. The following day, a customer asked if she could try on some of the clothes, and when he hesitated, she said testily, "Well if I can't return them, I'm certainly not going to buy them without trying them on first." He let her try on the clothes in the ladies' restroom.

As time passed, Darrell found that the clothing enterprise was creating additional minor problems that were adding up. Several times, a customer wanted to purchase clothes when the receptionist was on break, and Darrell or one of his trainers had to interrupt their work to attend to the front desk. Darrell lost count of the number of times customers complained about the weekly schedule board being moved out of its customary place in the front lobby. When the seasons changed, a new line of clothes would arrive, creating a disruption as Darrell had to recruit one of his trainers to help him rearrange the inventory. And when winter arrived, the lobby was plagued by traffic problems. Darrell's club was very close to a bus stop, and his customers who rode the bus chose to wait in his lobby rather than in the cold and snow. But now they really didn't have room to stand in the lobby with the clothing racks filling the space.

One day Darrell's early-morning receptionist, Eric, came to him and complained about selling clothes. Eric suggested that they not allow clothing sales until after 9:00 A.M. because he was so busy from 6:00 to 9:00 that he really didn't have time to deal with sales, or to answer questions from customers about the clothes—and he really didn't know anything about the clothes to begin with! Eric said, "I mean, really, are we selling clothes here or are we selling good workouts?"

Darrell looked at Eric and said, "You know what, Eric? You're absolutely right." The same day, Darrell called Amalia and started the process of canceling his agreement to sell the clothing. A month later, after the retail display had been dismantled, Darrell looked at the wall with the weekly schedule board hung back where it belonged and smiled. He was happy to be back in the business of selling good workouts.

EXERCISE 6

1. Write a mission statement for the personal training studio specializing in wellness for customers with diabetes.

2. Prioritize and select one part of the mission statement that differentiates the studio. Write a fairly detailed strategy to be employed for this part.

Mission	Strategy

---

key terms

review questions

1. Define mission statement.
2. Define strategy.
3. How are a mission statement and strategy related?
4. How are resources and capabilities related?
5. Create a mission statement for a local, regional, or national fitness facility that you know. Then go to its website and see if the facility has a mission statement online (check the About or Company sections). If not, look up another facility and craft a mission statement for it. How does what you wrote compare to the actual mission statement? What about the facility's mission statement makes it effective or ineffective?
6. Why is it important to identify the standard assets of a new business if the extraordinary ones are the assets that will provide the competitive advantages?
7. Think of a local fitness facility that you know. What are some of its extraordinary assets? Do a resource-based analysis of each of these assets (Rare? Easily substituted? Durable? Valuable?) to support your opinion.
8. Justify why a mission statement is important in terms of strategy.

individual exercises

1. Write a mission statement for your potential business.
2. Follow the three steps for identifying competitive advantages of your potential business.
3. Categorize your tangible and intangible assets into standard and extraordinary assets.
4. Evaluate the competitiveness of your extraordinary assets.
5. Develop a strategy using a table similar to Table 5.4 for your business.

group exercise

Break into groups of four or five. Suppose you are going into business together to start a local exercise facility that serves a midsized rural community. There are no other local facilities, but there is a large, franchised facility in the town about 25 miles away, where some of the local residents work. Together, design a mission statement for your new facility. Identify its competitive advantages, extraordinary assets, and strategies for the key part of its mission.

learning outcomes

After studying this chapter, you will be able to:

6.1 Recognize the fundamental importance of cash flow analysis.

6.2 Prepare a cash flow statement and a budget.

6.3 Identify other financial tools.

Your Financial Fitness

CASE STUDY

Studio 10 Personal Training

When Julius graduated from college his goal was to become a chef, not to help people attain optimal health and fitness. After graduating from hotel and restaurant management school, he spent 25 years working in some of the world's finest restaurants and hotels. Today, however, Julius is five years removed from the restaurant business and is the owner of Studio 10 Personal Training. The 3,300-square-foot business has been profitable in each of its first five years. But Julius had to be disciplined and clear-minded to keep his head above water when he was in start-up mode. Luckily, his past professional life provided him with some solid financial knowledge.

Several weeks before opening Studio 10, Julius met with a sales rep for a national fitness equipment company. Julius told the sales rep that he wanted to start small and purchase a minimal number of cardio machines. The focus of Julius's business was group exercise classes, and he thought that with the credit he had available, he could buy enough cardio machines to give customers a second reason to come to the studio. There was space enough to expand gradually into other areas as the business matured.

The sales rep worked with Julius in developing an order of 10 cardio machines, totaling just over $40,000, which was a bit less than Julius had budgeted. The following day, however, the rep called Julius to tell him that the equipment company had just announced a 65 percent discount on a line of weight machines that was being discontinued—for an additional $20,000, Julius could buy enough equipment to equip the area of his studio.

Julius was certainly tempted to take the plunge. He knew he would have to add the cost to his credit card, which would put him about $5,000 away from his credit limit once all his other start-up costs were expensed. And then Julius thought back to one of his first jobs in the restaurant industry. He had gotten a job as a line cook in a brand-new restaurant. Within three weeks of the restaurant's opening, the owner told the staff he could only pay half their wages for the next couple of weeks. He told the staff it was just "a minor cash flow issue" that would be resolved once the new month arrived. But when the calendar turned, Julius's pay was not restored. The owner did manage to install a sound system to pipe music throughout the restaurant. Julius scrambled to look for a new job and found one in a week. But he wasn't even able to give notice at the first restaurant—when he showed up for work, the business was shuttered, and he never heard from the owner again. Julius knew that the restaurant owner had overextended his credit and lost his business quickly because he could not maintain any cash flow in his opening weeks. He took that lesson to heart and decided to pass on the offer of the discounted weight machines.

At this point you have generated the basic concept for your fitness business, analyzed the potential of that business for success in the external environment, and determined what strategy the new business will use to compete in the marketplace. The next step in the due diligence process is to develop an actionable financial plan for the business. In fact, the next analytical step is perhaps the most critical in the due diligence effort, as the financial analysis of the business will most likely determine whether there is actual financial opportunity for your small business. Specifically, a new business must decide whether there will be sufficient cash flow for the proposed business to survive its early days and then thrive as an established entity. A good idea that is unable to generate minimally sufficient cash flow in some reasonable time is not a practical business idea.

Cash flow in the fitness business sense is money that comes into the business from operating activities, investment, and financial activities. This could include such things as accounts receivables and payable, investments, and sale purchase of stock. The cash flow statement identifies the cash that is flowing in and out of the business. When we discuss **cash flow,** it is important to understand that cash flow in a business is not the same as profit.[1] A facility obtains profits when its sales revenue is higher than its expenses, including depreciation of assets. However, generating profits does not put cash in the bank for a business. It is quite common to have products "sold" with no cash coming to the business. Credit accounts may have terms that range from 30 to 90 days, which means you will not receive payment for your services for 30 to 90 days. In fact, some percentage of these credit accounts will go past due and some will ultimately be uncollectible. Even simple items such as checks you receive from out-of-state banks may not be paid immediately, since a bank has the ability to hold them for up to 10 days after the check is deposited. Thus, you will not likely receive the money for your business immediately once you sell your services. On the other hand, a new business must generally pay in cash for its goods and supplies, as it has no credit history. Carrying inventory of any type results in payments for those supplies taking place long before any cash is received by the business. Thus, while many small businesses appear to be making a profit, they are suffering with a negative cash flow. Ultimately, the danger is that the small business will need to make payments in cash for its inputs but will have insufficient cash available from sales. In a manufacturing business, this cash crunch is actually exacerbated when sales are growing. A doubling in orders in a single month sounds great, but it means that twice the inputs must be paid for while there is no cash coming into the business to pay for the dramatic increase of inputs needed until those goods are paid for by the customer. A parallel example for a fitness club might be a club that has group-exercise classes for which clients pay upon arrival rather than in advance. A club owner may not be able to predict how many clients will show up and pay on a consistent basis. Meanwhile, the owner is committed to paying the instructor regardless of how many clients show up.

Cash flow is one of the most critical areas in the survival of a new business, and it is typically the absence of sufficient cash flow that is the main reason that a new business fails.[2]

LO 6.1 Understanding Cash Flow

The role of the cash flow statement developed in the due diligence stage of a fledgling venture is substantially different from the financial analysis developed for an ongoing firm. An established business will develop a series of

[cash flow]

Actual cash that flows into the facility, minus the cash that goes out of the firm.

financial reports for both investors and founders over some time period such as a month or a quarter. The data generated will include an actual cash flow statement, but will also include a balance sheet, an income statement, and a small series of industry-specific reports. Each of these financial statements provides a unique look at the operation of the business and each is valuable in its own right. We will briefly examine these statements in this chapter, and then in Chapter 9 we will provide a detailed examination of the means to use such financial reports once the business is up and running. For a proposed business, the financial analysis focuses almost exclusively upon its ability to generate positive cash flows in the shortest time possible.

This focus on cash flow is due in part to the fact that in the new business, the management of the facility will also be the owners of the facility. Profitability is applauded in the public investing community, where the members of management are generally not the majority owners and therefore there is a split in ownership and control. When there is a separation between management and ownership, profits are a useful measure to evaluate performance, as such firms are typically larger and have numerous slack resources. However, for owners of the small firm, the focus is on value and the viability of the business. Particularly for a new business, viability will be decided by cash flow, not profitability. The ability of the new business to generate strong profits on all services is indeed important; however, profit should not be the principal focus in the analysis of a potential new business. Profits have little to do with whether the business will be viable over the long term. The key to the success of a new venture (as simple and obvious as it seems) is its ability to bring in more cash each month than it spends and, more importantly, to bring that cash in on a cycle that is faster than the payout cycle.

One of the authors of this text assisted a start-up company whose founders had developed a device that sold for $199 and was used in the construction industry. The founders and their investors had invested almost $80,000 in the business (the firm's **equity**). The small business had been in operation for approximately four months when the founders asked him to come to the office for a celebration. Upon his arrival there were drinks and balloons to celebrate the first sale of the product produced by the firm. One of the founders proudly announced he had just made $100, a profit margin of about 50 percent on this first sale of their product. The owners were totally focused on that profit margin and had visions of a business that would now grow and provide them with a solid living for the rest of their lives. However, the owners had burned through almost $38,000 to make that $100. Total cash that had flowed into the company was $199; total cash outflow had exceeded $38,000, for a net cash flow of a negative $37,801.

Regardless of the profit margin of a company's product, there is a need to bring in sufficient cash to pay all of the bills. That small business was going to have to generate many more sales to have any potential for staying in business. Unfortunately, while the firm generated lots of interest and started to gain contracts for its product, it went through all of its cash reserves before it could bring in sufficient cash from sales for the firm to survive. This was another great idea that had lots of potential and a good profit margin but failed to produce a long-term business due to the absence of cash flow.

[equity]

Investment in a small business by the owners of the facility.

Of course the new businessperson wants to make a profit, but cash pays the bills and the payroll. As we stated earlier, a new small business will have to pay its vendors cash. Even after a small business is well established, it may have only 30 days to pay vendors, while its customers, particularly if they are large firms, may take upwards of 90 days to pay their bills. The small business has to cover that period of 60 days between when it had to deliver the product and when it receives payment. It may even be a longer period if your customer is a government entity of some type—for instance, if a trainer does combat or tactical training with local police or Army reserves.

This situation represents an important concept or term in cash flow analysis: **float.** This term reflects the difference between when the money goes out and when it comes in.[3] Banks commonly use float to their benefit. You as a business owner may deposit a check from an out-of-state buyer. For some period of time your bank account reflects no inflow to you. However, the bank generally receives the money for that check within 24 hours. This is because the bank is legally allowed to hold an out-of-state check for clearance for preassigned time periods. Thus, the bank has free use of the money during that period when it has received the cash but is not yet required to reflect it in your account. While the float from one out-of-state check may be very small, when those amounts are aggregated by large banks, they can involve millions or billions of dollars that they have the ability to use at no cost to themselves.

The small business owner can also benefit from float. Credit card charges (not including cash advances) are typically a free form of cash float, as the new business owner does not have to pay interest unless the bill is not paid in full each month. For anywhere up to 25 days a month, the owner has use of the funds without having any outflow to pay the bill. This is a positive cash flow situation for the small business owner.

An interesting fact, and one somewhat counterintuitive to most new business owners, is that one of the most dangerous situations for a new venture is rapid growth. Growth requires funds to provide services immediately, in a situation where the revenue from those activities will not be in hand until sometime in the future. The revenue from the sales can actually be far in the future, depending upon the nature of the business. As a result, the time lag during a rapid buildup of the business causes a cash crunch and is one of the leading sources of new business failure.[4] Active, accurate, realistic cash flow projections are critical to ensure that the new venture can survive by showing the founder of the new business what the cash flow should be over a given period of time.

Cash Flow versus Budgets

A cash flow statement is not a budget and should not be confused with a budget. A **budget** projects all the costs that will be incurred by the business over some period of time (a year, for instance) and allocates that expense evenly over the relevant time period. This is similar to what you might do for your household expenses as you set aside money each month to pay the annual life insurance payment or school tuition. At any one time the account for that expense usually has excess funds (except for the month in which the bill comes due). So for the life insurance payment, the annual cost might be $1,800; thus, the budget would reflect $150 per month.

An example budget for a fitness business start-up is shown in Table 6.1. This budget was what the business relied on as it started its business. It showed that the small business should have consistent positive cash balances. Note that many of the amounts in each category were the same from month to month.

[float]

The difference between when the money goes out and when it comes in. For example, if you deposit a check today in payment for some good, you typically do not receive cash when you deposit it. Instead there is a period of float before it is credited to your account.

[budget]

Statement that projects all the costs that will be incurred by the organization over a period of time and allocates those expenses evenly over the relevant time period.

Table 6.1
Example Budget for Start-Up Fitness Business

BUDGET		January	February	March	April	May	June	Total
Receipts	Training	$12,000	$12,000	$14,000	$14,000	$18,000	$22,000	$92,000
	Massage therapy	0	0	500	500	600	700	2,300
	Retail	400	500	600	600	800	900	3,800
Total Receipts		$12,400	$12,500	$15,100	$15,100	$19,400	$23,600	$98,100
Disbursements	Salary & payroll taxes	$4,900	$4,900	$4,900	$4,900	$4,900	$4,900	$29,400
	Benefits	350	350	350	350	350	350	2,100
	Contract labor	500	500	600	700	900	1,200	4,400
	Equipment	2,000	2,000	2,000	2,000	2,000	2,000	12,000
	Rent	4,000	4,000	4,000	4,000	4,000	4,000	24,000
	Insurance	450	450	450	450	450	450	2,700
	Maintenance	150	150	150	150	150	150	900
	Advertising	300	300	300	300	300	300	1,800
	Utilities	800	800	800	800	800	800	4,800
	Bookkeeping/ Legal	175	175	175	175	175	175	1,050
Total Disbursements		$13,625	$13,625	$13,725	$13,825	$14,025	$14,325	$83,150
Beginning Balance		$0	$13,775	$12,650	$14,025	$15,300	$20,675	
Equity Investment		$15,000						$15,000
Net Profit		–$1,225	–$1,125	$1,375	$1,275	$5,375	$9,275	$14,950
Ending Balance		$13,775	$12,650	$14,025	$15,300	$20,675	$29,950	

A cash flow statement does the exact opposite of a budget. In the example above of a life insurance payment, in each month in which no actual cash outflow occurs, the category receives a zero, and then in the month that the payment is due, the account will record a cash outflow of $1,800. While budgets are helpful for planning purposes, nothing brings home reality like the recognition that the company must have X amount of actual cash in order to pay this month's bills. Compare the fitness business's budget with its actual cash flow statement in Table 6.2.

The business developed this cash flow analysis after several months of operation, when it became clear that the budget document was not proving helpful in the management of its cash. The cash flow statement shows some shortfalls that should scare a business founder. The company (which started with $15,000 from the founders) was completely out of cash by March and had a negative cash position in April. The owner had to cover this shortcoming with credit card cash advances and was able to survive.

Table 6.2
Example Cash Flow Statement for Start-Up Fitness Business

CASH FLOW STATEMENT

		January	February	March	April	May	June	Total
Receipts	Training	$9,100	$9,425	$9,600	$13,330	$16,250	$18,000	$75,705
	Massage therapy	0	0	175	300	400	450	1,325
	Retail	390	475	400	525	710	790	3,290
Total Receipts		$9,490	$9,900	$10,175	$14,155	$17,360	$19,240	$80,320
Disbursements	Salary & payroll taxes	$4,000	$4,000	$4,000	$4,000	$4,000	$4,000	$29,400
	Benefits	350	350	350	350	350	350	2,100
	Contract labor	500	500	900	700	900	1,200	4,700
	Equipment	5,500	2,600	0	300	1,200	2,000	11,600
	Rent	4,000	4,000	4,000	4,000	4,000	4,000	24,400
	Insurance	0	0	970	1,700	0	0	2,670
	Maintenance	450	150	95	75	75	250	1,095
	Advertising	400	200	0	1,500	300	100	2,500
	Utilities	1,300	1,100	890	700	575	500	5,065
	Credit Card				500	2,250		
	Bookkeeping/ Legal	490	85	85	200	85	85	1,030
Total Disbursements		$17,890	$13,885	$12,190	$14,925	$14,635	$13,385	$84,160
Beginning Balance		$0	$6,600	$2,615	$1,100	$2,580	$5,305	
Equity Investment		$15,000						$15,000
Credit Card Advance				$500	$2,250			$2,750
Net Cash Flow		−$8,400	−$3,985	−$2,015	−$770	$2,725	$5,855	−$3,840
Ending Balance		$6,600	$2,615	$1,100	$2,580	$5,305	$11,160	

Note that the owners did not account for the interest on those advances that accrued from the date of the transaction—a cost they should have accounted for to better understand their financial standing.

One of the fundamental realities of starting a new business is that it takes a period of time for the new venture to ramp up sales and then to obtain cash from those sales. Much of the difficulty with this small business could have been avoided by completing a cash flow projection prior to deciding whether to pursue the business or not, and then using that cash flow projection to ensure an increase in the initial equity position of the new business.[5]

We utilize a rule of thumb (and it is only a rule of thumb) when examining the initial equity needs of a new venture that has proved to be very helpful in ensuring that the new venture has sufficient cash to achieve a market position. Calculate your entire cash flow projection without adding in any equity investment, and look for the point where the ending balance is at its lowest. Take that number and multiply it by 150 percent. We argue for multiplying by 150 percent because it always takes more cash than you expect. (It also takes more time than you expect.) That number is what we would recommend for the initial equity or equity-plus-debt investment.

For example, we took the exact cash flow statement from Table 6.2 and removed the equity-plus-debt investment from the projection to produce Table 6.3. Notice that in April the low point for the ending balance is

Table 6.3
Modified Example Cash Flow Statement for Start-Up Fitness Business

				CASH FLOW STATEMENT				
		January	February	March	April	May	June	Total
Receipts	Training	$9,100	$9,425	$10,100	$13,330	$16,250	$18,000	$75,705
	Massage therapy	0	0	175	300	400	450	1,325
	Retail	390	475	400	525	710	790	3,290
Total Receipts		$9,490	$9,900	$10,175	$14,155	$17,360	$19,240	$80,320
Disbursements	Salary & payroll taxes	$4,000	$4,000	$4,000	$4,000	$4,000	$4,000	$29,400
	Benefits	350	350	350	350	350	350	2,100
	Contract labor	500	500	900	700	900	1,200	4,700
	Equipment	5,500	2,600	0	300	1,200	2,000	11,600
	Rent	4,000	4,000	4,000	4,000	4,000	4,000	24,400
	Insurance	0	0	970	1,700	0	0	2,670
	Maintenance	450	150	95	75	75	250	1,095
	Advertising	400	200	0	1,500	300	100	2,500
	Utilities	1,300	1,100	890	700	575	500	5,065
	Credit Card				500	2,250		
	Bookkeeping/ Legal	490	85	85	200	85	85	1,030
Total Disbursements		$17,890	$13,885	$12,190	$14,925	$14,635	$13,385	$84,160
Beginning Balance		$0	−$8,400	−$12,385	−$14,400	−$14,670	−$9,695	
Equity Investment								
Credit Card Advance								
Net Cash Flow		−$8,400	−$3,985	−$2,015	−$270	$4,975	$5,855	−$3,840
Ending Balance		−$8,400	−$12,385	−$14,400	**−$14,670**	−$9,695	−$3,840	

−$14,670. Multiplying that number by 150 percent yields a recommended initial investment of roughly $22,000. With that number inserted into the initial equity investment for the facility, we see that the cash balance remains well above zero (Table 6.4). This provides a cushion to the new business, which enables it to pursue options it did not consider at founding, more easily handle rapid growth, and/or handle unexpected external shocks to the organization.

In developing a cash flow projection, the new business owner should contact vendors/suppliers to ask about payment terms and also check with

Table 6.4
Finalized Example Cash Flow Statement for Start-Up Fitness Business

CASH FLOW STATEMENT

		January	February	March	April	May	June	Total
Receipts	Training	$9,100	$9,425	$9,600	$13,330	$16,250	$18,000	$75,705
	Massage therapy	0	0	175	300	400	450	1,325
	Retail	390	475	400	525	710	790	3,290
Total Receipts		$9,490	$9,900	$10,175	$14,155	$17,360	$19,240	$80,320
Disbursements	Salary & payroll taxes	$4,000	$4,000	$4,000	$4,000	$4,000	$4,000	$29,400
	Benefits	350	350	350	350	350	350	2,100
	Contract labor	500	500	900	700	900	1,200	4,700
	Equipment	5,500	2,600	0	300	1,200	2,000	11,600
	Rent	4,000	4,000	4,000	4,000	4,000	4,000	24,400
	Insurance	0	0	970	1,700	0	0	2,670
	Maintenance	450	150	95	75	75	250	1,095
	Advertising	400	200	0	1,500	300	100	2,500
	Utilities	1,300	1,100	890	700	575	500	5,065
	Credit Card				500	2,250		
	Bookkeeping/ Legal	490	85	85	200	85	85	1,030
Total Disbursements		$17,890	$13,885	$12,190	$14,925	$14,635	$13,385	$84,160
Beginning Balance		$0	$13,600	$9,615	$7,600	$7,300	$12,305	
Equity Investment		$22,000						
Credit Card Advance								
Net Cash Flow		−$8,400	−$3,985	−$2,015	−$270	$4,975	$5,855	−$3,840
Ending Balance		$13,600	$9,615	$7,600	$7,330	$12,305	$18,160	

credit card companies to get exact information about when accounts will be processed and what percentage will be charged to the company for each transaction. These interactions also allow the new business owner to seek out the best terms possible from vendors and suppliers. In the next section of this chapter, we will suggest a specific series of items to be accounted for as you develop your cash flow statement. Once the venture begins operations, actual cash flow should be compared monthly to the projected cash flow statement in order to produce a **deviation analysis,** an analysis of how the predicted and actual cash flows differ. This will not only assist the new business owner in developing realistic forecasts for the business in the future, but also point out differences between actual performance and predicted performance at a point in time. Taking the time each month to examine this allows the new businessperson maximum flexibility in making changes to the business as it grows (a habit that will help keep the venture responsive as the venture develops). Chapter 9 will go into greater detail on such comparisons and how to analyze and respond to the deviations that are identified. To illustrate, Table 6.5 shows one month's cash flow deviation analysis from the fitness firm we have been discussing. This form may also be called a profit/loss form.

[deviation analysis]
Analysis of the differences between the predicted and the actual performance.

DEVIATION ANALYSIS

Table 6.5
Example Deviation Analysis for Start-Up Fitness Business

		January–Predicted	January–Actual	Difference
Receipts	Training	$12,000	$9,100	–$2,900
	Massage therapy	0	0	0
	Retail	400	390	–10
Total Receipts		$12,400	$9,490	–$2,910
Disbursements	Salary & payroll taxes	$4,900	$4,900	$0
	Benefits	350	350	0
	Contract labor	500	500	0
	Equipment	2,000	5,500	3,500
	Rent	4,000	4,000	0
	Insurance	450	0	–450
	Maintenance	150	450	300
	Advertising	300	400	100
	Utilities	800	1,300	500
	Bookkeeping/ Legal	175	490	315
Total Disbursements		$13,625	$17,890	$4,265
Beginning Balance		$0	$0	$0
Equity Investment		$15,000	$15,000	$0
Net Cash Flow		–$1,225	–$8,400	–$7,175
Ending Balance		$13,775	$6,600	–$7,175

EXERCISE 1

1. What is the greatest reason that a new business fails?
2. Name another leading cause of the failure of a new business, and explain how it causes failure (despite the fact that it seems counterintuitive).
3. Explain how cash flow and budget are different.
4. Identify the items that are compared in a deviation analysis. Summarize some of the benefits of creating a cash flow deviation analysis.
5. How would a fitness business's cash flow be affected by selling a package of five prepaid training sessions to customers? Is the effect on cash flow positive or negative?

In this example, the fitness business's revenues fell $2,910 short of the owners' predictions and their expenses were $4,265 more than they had expected. This type of cash analysis provides valuable information to the owners of this new company. Why were sales below expectations? Why was equipment expense so high? Note that the business spent relatively little on advertising; perhaps this is why sales were less than expected. Some expenses need to be made in order to increase the opportunity for success on the revenue side, so we are not suggesting that the new venture attempt to cut its way to success; instead we suggest a careful monthly analysis of all actual revenues and expenses.

LO 6.2 Developing Cash Flow Statements

There are several key issues that should be noted in developing a cash flow statement. The first is that a cash flow statement for a new business is substantially different from the typical corporate annual report that you may have seen. New businesses, unlike established companies, are unlikely to have either investing activities or financing activities (interest on notes/loans is included in the operations section of new business cash flow statements). New business ventures typically have only one type of activity: operations. Everything that involves cash in/cash out is related to the operation of the business.

The cash flow statement is used to describe all of the activities that provide and use cash during the period being examined (we would recommend that the statement be done monthly until the business is well established). Used effectively, this statement helps the owners accurately keep track of the overall cash position of the business and provides a well-respected and accepted means of displaying the ability of the company

ethical *challenge*

Positive cash flow is vital to a start-up business, so the pressure to bring in every dollar immediately upon rendering services is tremendous. Fitness clubs typically have cancellation policies for missed appointments—for instance, if a client does not cancel an appointment at least 24 hours before it is scheduled, she will be charged 100% of the fee if she does not show up. Also, most health and fitness facilities state cut-off dates for buying discounted multiple-session packages up-front. These can be touchy subjects with clients, especially for a new business trying to woo new clients. Many clients think these policies are just formalities and may expect them to be waived. Some clubs do waive these fees on a case-by-case basis. You want to be flexible and accommodate your clients' wishes if only to keep them happy and returning to your club; on the other hand, you have a responsibility to maximize your cash flow and make sure that every open time slot in your calendar is producing revenue. So if a new client asks for these fees to be waived, how do you respond?

to meet its obligations. As the business grows, a well-developed, accurate long-term track record of cash flow statements and their comparison to plan will go a long way toward assisting the company with loans, credit lines, infusions of equity capital, and even valuation, should the business-person want to sell the company.

Generating the cash flow statement should actually begin with the expenses of the organization, for the very simple reason that they are easier to accurately forecast than are revenues. Expenses fall into a number of categories that are inclusive of, but not limited to, the following list:

- Salaries
- Basic Benefits
- Taxes/Fees
  - Payroll
  - Income
  - Local
  - State
  - Business
  - Licenses
- Cost of Goods Sold
  - T-shirts
  - Nutritional Supplements
  - Direct Labor
- Utilities (Electricity, Gas, Phone Service, etc.)
- Security Systems
- Equipment
- Office Supplies (a big and often underestimated expense)
- Travel
- Insurance
- Advertising
- Furniture/Computers
- Telephones
- Maintenance of Equipment
- Cleaning (either a service or supplies for your use)
- Rent/Mortgage

In short, all actual expenses must be accounted for in the cash flow statement. If your specific business has unique expenses that do not fit into these categories, note that you also need to add those expenses to this list.

Revenues (cash inflows) should be separated into as many categories as possible in order to provide maximum insight to the owner. Separating out revenue lines aids both in predicting where the firm's revenues will come from and in analyzing the actual revenue sources for the business. The following are some of the revenue categories that a fitness business might include on its statement:

- Personal Training
  — James
  — Marcia

- — Monique
- — Alexa
- Group Exercise
  - — James
  - — Marcia
  - — Nathan
- Pilates
  - — James
  - — Monique
- Yoga
  - — Benita
- Retail/Snack Bar
  - — Clothing
  - — Equipment
  - — Supplements
  - — Food
  - — Beverages

Once there is a fine-grained understanding, categories can be collapsed together if a more general-level categorization is desired.

As the examples above suggest, generating a cash flow statement should be tailored to the information needs of the new venture. The lists above are not meant to be exhaustive. In general, we recommend that each unique area of the business that generates income should be given a separate revenue line item.

A final comment regarding cash flow statements concerns the development of a **sensitivity analysis.**[6] The cash flow statement developed above could best be labeled a "most-likely-case" scenario. It is also quite prudent to look at a worst-case and a best-case scenario to examine the sensitivity of the potential cash flow to dramatic changes in the revenue or cost stream when conducting due diligence on a business idea. The sensitivity analysis is a judgment call by the new businessperson about whether the business could survive the worst-case or successfully carry out the best-case scenario.

To better understand your financial situation, our advice is that you take the revenue figures developed in your most-likely scenario and create two new cash flow statements (see Table 6.6). One increases monthly revenue by 25 percent and the other decreases monthly revenue by 25 percent. What is the effect upon your net cash flow? Could your new venture survive either of these situations? What changes might you make to accommodate the new outcomes?

The owners of a full-service health club developed best- and worst-case scenarios in their cash flow projections. The worst-case scenario painted a picture of events that the founders of the small business could not survive. This did

[sensitivity analysis]
An examination of the best- and worst-case cash flow scenarios.

EXERCISE 2

1. Construct two lists of categories and line items, one for your proposed business's expenses and one for its revenues.

2. Create a six-month projected cash flow statement using the lists you just created. Use the most likely scenario, and DO assume that you would receive an initial equity investment.

3. In conducting due diligence on your business idea, hypothesize about and list events that could dramatically change the revenues or expenses in the cash flow statement you just created. These dramatic changes may have a positive or negative effect on revenues or expenses.

4. Considering the information you just listed, construct a projected cash flow statement for a best-case scenario and another one for a worst-case scenario.

Table 6.6
Revenue-Side Cash Flow
Statements: Best Case/
Worst Case

BEST CASE

	January	February	March	April	Total
Receipts					
Personal Training	$10,100	$10,000	$12,100	$12,000	$44,200
Group Exercise	13,500	12,700	12,250	11,500	49,950
Pilates	6,000	6,900	5,900	6,000	24,800
Yoga	6,600	6,150	6,850	6,650	26,250
Retail/Snack Bar	3,550	3,700	3,650	3,900	14,800
Total Receipts	$39,750	$39,450	$40,750	$40,050	$160,000

WORST CASE

	January	February	March	April	Total
Receipts					
Personal Training	$6,900	$6,500	$6,100	$6,500	$26,000
Group Exercise	9,000	9,000	8,500	8,100	34,600
Pilates	3,550	3,500	3,000	3,500	13,550
Yoga	3,150	3,000	4,000	3,500	13,650
Retail/Snack Bar	2,000	2,000	2,200	2,000	8,200
Total Receipts	$24,600	$24,000	$23,800	$23,600	$96,000

not lead the entrepreneurs to give up. Instead, they worked to control their immediate costs through methods such as negotiating with their landlord to pay lower rent until they reached the break-even point. The result was that the founders were able to revise their cash flows such that even a worst-case scenario would be survivable.

LO 6.3 Other Financial Tools

The focus thus far in this chapter has been exclusively on cash flow. This focus is consistent with the view that cash is king in small business. However, there are other financial tools that are very helpful in analyzing a new business idea. Specifically, an income statement is a necessary tool.

Income Statement

An **income statement** projects the income of the business, focusing on profit rather than cash flow. While we emphasize cash flow as a foundation for analyzing the potential viability of the new business, we believe an understanding of profit allows the projected business to understand its overall cost picture. It is not unusual for a new business to take a significant amount of time to reach overall profitability.

[income statement]
Revenue of the firm minus expenses.

One of the keys to developing an income statement is predicting sales for the organization. While there is much more art than science to this process, there are some techniques available to assist the new businessperson. The new owner should initially look to similar enterprises and attempt to estimate or research their sales levels. If a club with a similar format to yours is available, for example, you can estimate its sales by taking the average membership price and multiplying that by the traffic flow through the club. You can estimate traffic flow by sitting in the parking lot and keeping a count of how many clients go in the door. Talking with entrepreneurs in the same domain against whom you will not compete was cited in Chapter 3 (identifying the idea) and in Chapter 4 (external analysis) as an excellent source of information. These same individuals will have considerable expertise on what sales levels could be expected at various stages in the new business's growth. The key is to be conservative because the reality is that things never happen as fast or as smoothly as you would hope in founding your business.

The entrepreneur may come to the conclusion that there are 25,000 people who live in the area around his fitness club who are potential customers. The owner cannot (and should not) assume he will get all or even a majority of those people as customers. It is better to be very conservative and underestimate demand for a product or service than to overestimate demand. What percentage of the general population uses personal training on a weekly basis? What are the demographics of the typical personal training customer? How far will the typical customer drive to see a personal trainer two to four times per week? What are the primary drivers for joining a personal training club versus the closest large commercial gym that also has personal and group training? How is the industry tracking? These and many other questions will assist the new businessperson in estimating the potential sales of his new venture. Additionally, the entrepreneur needs to realize that sales growth is a function of time and should not assume that the new venture will reach an established company's sales volume in the short run. The new business venture needs to make conservative predictions regarding demand. Again, successful entrepreneurs are the new businessperson's best resource.

The income statement provides both the gross and the net profit figures for the company. In its simplified form, gross profit generally equals the sales of the organization minus the cost of goods or services sold. The facility then calculates all other expenses, such as salaries and benefits, to reach a total expense for the firm. Gross profit minus all other expenses yields net profit before taxes. Lastly, estimated taxes are calculated and subtracted from net profit to determine the company's net profit after taxes. A sample income statement for the fitness business discussed previously is shown in Table 6.7. Note that the cost of goods and services sold is very small, as providing fitness training requires virtually no production costs. If this were, for instance, a restaurant, the cost of goods sold would be much higher.

Break-Even Analysis

It is time to look at one additional analytical tool. The initial effort to project cash flow is critical. However, the start-up business needs to extend this analysis. Specifically, what are the opportunities for the new venture to really generate significant returns for the owners? Individuals have

Table 6.7
Example Income Statement for Fitness Business

		January	February	March	April	May	June	Total
Receipts	Training	$9,100	$9,425	$9,600	$13,330	$16,250	$18,000	$75,705
	Massage therapy	0	0	175	300	400	450	1,325
	Retail	390	475	400	525	710	790	3,290
Total Income		$9,490	$9,900	$10,675	$14,155	$17,360	$19,240	$80,320
Cost of Goods and Services Sold								
	Retail inventory	$3,200	$2,000	$1,500	$1,500	$1,500	$1,500	$0
Gross Profit		$6,290	$7,900	$9,175	$12,655	$15,860	$17,740	$80,820
Disbursements	Salary & payroll taxes	$4,000	$4,000	$4,000	$4,000	$4,000	$4,000	$29,400
	Benefits	350	350	350	350	350	350	2,100
	Contract labor	500	500	900	700	900	1,200	4,700
	Equipment	5,500	2,600	0	300	1,200	2,000	11,600
	Rent	4,000	4,000	4,000	4,000	4,000	4,000	24,400
	Insurance	0	0	970	1,700	0	0	2,670
	Maintenance	450	150	95	75	75	250	1,095
	Advertising	400	200	0	1,500	300	100	2,500
	Utilities	1,300	1,100	890	700	575	500	5,065
	Bookkeeping/ Legal	490	85	85	200	85	85	1,030
Total Expenses		$17,890	$13,885	$12,190	$14,925	$14,635	$13,385	$84,160
Profit Before Taxes		−$11,600	−$5,985	−$3,015	−$2,270	$1,225	$4,355	−$3,340
Taxes		$1,200	$1,200	$1,200	$1,200	$1,200	$1,200	$7,200
Profit After Taxes		−$14,700	−$9,085	−$6,115	−$4,870	$375	$1,255	−$21,940
Ending Balance		$1,200	−$7,885	−$4,915	−$3,670	$1,575	$2,455	

numerous alternatives to starting a new venture, and we want to suggest that a **break-even analysis** of the projected position of the company will go a long way toward determining not only the viability of the new venture, but also the realistic assessment of whether this is the best path for the entrepreneur to embark upon. A break-even analysis provides some judgment about when the firm will reach a point of being self-sustaining after the business is begun.[7]

The break-even analysis recognizes that the growth in sales does not occur all at once. Instead, the sales of the business will grow incrementally. However, many of the expenses of the facility will start months before

[break-even analysis]

Tool for the estimation of when a business's income exceeds its expenses.

the first sale. Specifically, there are **fixed costs** (rent, utilities, equipment leases, etc.) that must be paid regardless of the sales level. There are also **variable costs** that will fluctuate according to how many goods are produced. For example, if a company manufactures something packaged in plastic bottles, the company will have increasing costs as it produces more products, as it will need more bottles.

The traditional Fortune 500 approach to break-even analysis would suggest that once revenues exceed the total of the fixed costs plus the variable costs, then the business has reached the break-even point. In this approach the profit margin from each sale adds to the net profit for the facility. For businesses operating in a project-by-project environment, this type of analysis is relatively effective. These facilities are simply trying to compare investment in one project to investment in another, as shown in Figure 6.1.

However, entrepreneurial ventures need to operate in a fundamentally different manner, and we calculate break-even using cash flow rather than profit. The initial investment in the new venture is an item of concern that is not normally included in most corporate cash flow analyses. Accounting for the initial investment allows the new facility to discuss the true economic returns, or economic benefits, from the business. (Recall that we discussed earlier that the small businessperson wants to be sure that her business is providing the economic return she envisioned and that she is not working essentially for free.) Figure 6.2 demonstrates this relationship. We begin this diagram with an initial investment level. As the new business begins operations, it is burning cash (from both a fixed and a variable cost standpoint) and reporting a negative net cash flow. Depending upon the venture and the industry in which it is operating, this negative cash flow can go on for some time. However, at some point a successful business turns the corner and begins producing positive cash flows. This has been called the break-even point for the company—that is, when the firm's costs equal its sales. However, we believe that until the new venture's positive cash flows

EXERCISE 3

1. Brainstorm some ways in which you can predict sales for your proposed business. Predict potential sales for your business using some of these methods.

2. Create a six-month projected income statement for your proposed business.

3. Determine the fixed and variable costs for your proposed business.

4. Perform a break-even analysis using the costs and the projected income you just determined. Based on this analysis, appraise whether or not your proposed business will break even within the six-month time frame. Explain why or why not.

Figure 6.1
Classic Break-Even Diagram

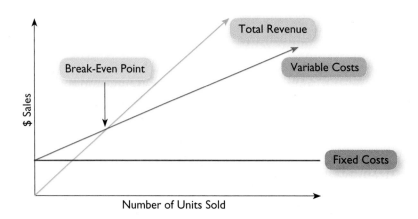

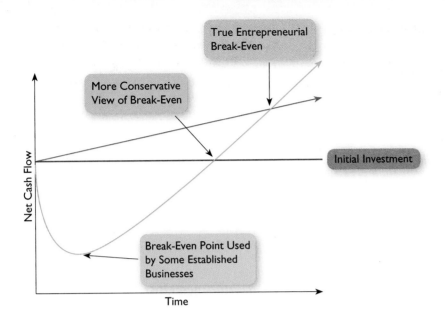

Figure 6.2
Entrepreneurial Break-Even
Diagram

True Entrepreneurial
Break-Even

More Conservative
View of Break-Even

Initial Investment

Net Cash Flow

Break-Even Point Used
by Some Established
Businesses

Time

exceed the initial investment, true break-even has not been achieved. This analysis can be further enhanced by taking into consideration the issue of time value of money.[8] There are other uses of your investment dollars and your raw time. With inflation, $1,000 received today is far more valuable than $1,000 will be if received 10 years from now. Thus, if you invest in a business today, you will want it to produce a return that is greater than the return you could have made if you simply had put the money in a savings account. Calculating the **time value of money** gives the initial investment line in Figure 6.2 an upward slope and creates an entrepreneurial break-even point that is farther out, but infinitely more realistic from an investor point of view.

[time value of money]

The value of money over time at a given rate of inflation or other type of return. Calculated as the value of your investment in time and money if you did not do the proposed venture.

key terms

break-even analysis 99
budget 88
cash flow 86
deviation analysis 93

equity 87
fixed costs 100
float 88
income statement 97

sensitivity analysis 96
time value of money 101
variable costs 100

review questions

1. Define cash flow.
2. Name a positive cash flow situation for a small business owner, and explain how it works in terms of cash inflow and outflow.
3. Define budget.
4. State in your own words why profitability is more important to a public investor and cash flow is more important to a small business owner.

5. How could keeping well-developed, accurate, long-term track records of cash flow statements and deviation analyses help your business with regard to its financial health?
6. How often should a new business owner create a cash flow statement and deviation analysis?

7. Succinctly interpret revenues and expenses in terms of cash flow.
8. Propose how an income statement can be used by a new business owner.

9. Justify why a break-even point should be considered to be reached when revenues exceed costs rather than when revenues equal costs.

individual exercises

1. Create a cash flow statement for your proposed business that does NOT include any equity investment.
2. What is the lowest ending balance in the cash flow statement?
3. Multiply that number by 150 percent to calculate the required initial equity investment.
4. Finalize your six-month projected cash flow statement using the required equity investment you just calculated. Can you realistically obtain the required initial equity investment?
5. How does the final statement you created affect the best-case and worst-case scenarios you developed?
6. Using the income statement you previously generated and the final cash flow statement you just created, perform a break-even analysis.

group exercise

Find a partner and choose one of the following scenarios on which to work together.

A. You and your partner are starting a mobile personal fitness consulting business, doing training in clients' homes. You have an initial equity investment of $20,000. Develop a one-year projected cash flow statement (most-likely scenario) and a one-year projected income statement. Perform a break-even analysis.

B. You and your partner are starting a small fitness center in a strip mall. You have an initial equity investment of $50,000. Develop a one-year projected cash flow statement (most-likely scenario) and a one-year projected income statement. Perform a break-even analysis.

Establishing the Business

After studying this chapter, you will be able to:

7.1 Discuss the various legal forms of business in order to determine the best design for a proposed new business.

7.2 Explain the nature of independent contractor status.

7.3 Explain the basics of contracts.

7.4 Define the role of leases in the legal formation of the new business.

7.5 List how laws, rules, and regulations benefit new businesses.

7.6 Demonstrate the appropriate standard of care and scope of practice for personal trainers.

7.7 Define the role that insurance plays in the risk portfolio of the new business.

7.8 Explain the basics of the legal system.

The Legalities of Your Personal Training Business

CASE STUDY

Susan had been running Basic Fitness, a women's-only fitness center in an urban area, for eight years. In order to compete with other local businesses, Susan decided to shift the focus of her business and start offering various fitness-related services such as group and one-on-one personal training, massage therapy, and esthetic and chiropractic care. To search for potential employees, Susan placed a number of ads in the local newspaper and on several websites, which garnered a large number of candidates for the services she wanted to offer. Susan was impressed with the range of talents in the pool of applicants. As she continued exploring the talent pool, Susan began projecting the additional revenue that her expanded business would generate. After numerous interviews, Susan decided to employ five personal trainers, a chiropractor, an esthetician, and a massage therapist who would work in conjunction with the chiropractor.

About a week after he started working at Basic Fitness, the massage therapist, James, came to Susan's office and asked about her liability coverage. He apologized for not remembering to ask about this upfront during his recruitment, but it just came to mind. Susan, too, suddenly realized that she had failed to investigate how her legal liability had changed given her new services. Susan started making phone calls to her peers and colleagues, and after considerable research, she realized that she did not have adequate risk management policies and procedures in place and that she also needed to investigate the issue of legal liability.

As she did this work in panic mode, Susan began to wonder what other tasks she had left undone in preparing her business for expansion. She wondered if she would have to pay higher liability insurance than she had anticipated. She did not know if there were additional licenses that she needed to apply for. To allow her business to thrive, Susan should protect herself legally, ethically, and morally.

Legal issues are critical for a small business to consider. The information in this chapter is not meant to be definitive or exhaustive of all the legal concerns for starting a new business. The material is factually correct; however, we strongly believe that you should hire a qualified attorney to assist you in building the foundation of the new business. The laws in each state vary, and the consequences are often serious enough that you will want to ensure you have a full and complete understanding of the legal issues related to the business.

In the previous six chapters, we have set out a means for you to develop the type of business that you want to create, determine its strategy/mission, and perform a detailed analysis of the potential cash flow position for the new facility. However, prior to the beginning of any actual operations, the founder must ensure that the proper legal foundation is established, and that all legal procedures, licenses, and authorities are granted or obtained.

Mature economies are based upon laws.* To fully appreciate the reliance in the United States on its legal institutions, one need only compare the United States to China.[1] There is a legal system in China, but in most cases this system can best be described as chaotic. Similar laws may exist in many nations, but the key questions are how are those laws enforced, and what are the penalties for violations of those laws? These two answers will vary widely between different provinces and even between different cities in the same province in China. Whether laws and their enforcement are the concern of the central government, province, or city is often unclear; instead, there are competing authorities who may interpret the laws very differently. To work in this environment, a business survives by developing good relationships with administrators, regulators, and/or the police. The relationships between these individuals and the small businessperson will determine whether the laws are enforced and, if so, how they are enforced.

These relationships may originate from a variety of sources, such as being related by blood or marriage, going to school together, or making a payoff, but without such relationships the small businessperson will most certainly find that she has significant legal problems.[2]

By contrast, the laws of the United States and some other economies are relatively clear and reasonably well enforced, and the amount of corruption is among the lowest in the world. As a result, your legal conflicts are decided based on the facts, not on whom you know. While this may indeed be the fairest way to decide business issues, the American legal system is still a source of irritation to some businesspeople. The abilities to collect money owed to you, to trust that contracts will be honored, to operate without fear of being arbitrarily shut down, and to insure your business against ruinous interventions by the government are all the result of laws. Indeed,

---

* The law present in a country is referred to as an institution. Other issues such as culture and ways that a given profession may conduct business are also institutions. These institutions shape the way business is conducted in subtle and pervasive manners. To fully understand how business is conducted in a given area, such institutions must be understood.

in a developing country or one recently ravaged by war, one of the first major steps in building the nation's economy is to establish the police and the courts so that basic business can be transacted. Our view is that small business owners need to acknowledge the central role and importance of the legal system, recognize how it will impact their business lives, and be prepared to compete in that arena. The businessperson cannot ignore legal issues.

If a supplier or customer does not live up to an agreement in China, you might go see a powerful person who will mediate the dispute between you and the other party using his judgment and experience as a guide. However, if your relationship with that person were poor or the other party's were very strong, you would likely lose. In the United States, the entrepreneur has the ability to use the court system for a legal remedy that is bound by precedence and the Uniform Commercial Code. The nature of business is that there will be disagreements, and as a result, you as a small business owner are likely at some point to be in court. While this may not be the ideal, it is better than the alternative of no legal system, or a weak one.

An important part of operating a business is having a fundamental understanding of the basics of commercial law and the potential remedies when there is a dispute. The establishment of a basic legal foundation will help the small business owner navigate the legal environment much more easily. If Susan had a more solid understanding of liability prior to recruiting her new staff, she might have known how to handle most legal issues that came up.

As has been noted, the legal environment can have a significant impact upon the operation of a business. Significant time and effort can be saved in the long run with some careful thought at the founding of a new venture.

ethical *challenge*

Paula had recently started her business as an independent-contractor personal trainer and was looking forward to training individuals in their homes. Her first client, Joyce, had prepaid for 12 sessions, which were to take place three times a week. The sessions would be a challenge due to Joyce's physical infirmity, but Paula knew she was up to the challenge. At their first session, as Paula went over the standard paperwork with Joyce, Paula realized that she had failed to include an assumption of risk and liability waiver. After a short discussion, Paula and Joyce decided to proceed with the initial workout without having Joyce sign the waiver and assumption of risk form; she could sign the form before the next session.

For this first session, Paula decided to do a series of fitness assessments with Joyce, one of which was the three-minute step test. One minute into the step test, Joyce stepped awkwardly and rolled her ankle. After taking a break, Joyce said she felt fine, and they completed their session.

The next day, Paula called Joyce to confirm their next session for the following day. Joyce told Paula that her ankle had been bothering her all night and now it was swollen. Paula canceled the session and told Joyce to call her back when she was feeling better. Paula noted in her records that the client was too injured to participate.

Paula was very busy over the next few days with other clients and realized a week later that she hadn't heard from Joyce. After leaving several messages over several days, Paula decided to drive to Joyce's house to check on her. When Joyce opened the door, she seemed surprised to see Paula and asked that she remain at the door while she went and got something. She brought back a demand letter from an attorney stating that because of negligence, Joyce was requesting a refund of her prepaid fee. Is Joyce entitled to the return of any or all of the fee? If so, what is the determining factor?

This chapter will examine a number of legal issues that impact the founding of the new business, including the following:

- the forms of business
- contracts
- leases
- regulations, including licensing requirements
- copyrights/trademarks/patents
- insurance
- the legal system
- board of advisers/directors

LO 7.1 Forms of Business

There are three basic types of business: sole proprietorship, partnership (including both general and limited liability), and corporation (C, S, and limited liability company). Each of these will be examined below.

Sole Proprietorship

[sole proprietorship]

The simplest form of business organization, characterized by the fact that the person who owns the business and the business itself are treated as the same entity.

A **sole proprietorship** is the simplest form of business to establish and in the personal training industry, one of the most common. In a sole proprietorship, the person who owns it and the business itself are treated as the same entity. On the principle that small business is good for the economy and should be encouraged, most communities have made the process for obtaining a sole proprietorship license quite simple. A quick trip to the local courthouse or public administration building, filling out a simple form, and paying a small fee are usually the only steps required to establish a sole proprietorship. Communities are making this process even simpler with online applications. All of your business income and losses are treated as part of the individual's overall income and are reportable on Schedule C of your 1040 tax form. Absent other licenses that may be required to operate your business (a topic that we will cover in more detail later in this chapter), the establishment of a sole proprietorship allows an individual to legally transact business.

The major benefit of this form of business is that it is very easy to form and easy to dissolve. There is virtually no separation between the founder and the business. There are strict rules regarding record keeping, and it is important that the founder maintain a firewall between personal and business expenses; however, you may deduct business expenses from your income.

The drawbacks to this type of business are numerous, and for business-people who develop a substantial business, these drawbacks will outweigh the ease of establishment. The first disadvantage is that a business involving more than a single founder cannot be a sole proprietorship. The law does not recognize other equity investors in this type of business. This limitation is a significant drawback for the growth potential of a new business not only from an initial investment perspective, but also because as the business develops it may need additional outside investment, which often is in exchange for part ownership of the business. Such investment would be virtually impossible in this legal form. This inability to have additional owners also means that equity incentives to attract top employees/executives are not possible. This leaves the founder with two options: either obtain all new monies as **debt instruments** or go through the process of changing the legal form to a more robust one.

[debt instruments]
Written promises to repay debts.

This brings up a second significant disadvantage of a sole proprietorship, that of liability. In the sole proprietorship form of business, all the liabilities of the sole proprietorship are the direct responsibility of the owner of the business. Thus, a debt for the facility is a personal debt for the business owner. The result is that if the business does something relatively risky (such as adding a pro shop), or even something mundane (such as increasing nutritional supplement inventory), then those debts of the business are treated as debts of the owner.

A third issue is one of legitimacy with suppliers and customers. Due to the fact that this legal form is so easy to dissolve, suppliers typically require personal guarantees for debts, and the value of the business is only as good as the reputation of the founder.

Thus, a sole proprietorship is very popular among individuals such as the following:

1. Those who are unsure of their business idea and just want to see what might happen (if the business proves successful these individuals often re-form the business later, using another business form).

2. Those who have a small business in which the time limitations of the founder will keep the business from growing significantly.

3. Those who have a small business in which the costs of equipment are low and, therefore, so are the risks. For example, a small business that embroiders names on shirts and hats can have relatively low costs and low risks.

Partnerships

A more complex business form is a **partnership.** There are two types of partnerships: general and limited. The two differ significantly from each other and will be reviewed separately.

[partnership]
A type of business formed between individuals directly. It includes both general and limited varieties.

General Partnership. If two or more people are involved in the founding of an organization, they can form a partnership. Similar to the founding of a sole proprietorship, the means of forming a basic partnership is relatively simple; however, it does involve an extra step beyond that of a sole proprietorship. When filing for a partnership, most local communities require a partnership agreement. While there is no set form that this agreement must take, these agreements generally specify who is involved; what each party is expected to contribute to the founding of the business (whether it be cash, services, or property); how profits, losses, and **draws** by the partners are to be treated; how one partner can buy out the other(s) if she decides to leave; how new partners are brought into the partnership; and how disputes are to be settled.

[draw]
A distribution of funds from the business. It is usually in the form of a cash dispersion in advance of salary, bonus, expected year-end distribution, etc.

We periodically hear from potential partners that they simply do not need such items to be specified. These individuals may have known each other for years and feel very comfortable with each other, so that they trust each other and are ready to tie up their combined financial wealth. However, recall what we stressed at the beginning. This is a legalistic society, and a business is fundamentally a financial transaction that should be treated as such. The time to prevent problems is early in the relationship, prior to any conflict (which, by the way, is inevitable in any interaction between two or more people). We recommend the early establishment

of clear and legally binding dimensions of the partnership. Thus, our advice is to get aid from your accountant or lawyer in drawing up such an agreement.

To illustrate the importance of this process, we will describe a partnership we worked with that had been formed to develop a landscaping business. The business developed quite well for several years and grew to where it had more than 50 employees and annual revenues in excess of several million dollars. When the partners began, both were married, had known each other for years both personally and professionally, and attended the same church. One partner worked in the field operations while the other attracted new business for the company and managed the office operations. The wife of the partner who worked in the field was the in-house accountant for the business. Unfortunately, after several years it became clear that the partner working in the office and the wife of the field partner were having an affair. During the next few months, both partners filed for divorce and the pair having the affair moved in together. The rift in the business became obvious to customers, suppliers, and the employees of the business to the point that the business was on the verge of collapse.

The two partners had developed a short partnership agreement when they formed the business, but it was based on one they found in a how-to book from the local bookstore, and they had simply deleted passages that they did not want to address. The document they had generated was not clear on how they were to split the business if either partner wished to terminate the agreement. The result was that the case ended up in court connected to two messy divorces. As you can imagine, the business continued to suffer. Employees left, customers chose other landscaping companies, and suppliers changed their credit terms for the business, as they were concerned about the dissolution of the business. The result was a costly battle for each party, with the field partner retaining the business and the office partner receiving a cash payment. Unfortunately for the partner who got the business, there was no **noncompete clause** in the partnership agreement, nor in the settlement. Once the legal case was over, the partner that left with the cash payment began to set up a new business. In this business he immediately began to seek the best customers of the partner who had received the business in the termination of the partnership. In general, divorce has a negative impact on small business.[3] However, a better-constructed partnership agreement could have allowed for a fair and less costly dissolution of the partnership, plus it could have protected the existing company as it continued in operation.

If a partnership agreement is not developed and signed, the partnership will be governed by either the Uniform Partnership Act or the Revised Uniform Partnership Act. These partnership laws were developed as suggested formats and adopted by each state. Thus, while there is some variation among the states, they are nonetheless a relatively effective means to handle the basics of partnership. Although the laws vary somewhat from state to state, there are certain standards that are in place in the absence of a pre-formation agreement. The rules in the acts are reasonable, but they

[noncompete clause]

An enforceable agreement that prohibits an employee from working for a competing company.

rarely match exactly what most individuals would like to do. For example, in these acts all assets are treated as equal for the partners. However, we find that rarely is there a 50–50 partnership. Inevitably, one or more partners contribute more capital or take more of a role in running the business than the other(s). Given this situation, small business owners would likely want to write a partnership agreement that recognized the larger contribution and perhaps provided a larger ownership stake. Similarly, issues such as noncompete agreements are not covered in these acts. Having one partner leave the business and set up a competing business is such a negative event that it is highly preferable to have a signed partnership agreement in place with a rich set of contingencies specified.

A partnership has many of the same characteristics as a sole proprietorship. The owners report their shares of losses or profits on their own personal income tax returns in proportion to their interest in the facility. Business expenses have some flow-through to personal tax forms, but the restrictions are significant. Partnerships require little more in the way of formal paperwork than sole proprietorships, and dissolution can be quite easy, although it does require a formal record with the local authorities.

Some of the drawbacks are the same as with a sole proprietorship. Liability is usually a bit more of an issue than with a sole proprietorship. Partners are generally held to be jointly liable for all debts incurred by the partnership. This means that a debt agreed to by your partner for the business becomes your total responsibility if the partner fails to meet his obligations. Each partner is assumed to be involved with all decisions, which translates into a fiduciary relationship between partners. In other words, partners have the responsibility to watch out for the best interests of the other partners.

While a sole proprietorship virtually eliminates the business's ability to bring in new equity investment, a partnership opens this door just a bit. In order to accept new equity investment in a partnership, each established partner must surrender a portion of her ownership position. This is usually a process in which the new "partner" buys out a portion of each of the existing partners in a transaction that also adds some financial muscle to the organization. A new partnership agreement is required each time this process occurs, and there are limits in some communities as to the number of partners in a business.

Limited Partnership. Some of the drawbacks to a basic partnership encourage the development of another type of partnership: a limited liability partnership, or **LLP.** In an LLP there are still at least two individuals who are partners in a venture (although, technically, one person can form an LLP and declare a full pass-through [of all income] on his federal taxes); however, there are two classes of partners in such a venture. The first is a **general partner.** This individual is considered the manager of the business and, as such, has unlimited liability for any debts or judgments against the business. In contrast, the other partners are considered to be passive investors, and, as such, their liability is limited to their investment in the business. The other partners are called limited partners and can work for the business but must not be active in the management of the organization. Active management makes that partner a general partner. The only requirement of an LLP is that at least one partner is considered to be a general partner. Otherwise, the positives and negatives discussed in the previous section for general partnerships also apply to LLPs.

[LLP]
A limited liability partnership.

[general partner]
In an LLP, the individual considered the manager of the business, who, as such, has unlimited liability for any debts or judgments against the business.

Corporations

The result of forming a sole proprietorship or a partnership is that the business debts flow directly to the owner(s), meaning that all owners are responsible for any debts of the business that arise. Thus, owners can have their life savings disappear if the business goes poorly. The critical issues of personal liability and the desire to limit exposure to the original equity investment led to the development of other forms of organization. A corporation addresses both drawbacks by viewing the business not as synonymous with the individual but as a separate entity.[4] If a corporation suffers substantial losses, the founder(s) will lose only their investment in the business.

What Are the Advantages of Working for a Corporation?

There are a variety of different types of corporations that have been developed, and we will address the three most common forms. Historically, a small business formed a simple, protected corporate form known as a Subchapter S corporation, while a business that was large or one that was developing into a large business formed a Subchapter C corporation. These corporation types take their names from subchapters in the Internal Revenue Code. However, since its development, the limited liability corporation (LLC) has become one of the predominant forms of business formation in the United States. We discuss S, C, and LLC corporations in greater depth next.

[Subchapter S corporation]

An organizational form that treats the business as an entity separate from the individuals. This allows the owner(s) to treat the income as they would if the business were a sole proprietorship or a partnership. It has limitations in the number and type of shareholders.

Subchapter S Corporation. As with all corporate forms, the Subchapter S has the benefit of protecting the owner(s) by treating the business as a separate entity. Thus, the liability is generally limited to any investment the owner(s) might have in the organization. However, a Subchapter S allows the owner(s) to treat the income as they would if the business were a sole proprietorship or a partnership. Thus, the owner(s) report their income or losses on their own 1040 income tax forms. The business must file informational tax returns that report each shareholder's portion of the business.

Therefore, the benefits of a Subchapter S can be summarized as follows:

1. Limited liability.
2. The potential to consolidate financial statements for the tax benefit of the owner(s).
3. Relatively easy formation compared with a Subchapter C corporation.
4. Legitimacy in the market as a more established form of business (the ability to put "Inc." after your business name).

However, there are negatives to this form of business as well. While forming this type of organization is substantially easier than forming a Subchapter C corporation, it is nonetheless quite cumbersome and expensive when compared to a sole proprietorship/partnership form. We strongly recommend that founder(s) wishing to form a Subchapter S corporation hire an experienced professional (lawyer or accountant) to process the paperwork. A second consideration is the limitation to the number of shareholders in this type of organization. Historically, a Subchapter S corporation has had a numerical limit to the number of shareholders. Currently that limit is set at a maximum of 100 shareholders. This limitation is fine for a closely held or family corporation, but is a significant limitation to a rapidly growing organization or one that has any thought of going public in the future.

Subchapter C Corporation. Subchapter C solves some of the issues raised regarding Subchapter S corporations, while creating others. Subchapter C corporations also have limited liability for the owner(s), but the corporation pays an income tax.[5] This leads to the corporation paying a tax on its profits. Then those profits after taxes can be paid as dividends to the owner(s). However, the owner(s) will have to pay taxes on their personal tax returns for that income. This is the double taxation situation that is often discussed in the United States.

However, it is possible for the developing new business owners to mitigate this cost. The owner(s) are also employees of the corporation and as such are paid salaries and bonuses. These salaries and bonuses are expensed as costs. Thus, the owner(s) can pay themselves virtually all of the profits each year, so that little actual profit is reported and therefore little corporate tax is owed. Profits that are not paid out for such items as salaries, bonuses, and/or dividends are then retained by the corporation for future expansion. A Subchapter C corporation also has the advantage that fringe benefits that are paid out are not treated as income for employees. Thus, owner(s) can have their health insurance and other benefits paid by the corporation, which then expenses each of these as a cost of business.

A nice feature of a Subchapter C corporation is that there are no limits to the number of shareholders that the organization may obtain. The only real limit is the number of authorized and distributed shares in the organization. Shares in the business must have an initial value at which they are offered, a "par" value. Thus, the corporation has a floor value that is equal to the par value times the number of shares distributed, and this will be equal to the shareholder equity of the business. We recommend that the par value be set very low so that the new company can authorize a very large number of shares (millions or even tens of millions). In both Subchapter C and S corporations, authorizing more shares; annual board meetings; and reporting standards to local, state, and federal authorities are among the issues that must be formally addressed. A Subchapter C corporation requires a rather detailed corporate charter, and while packages are available to guide the new businessperson through the process, we strongly recommend that she again seek professional advice. At a minimum the entrepreneur will have to have the following:

1. A corporate name—the new organization cannot choose a name that is considered a replication of another company's name. Patent/trademark attorneys offer services that include detailed searches of company names (and that allow business owners some level of comfort with their choice) all the way to obtaining a nationwide trademark on the name.

2. Location of the corporate headquarters—for a new business this is generally the same as the business address.

[**Subchapter C corporation**]

An organizational form that treats the business as a unique entity responsible for its own taxes. There are no limitations to shareholder participation and the "owners" are protected beyond their equity investment.

At the New York Stock Exchange, shares of public corporations' stock are traded.

3. General nature of the business, specified for the filing.

4. Names, addresses, and titles of all corporate founders and initial investors.

5. A so-called time horizon for the business's existence—for all intents, this is usually "in perpetuity."

6. Authorized stock and capital—the par value times the number of shares issued is considered the initial capital of the organization. Some states require the company to have that amount on deposit in a business account with a bank.

7. Bylaws of the organization. These are the basic rules that will govern activity in the new company.

Limited Liability Corporation. In recent years the limited liability corporation (**LLC**) has become one of the most popular forms of incorporation for small businesses.[6] This business form is still relatively new; for example, it was only in 1994 that California passed the law to allow such entities. The limited liability company has many similarities with the Subchapter S corporation. There is the limited liability feature, which exposes each shareholder to the amount of his investment. However, the LLC allows the new venture to have more than 100 investors, and it allows other corporations to hold stock in the company (a feature not available to Subchapter S corporations). An LLC may have as few as one individual listed as an officer of the company, referred to as a "member" of the corporation. The LLC is similar to a C organization in that all of the information required is the same, but is unlike a Subchapter C corporation in that profits from the organization can be handled flexibly. The owner(s) are allowed to flow the profits through to their personal returns to avoid double taxation, which occurs with a C corporation. Furthermore, there is substantial flexibility (unlike with a partnership) regarding the amount of income that is designated for each individual. It does not have to be in proportion to that owner's holdings.

While the cost of formation is very low, this type of organization is formed by submitting the paperwork to the state government and having a charter issued prior to beginning operations. Therefore, dissolving these organizations is somewhat expensive and a relatively drawn-out process. State governments establish how this business entity is formed and a few states, such as New York, also require that the founder of the new business publish notice of forming the limited liability company in the local newspaper. Some states limit their use and will not allow professionals such as accountants and lawyers to form such business entities. As we have stated before, professional advice in regard to what is appropriate within your state is money well spent.

[LLC]

A limited liability corporation.

EXERCISE 1

1. Name the three forms of business that a new enterprise can take.

2. Describe the two types of partnership: general and limited.

3. Describe Subchapter S corporations, Subchapter C corporations, and limited liability corporations in terms of liability, taxes, and shareholders.

[independent contractor]

An individual who performs services for another person or business but is not an employee.

LO 7.2 Independent Contractor Status

Many fitness professionals set themselves up in business as **independent contractors** and do not formalize their business status any further. Independent contractors are those who work under contract or on an as-needed basis. By definition an individual is an independent contractor if the person for whom the work is being performed has the right to control or direct only the result of the work, and not what will be done and how it will be done. Independent contractors limit a business's liability and employee costs. Most clubs who use personal trainers hire them as independent contractors.

In this scenario, some trainers pay the club a set fee, from $100–$800, for "rent" or use of the space or facility. The alternate scenario is when the trainer pays a percentage of his fees to the club. Some clubs do a 60/40 split, which means that out of a client's fees, the trainer keeps 60 percent and the club gets 40 percent. (Example: Bob charges $60 per session; he keeps 60 percent of that, or $36, and the club keeps 40 percent, or $24.) Being an independent contractor means several things must happen that you and only you control. There are several advantages to being an independent contractor. Some include:

- You are your own boss.
- You may be paid more than employees.
- No federal or state tax is withheld from your pay.
- You can take increased business deductions.

Some disadvantages include:

- You have no job security.
- You might not get paid.
- You must pay self-employment taxes.
- You may be personally liable for business debts.
- You have no employer-provided benefits.
- You have no unemployment insurance benefits.
- You have no employer-provided workers' compensation.
- You have very few labor law protections.

Taxes and insurance are two of the most important considerations. When it comes to taxes, independent contractors are unlike employees, who are subject to federal and state income taxes, Social Security tax, and Medicare taxes. These taxes are withheld from employees' paychecks, whereas independent contractors are required to pay their own taxes. This means that the independent contractor must set aside enough money to pay his estimated taxes every quarter. According to the IRS, all independent contractors who make more than $400 per year from business activities must report their business income to the IRS.

Because independent contractors are not considered employees of the facilities where they perform their work, it is common for personal trainers to purchase insurance. An independent contractor must be aware of the two

EXERCISE 2

1. Identify some advantages and disadvantages of being an independent contractor.
2. Distinguish general liability insurance from professional liability insurance.

types of insurance needed to fully protect him against possible legal action: general liability and professional liability. General liability insurance typically addresses claims of bodily injury or property damage liability. General liability is commonly looked at as an all-encompassing, umbrella policy that covers everything. Professional liability insurance differs from general liability in that it pertains to negligence associated with your professional services. The damage is usually financial rather than physical and is crucial to have in addition to general liability insurance as it covers the indirect consequences of your conduct.

LO 7.3 Contracts

[contract]

An agreement between two parties to perform certain activities for some consideration.

Beyond the legal form of the new organization, there are a number of other legal issues that should be considered prior to beginning operations. A **contract** is an agreement between two parties to perform certain activities for some consideration. A contract does not have to be written, but consistent with the theme presented in this chapter, we strongly recommend that the small business founder employ formal written contracts whenever she has an agreement with another party.

A contract should include several items that are reasonably straightforward, including the following:

1. Who the parties are in the contract. This preamble briefly describes who the parties are so that it is clear who is involved and in what manner.
2. What each party agrees to do and for what consideration (i.e., their cost, pay, product received, etc.).
3. When the transaction is to take place.
4. The timing of payment, if other than immediately.
5. When the activity is to take place and how long the contract is in place.
6. Warranties.
7. How the contract can be terminated. There may be damages specified.
8. Whether the contract can be transferred.
9. If the businesses are in different states, which state's law applies?

EXERCISE 3

1. Construct a list of points to be covered in a contract between a personal trainer and a client. Write some terms of agreement on each of the points on your list.

LO 7.4 Leases

One of the most significant contracts that a new business is initially involved in is the lease for the location where the business will operate. Lease contracts may be of any term length that is agreeable between the parties. Whatever the length of the lease, there are several issues that the new business owner should consider as he examines such contracts:

1. What exactly is the new business owner leasing? Beyond the basic address and exclusive access to the premises, leases should address utilities; access to parking (either exclusive or shared); responsibility for the external premises (including lawn care, painting, etc.); structural repairs/improvements; approval of leasehold improvements; and responsibility for permanently installed equipment (heating/air conditioning, plumbing, electrical, etc.).

2. Is there an ability to renew the lease? The lease should specify how long the lease is in effect and if there is the opportunity to renew the lease. The actual space that is leased may not be critical for some types of businesses, but for a small personal training studio, a consistent presence in the same location could be a crucial marketing advantage. Does a personal training studio need 10,000 square feet or even 6,500 square feet? Regardless of the type of business, it is simply expensive to keep moving operations.

3. Who is responsible for improvements? Who has responsibility/authority for physical plant improvements? A lease that includes the responsibility for making improvements to the facility should be accompanied by a lower lease payment. One entrepreneur bought an existing barbershop and negotiated what he believed was a reasonable lease with the landlord. During the first summer that he occupied the building, the air conditioner stopped working, and the lessee found out that he was responsible for replacing the air-conditioning unit; however, the landlord had to approve the unit. The landlord wanted a top-of-the-line unit to replace the old unit, while the lessee just wanted to install a functional mid-priced unit. The decision had to be made quickly, as it was midsummer in the southwest United States, with temperatures over 100 degrees. The owner of the business had no choice but to put in the unit the landlord wanted. The unit and the related improvements cost over $15,000.

4. Who has responsibility for maintenance and other facilities issues? Who has responsibility for issues such as the utilities, landscaping, janitorial costs, trash removal, parking lot maintenance and security, window washing, and real estate taxes? Can you place the signage you want, or are there restrictions?

5. Who has to carry the liability insurance and at what level? Many leases require the tenants to carry insurance not only for themselves but also to cover any liability of the landlord. Insurance can be expensive and it merits particular attention to be clear who has what responsibility for insurance.

6. Can your landlord enter your place of business? Most leases give the landlord some rights to enter your business to inspect it. The landlord wants to make sure you are taking care of the rental location and that nothing illegal is occurring. However, it can feel like an invasion if the landlord comes into your business whenever she wants.

7. If there are problems, what are the procedures for addressing and resolving them? If you cannot use all of your space and have a financial need, can you sublet some of your leased space to others? Many leases prohibit such subleasing. Most leases also do not allow you to cancel the lease unless you meet the specified conditions in the lease. To illustrate, recently a small business was looking for a location for a new retail store. There appeared to be a number of good opportunities in buildings with empty space. Unfortunately, the business owners found that one space they really liked was already leased by a business that no longer existed. The lease had been written with the personal guarantee of the small business founder. Most states do not allow a landlord to charge two individuals for rent on the same space. Interestingly, the landlords chose to leave the space empty and collect full rent for the remainder of the old lease rather than rent the space to the new start-up at a lower rate. The individual who had personally guaranteed the lease before going out of business could only get out of the lease by filing personal bankruptcy, which he was not willing to do. If there are other problems and disagreements between the landlord and the business owner, how will these be solved—mediation, arbitration, or other means? If there are problems, can you withhold your rent?

Hopefully you can see that a lease is multidimensional and should be carefully crafted before signing. Consistent with our belief stressed in this chapter, small business owners can prevent many problems by ensuring that legal issues are thoroughly investigated and that they employ experts where needed.

EXERCISE 4

1. Would you sign a standard lease? Why or why not?
2. What do you think are the three or four most important considerations when negotiating a lease? Write your answers in the left column of the table below.
3. What is your minimal acceptable negotiation position for each consideration? Write your answers in the right column of the table below.

Important Considerations	My Minimal Acceptable Negotiation Positions

---

LO 7.5 Regulations

Small businesses generally deal with fewer regulations than do large businesses. There are many regulations enacted by the federal government that do not apply to businesses with fewer than 50 employees (this number varies with the regulation). Some industries are highly regulated regardless of size, whereas others are only loosely regulated even for the large, well-established organizations. The fitness industry is a highly unregulated industry; most facilities or employees are not bound by a vast number of regulations. Most of the regulations deal with spacing of equipment, temperature of the facility, and other health and safety concerns.

There are some basic regulations that cut across the spectrum of businesses. If a small business has employees, then the business must have an Employer Identification Number. Additionally, the business will be required to calculate and deduct various taxes for federal, state, and, in some cases, local authorities. The payroll requirements are specific and well developed. Thus, an entrepreneur can simply purchase a canned package for doing payroll and should be able to meet all of these various requirements.

Many states, such as California, have much more expansive laws governing small business practices. While environmental regulations at the federal level are typically designated for large businesses, in some areas the states will also apply those laws to small businesses. Similarly, specific cities may have unique sets of special regulations. A city like New York has extensive additional regulations for small businesses. For instance, a restaurant in the city has to post information on the calories and fat content in all of its products and also deep fry its food only in particular types of oil.

Obviously, the special rules and regulations for your industry and location should be explored before you start your business to ensure that you are meeting all requirements. Excellent sources of information regarding regulatory requirements are the Small Business Assistance Center (run by the Small Business Administration) in your area, the state or local department of economic development, and the local chamber of commerce. Most states and cities are critically aware of the role small business plays in their economic viability. The result has been the establishing of offices to help new small businesses to navigate these laws and regulations.

[ADA]
Americans with Disabilities Act.

One set of regulations that bears particular mention is the Americans with Disabilities Act (**ADA**). This law applies fully to any business with more than 15 employees. Thus, many more small businesses will be affected by this law than by other federal laws. The law requires that there be no discrimination in the hiring, management, or dismissal of employees with disabilities. If the business has someone with a covered disability, the business must make reasonable accommodation for that individual. Additionally, virtually all retail and most office businesses need to make their places of business accessible to people with physical disabilities.

Licensing

Related to the topic of regulation are the licenses that the business must obtain to operate. A license can be as simple as a business license that is used by communities to track business performance (and thereby tax income), or it may be specifically related to the fundamental operations of the business. Examples of licenses/permits include the following:

1. Zoning permit

2. Occupancy permit

3. Business license (from the local authorities)

4. Sign permit

5. OSHA permit for food handling

6. Fire safety permit

7. Licensing and certification of fitness staff (personal trainers, group exercise instructors, etc.)

At a minimum, most businesses must acquire a license to do business in the county/city in which they will be operating. This type of license is quite simple to obtain, as it normally requires only that one of the principals of the business fill out a form, pay a set fee (usually less than $100 and often quite a bit less), and agree to report basic information about the business's performance on a set schedule (again,

EXERCISE 5

1. Using the Internet, search for federal regulations for fitness facilities. What set of federal regulations, besides ADA, must also be considered by a fitness facility?

2. Using the Internet for your research, describe the differences between an EIN and a Social Security number (SSN). What type(s) of business may use an owner's SSN as a company identifier?

usually quarterly at the most). While completing this procedure, which is normally transacted at a courthouse or government agency building, we suggest that the new businessperson inquire as to other licenses that might be required for his operation. Lack of knowledge is no excuse for failing to have the proper licenses, so we always recommend talking with current business owners concerning the procedures and licenses required in each locale. For those facilities that are facing more challenging licensing, such as liquor businesses, it is best to visit with a lawyer.

LO 7.6 The Standard of Care and Scope of Practice

The ability of a trainer to provide one-on-one specialized care is just one of the skills that makes a personal trainer just that—personal. As a trainer, the **standard of care** and the **scope of practice** play into how well you will do in your profession. The most important professional standard to maintain is your scope of practice as a personal trainer. The proper scope of practice includes assessing, motivating, educating, and training clients to help them achieve their fitness and health goals; it does not entail diagnosing, treating, or counseling, which are the responsibilities of licensed health-care providers.

Personal trainers have a general understanding and concept of a scope of practice based on their education and the foundation laid by other pioneer trainers in the field. Upon being certified, a personal trainer should be proficient in leading and demonstrating safe and effective methods of exercise by applying the fundamental principles of exercise science. If you at any time do not adhere to these guidelines, you are outside of your scope of practice.

Trainers sometimes make the mistake of "counseling" clients. While it is acceptable to listen, it is best to not give out any type of psychological advice—that would be considered outside a personal trainer's scope

[standard of care]

Care that a reasonably prudent, professional, and responsible trainer would provide in a given situation. This includes the standards of practice that are developed and published by professional organizations.

[scope of practice]

The appropriate extent to which personal trainers assess, motivate, educate, and train clients.

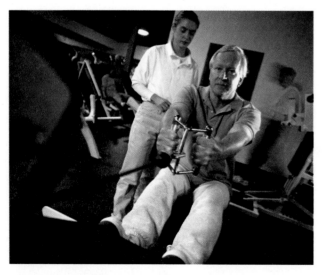

of practice. You will no doubt find that clients will bring outside problems into their training sessions. You must remember that you are walking a fine line when you allow clients to share personal problems with you. You should remain professional at all times. There are polite ways to steer the conversation back to the topic at hand, which should be their fitness goals. Sometimes, a client will enter a training session having had a bad day and start "venting." A caring, compassionate trainer may instinctively listen, but it's easy to allow the client to take up too much time talking while not using that time to exercise. Although it is good to listen, we still have to get them back on track by using some type of diversion method.

The standard of care for a personal trainer is similar to the scope of practice, but the scope of practice is a defined set of criteria that detail the appropriate duties of a personal trainer. When the standard of care is not followed, the trainer is potentially negligent. (We will explain how to prevent and to deal with negligence later in this chapter.) The scope of practice is a broad spectrum, but the standard of care refers to practices that all personal trainers—especially efficient and effective ones—engage in at all times. For instance, having clients fill out proper informed-consent forms and health and medical questionnaires is part of the standard of care. These forms provide documentation in the event that records are reviewed. In tort law, the standard of care is the degree of prudence and caution required of an individual who is under a duty of care (your client). A client would need to prove a breach of the standard for successful legal action against a trainer.

EXERCISE 6

1. Suppose a client enters a training session with you on the verge of tears. About 10 minutes into the session, he breaks down and starts crying, saying that he has done something unethical at work and a whistleblower is about to turn him in to management. He looks at you and asks how you would handle such a situation if you were in his shoes. What do you do or say in response? Do you continue the session? Why or why not?

2. Compose a list of three standards of care for a personal trainer.

LO 7.7 Insurance

A topic related to the legal concerns of all types of business is insurance. One of the key concerns that should have been clear in the discussion of the form of organization is that the small business chooses the level of liability it is willing to risk. One means to limit liability concerns is through the effective application of insurance.

There are several basic types of insurance, including property, general and professional liability, employee bonding, and workers' compensation. Property insurance covers the building, fixtures, and inventory in all of the buildings in which the business has a function. One key concern is whether the insurance covers replacement cost or current value. For example, you may have equipment that has only limited value in a resale market, but that would be very expensive to replace if you had to buy new equipment. The business must decide what types of risks it will accept and cover itself versus those that it will purchase insurance to cover. It is fairly standard to obtain coverage for fire, windstorms, hail, and smoke. However, the businessperson may also wish to obtain a special form of insurance that covers natural disasters such as floods and earthquakes. The greater the insurance coverage obtained by the small business, the greater the cost. Thus, each businessperson needs to balance risk and cost.

The business can also obtain liability insurance, which covers lawsuit judgments. Such insurance does not cover intentional acts of malice; however, it does cover the business for accidents. General liability insurance and professional liability insurance are both essential for a fitness facility owner. General liability insurance typically addresses claims of bodily injury or property-damage liability. Most companies have and are familiar with general liability coverage, as it includes protecting businesses from any

Liability insurance can protect a professional fitness trainer against damages if a client becomes injured during a training session.

financial losses due to injury, environmental impact, casualty, and property damage. Professional liability insurance differs in that it pertains to negligence associated with professional services. The damage is typically financial, rather than physical. This type of insurance is especially important for those who are sole proprietors or independent contractors. Example: You as the trainer are in the gym that you rent space from and are training your client during a busy time of the day. For her exercise, your client is doing a dumbbell chest press. The end of the dumbbell falls off and onto the client's nose, breaking her nose. Your client decides to file a lawsuit against you, your gym, and the dumbbell maker. This insurance claim falls under general liability because it is an equipment malfunction. If we take the same scenario in which your client is performing a dumbbell chest press, suppose you leave to retrieve another set of weights and her weight falls on her. You as a trainer have failed to spot your client and have now caused that client potential harm. This negligence claim now affects the professional liability portion of your insurance contract.

A small business should also explore whether it needs to have its workers bonded. Bonding is a type of insurance in which the business is covered in case the workers cause any damage in the performance of their work. To illustrate, a plumber may hire an assistant that makes some of the calls on customers. The assistant may make a mistake that leads to a pipe's breaking and flooding the house or apartment. The damage done can be very costly and perhaps even cause bankruptcy. However, through bonding, the insurance company agrees to pay for such damages. In an office setting you can also get bonding to cover losses from employee embezzlement.

Workers' compensation insurance covers liability for workers that are injured on the job. In many states, workers' compensation insurance is required and can represent a major expense for a small business.

We suggest that insurance is such a critical issue that it merits spending time with an insurance agent, or multiple agents, to discuss the needs of the new business. Discussion with multiple agents will allow the new businessperson to obtain different viewpoints on the issue. The new business owner should seek out agents with expertise in the industry in which the small business operates.

EXERCISE 7

1. Create a mini-plan for the types of insurance you would want to purchase for your fitness business. Provide a reason for including each type.

2. Imagine a scenario in which your personal trainer, who trains you at his house, is negligent and does not prevent you from being injured during your session. The trainer has no professional liability insurance. What would you do? Why?

LO 7.8 The Legal System and Fitness Facility and Personal Training Businesses

As stated earlier, it is not a pleasant thought, but small business owners should realize that over the course of time, most businesses wind up in court for one reason or another. It's best to be aware of the general nature of legal proceedings as they relate to fitness businesses.

Court jurisdiction mandates where certain cases have the potential to be tried or heard. Federal courts have several levels, the highest level being the Supreme Court. Other levels in the federal court are district court and appeals court. On the state side, there are several court systems in place.[7] This includes trial courts, the court of appeals or state appellate, and the state Supreme Court. There are also courts on the municipal or city level, which primarily deal with ordinance violations and issues in which the legal rights of individuals are safeguarded and public interest is protected (such as small claims court).

The legal system is a complex, unique world involving many principles. Common law, the body of recorded decisions that courts refer to and rely upon when making legal decisions, sets the tone for most of our legal decisions today. Case law covers the effects of court decisions that involve the same or similar facts. Entrepreneurs should be aware of both of these types of law when operating a fitness business.[8] Other classifications of law that the fitness facility owner should be aware of include civil law, the study of the rights and obligations of individuals, which includes the law of property; the law of contracts; and tort law, which deals with the violation of the rights of an individual or business that has been wronged either intentionally or by negligence.[9]

Perhaps the most common types of law that the facility owner or personal trainer might encounter are three types of tort law: intentional torts, reckless misconduct, and negligence.[10] The most common tort in the health and fitness industry is the negligence tort.

Negligence

Negligence is defined as the failure to use reasonable care. It can include doing something that a reasonably prudent person would not do or the failure to do something a reasonably prudent person would do under like circumstances. There are several degrees of negligence, but the most damaging is gross negligence.

There are several elements that make up negligence, and all elements must be evident to prove negligence:

- duty of care
- breach of duty
- factual causation
- damages

Duty of Care. When you enter a relationship with a client, you are actually in a contract to provide the client with personal training services. You must train clients with the same standard of care and with the same duty of care that all other competent personal trainers follow. Duty of care is the standard of care that the law has established for the protection of others.

The law of negligence does not require that you ensure the safety of every person using the facility from every conceivable injury; it merely requires that you do not create an unreasonable risk and that you protect people from risks that are foreseeable.[11]

Breach of Duty. A breach of duty occurs if you have injured your client or if you have continued to allow harm to that client in some way. For instance, if you allow a client to lift weights that are beyond her capacity and she becomes injured, you have committed a breach of duty. (If you realize your client is harmed and you allow the harm to continue, then you may get yourself into the realm of "gross negligence.")

Factual Causation. There must be some sort of "hard" evidence or facts behind the personal trainer's actions. For instance, a written log of a workout routine could prove that a trainer committed a breach of duty.

Damages. The monetary amount awarded to the plaintiff for breach of duty that caused the negligence is called damages. The most severe type of damages are punitive damages, which serve to inflict punishment. Punitive damages are awarded when there is intentional or malicious wrongdoing—most often causing the death of the victim. Punitive damages are also often awarded to plaintiffs in lawsuits against large corporations such as tobacco companies. As you can imagine, punitive damages are rare in fitness-related legal cases. More typically, non-punitive damages in a fitness-industry negligence case will be a monetary reward meant to deter people, groups of people, or businesses from performing the same act that caused the negligence in the first place.

EXERCISE 8

1. Suppose a client new to exercise comes to you for personal training, explaining that she wants to lose 75 pounds. At the start of your first session together, you tell her to work out on a treadmill for half an hour while you go and take care of some unrelated paperwork for your business. Fifteen minutes into the workout, the client has a heart attack and becomes unconscious. You are able to perform CPR, which you are certified to do, in time to save the client. Provide an argument for why a case of negligence is apparent.

2. Could the unauthorized release of information that a client gave to you in confidence be considered grounds for a lawsuit against you? Justify your answer.

---

key terms

review questions

1. What is a sole proprietorship? Name one advantage and one disadvantage to owning a sole proprietorship.
2. Define limited liability corporation.
3. Define tort.
4. Explain the benefits for club owners of hiring independent contractors.
5. Using the Internet, study local and state regulations and licensing requirements for fitness professionals or fitness facilities (your choice) in your area. Formulate a paragraph describing how you would implement these regulations and licensing requirements.
6. Would offering advice on diets for weight loss be within the scope of practice for a personal trainer? Why or why not?
7. Justify why it is imperative for a personal trainer to have professional liability insurance even if incorporated as a limited liability corporation.
8. Assess the phrase "reasonably prudent person." What makes a "reasonably prudent" fitness professional?

individual exercise

Compile a list of legal issues that you might have to deal with in your own fitness-related business. Consider the form of your business, contracts, leases, regulations, licenses, and insurance. Also consider costs. You may choose to make a table to organize this information.

group exercise

Break into groups of four or five. Together, design a waiver of liability for a local fitness club that offers both personal training and group instruction. Samples can be found online. Debate why you should or should not include certain features. Discuss why having clients sign such a waiver does not necessarily release the club from all liability, and determine what types of insurance will help to protect the club.

Establishing Operations

After studying this chapter, you will be able to:

8.1 Describe how location can be used as a competitive advantage.

8.2 Discuss the important issues in the financing considerations of new firms.

8.3 Distinguish between the various methods with which a new firm establishes legitimacy in the market.

8.4 Describe the importance of quality as a competitive tool.

8.5 Assess and evaluate technology best suited for a new business.

8.6 Discuss the type and condition of equipment needed at start-up.

8.7 Demonstrate proper facility and equipment layout.

8.8 Demonstrate proper equipment placement to reflect user space and safety cushions.

8.9 Explain how timing is a competitive advantage.

8.10 Recognize the issues related to time management in the starting of a new business.

CASE STUDY

Jeff and Aiko were a married couple who planned to open their own business. Jeff was a personal trainer, and Aiko had worked as a manager in a variety of businesses. In their new business, Jeff would run the training services of the business, and Aiko would oversee the business side.

The couple had been talking about opening the business for a couple of years, but the idea suddenly gained urgency when they discovered a vacant commercial space that they fell in love with. The location was in a strip shopping center with very inexpensive rent. It was located about five minutes from the high school the couple had graduated from 10 years before. Jeff and Aiko thought it would be wonderful to open their business in their old neighborhood and maybe even move out there from their downtown apartment and start a family.

Jeff had cobbled together a following of about 25 clients working in several different clubs in the downtown area.

Although they would have to make a 20-minute drive, Jeff was convinced that his devoted clients would follow him to his club. And because there was no other fitness club in the suburb, he was sure he could drum up more business.

When the landlord sent Aiko the lease to review, she faxed it to her cousin, who was a real estate lawyer. He started asking questions about the shopping center and did not like the answers Aiko was providing. In particular, he was not happy that the center was located so far from Jeff's client base. Also, the center was a five-minute drive from the highway, so he was concerned that there would be very little exposure to drive-by traffic. Most of all, he was disturbed that most of the storefronts in the center were vacant. "It has eight units and only two are occupied? No wonder the rent is so cheap!" he commented. He urged Aiko to do some more research and make sure this location was right for their business.

Aiko did do research, and she was disturbed by what she found. The shopping center had never been 100 percent occupied in its five-year history. None of the businesses that had opened at the center had lasted more than a couple years. The current tenants were a dollar-discount store and an appliance repair shop. She drove past the center at different times of day and never saw more than a few cars in the lot—probably those of the employees, she realized.

One day as she drove to the shopping center, she was getting off the highway and realized there was another strip center of a similar size just off the exit ramp. Out of curiosity, she drove there and found the parking lot was full of cars. And every unit in the center was occupied.

There was a pizza shop, a dry cleaner, a manicure/pedicure shop, and more.

That night, Aiko and Brian had a long, difficult discussion. Aiko said she thought they were about to make a huge mistake with this location. Brian acknowledged it would be a challenge, but he insisted he could make it work once his clients started coming to the new space. The club would be so popular that it would help turn the strip center into a destination, he said. Brian saw it as an opportunity. Aiko saw it as a dead end.

In the end, Aiko convinced Brian that they should not sign the lease and instead continue to look for another location.

Planning is the first step in the small business development process. A great many individuals do little more than this initial investigation. During this process they find a fatal flaw, decide that the business is not nearly as lucrative as they had originally thought, or simply determine that they do not want to take the risk. The decision to not pursue the business is completely legitimate, and it is better to make it early if you believe that the business does not present the right opportunity for success. The process provided in this book, in fact, is designed to encourage the student to fully examine the business opportunity prior to actually starting a business.

However, at some stage the small business researcher must decide that she has investigated the idea sufficiently and that it is time to actually begin operations. While we would advocate good research and examination of your idea, the critical point of difference between an entrepreneur and someone with an idea is *action*. This chapter examines the practical, process-based actions that must occur to actually begin operations.

LO 8.1 Location

One of the most important steps in planning a new business will be the identification and purchase/lease of a location for the new business. The old axiom from marketing is that the three keys to business success are location, location, and location. While this might be a bit overblown, we certainly agree that location is a critical item in the successful operation of a new business.[1] How do you decide upon the best location for the money? The method that we utilize involves breaking the business down into the critical design features of the business. You may recall from Chapter 5 that you should develop a list consisting of all the resources/capabilities of the organization. These should then be divided into two categories representing the ordinary and extraordinary points of competition for the new business. Your location decision should address all of the orthodox points required for your industry and should enhance

Many criteria must be considered in choosing a location, including the proximity to competing businesses.

the unorthodox points. For example, an orthodox location for a restaurant is one that is visible and easily accessible to your target customers, while an unorthodox location may have a stunning view of the downtown skyline.

It is very easy to simply fall into the trap of trying to locate a business based upon the capital available or some convenience factor that has little to do with the actual strategy of the business. This is a mistake that can, by itself, send all of the other planning down the drain. In the example of Brian and Aiko's fitness business, the couple made the mistake of falling in love with a location for sentimental reasons that had nothing to do with a critical analysis of their business. They nearly committed to the location before examining its qualities in an objective manner.

While there are many very sophisticated methods for performing a location analysis, in more simple terms locations can be graded by the type and amount of traffic that the particular location draws. If you are setting up a warehouse, then you neither need nor want an "A" location in a mall, on a busy street, or in a tourist-heavy downtown area. Match the type of business, its needs from both an orthodox and an unorthodox perspective, and the amount of money that you wish to invest in the first years of operation. Take the time to analyze the long-term as well. If you will need to move within a short period of time because you achieve all of your targets and outgrow your space, then you may want to consider a location that includes an option to allow for expansion.

To illustrate the rich options that a business owner can pursue, consider the following small business, which for the sake of this example we'll call Yoga X. Yoga X starts out as yoga instructors who go into business together by renting vacant studio space in a suburban dance center. The dance center's owner also owns the building, which has five different studios plus office space on two floors. Yoga X starts by renting one of the studios two days a week. But the dance studio's business is struggling, which allows Yoga X to rent more and more of the studios as their business expanded. Within 18 months they were renting the entire second floor of the building and approached the dance center's owner about taking over the entire building and setting up a lease/purchase agreement. The dance center owner has been contemplating retirement anyway, and so she sells the building to Yoga X. Having established a client base, the Yoga X partners really want to hold onto their location, and through a confluence of good business practice, luck, and investment, they not only hold but own the location. As will be discussed later in this chapter, location is one of the things that provide a business with legitimacy. If you have a location and maintain it for some period of time, then you are more accepted and acceptable with potential clients and suppliers, as your business appears to be more stable.

Commercial real estate firms are a source of unparalleled information for new business owners trying to locate their business. The websites for commercial real estate firms provide much more information than want ads. Many sites allow you to download demographics for an area, preview the building's parking setup, and view car and foot traffic patterns. Building owners pay agents in a leasing agreement that is usually based upon a percentage of the first year's lease and the signing of a two-year lease. While commercial real estate agent income can

EXERCISE 1

1. State why locating a business based mostly on available capital or convenience is not appropriate.
2. Name three possible steps in performing a simple location analysis.
3. Investigate a commercial real estate website. What are some of the things you see there that would not typically be available in a real estate print ad?

Location is a critical choice for a fitness business. Some entrepreneurs become completely enamored with what they perceive to be the perfect location. It is difficult for these people to see any way that the business can succeed unless they can operate in that one location. The same goes for the perfect piece of equipment, the rights to a critical license for the business, or any number of things or events.

1. What would you do to obtain something that you deemed to be critical for your new business?
2. What if you were prevented from obtaining it by someone you felt was just being vindictive?
3. Would paying double the true value of something be acceptable to you?
4. What if you had to sell part of your business in exchange for that perfect location?

be quite substantial, the commercial real estate market is relatively small and an individual's reputation is critical to future bookings. Therefore, agents focus extensively on ensuring that the new business signing the lease is successful. The fact is that the cost for all this expertise is paid by the building owner, and a successful business that pays its bills is very desirable. Thus, commercial agents can be a valuable asset to new business owners as they seek to locate properties that match their needs.

LO 8.2 Financing Considerations

While not addressing the details of financing operations here (we will cover those issues in depth in Chapter 9), we nonetheless want to acknowledge the gamut of financial issues related to the operational start-up of a new business. Financing the initial operations begins with the variety of initial payments and the process of setting up the business, and ends with the first completed sale. The new organization has to be in a position to make initial payments for the following:

Purchasing equipment and supplies must be considered while planning the opening of a fitness club.

1. Security deposits
2. Utility set-up fees
3. Purchase/lease of initial equipment and installation and monthly maintenance
4. All licenses and inspections
5. All initial supplies such as computers, printers, letterhead, business cards, office supplies, fitness management software (this is a significant and often-overlooked expense)
6. Hiring and training of initial staff
7. Initial advertising expenses
8. Bank set-up fees

9. Business licenses and permits for different services, such as massage therapy or body work

10. Legal assistance in writing contracts, waivers, and trademarking and copyrighting

11. Accounting set-up and monthly or bimonthly assistance

12. Cost of liability insurance

These costs can be substantial and the new business must ensure that it has the proper resources to conduct such activities. If one element, such as purchasing of some key inputs, must be delayed due to a lack of resources, the impact can place the entire development of the new business's operations behind schedule.

Point number 8 in the list of financial considerations on page 130 brings up the issue of establishing a bank relationship. The new business is well served to establish a variety of financial relationships with its bank. Some of these key issues include establishing a revolving line of credit (working capital), acquiring a business credit card account, and setting up a basic business checking account. These accounts should have a primary signatory and a confirmation signatory as an audit safety condition. No one individual should be able to write checks for the business in excess of a specified amount (usually $500) without a countersignature.

Picking which bank to work with is more than a choice of which branch is closest to you. Working with small businesses is a specialized skill that all banks will say they possess, but which in fact may be very limited at a given institution. Some banks develop expertise in large commercial accounts such as Fortune 500 customers. Other banks have an expertise in retail banking, primarily serving individuals. Still other banks have their principal focus on small and medium-sized businesses. A bank may have a range of customers, but you want to ensure that it has an expertise in your type of business and understands issues such as timing of payments from customers. If you have a small personal training facility, you may need large draws on your lines of credit to acquire the necessary equipment to compete with other facilities. Or you may need funds for a seasonal marketing push. Whether your bank can work with such issues is an important question for a new business owner. The expertise of other successful small business owners in your area provides valuable insight into these issues. Don't limit yourself to just understanding other gyms and health and fitness facilities when studying those successful businesses. You can gain valuable insight into customer service skills and integration of technology from businesses such as hotels, restaurants, and retailers.

> ## EXERCISE 2
>
> 1. Without referring back to the list in this section, name as many initial financial payments that a business must make as you can, then check your responses to see which ones you might have missed.
>
> 2. List at least three things that a business owner sets up with a bank to establish a relationship.
>
> 3. Identify several banks in your area. Which banks focus on small and medium-sized businesses? Which have the type of expertise your future business might need?

LO 8.3 Legitimacy

A topic rarely discussed in the establishment of a new business is the issue of legitimacy. **Legitimacy** is the term that we use to discuss acceptance by key stakeholders, such as customers and suppliers, that you are a genuine business that will still be in operation next year. Developing the perception of legitimacy for both customers and suppliers can be difficult, although it is critical to the long-term survival of the business.[2]

[legitimacy]
The acceptance by key stakeholders such as customers and suppliers that you are a genuine business that will still be in operation next year.

The new business will need to look and act like an operation that will be in business for the long run in order to achieve some level of legitimacy. Customers and suppliers want to do business with someone who will still be in business next year. If a customer buys a six-month package of personal training sessions and the trainer is out of business in two months, to whom does she turn? When an equipment supplier gives a five-year lease or sells equipment on terms of 90 days, where will that firm get its payment if the fitness club that bought the goods cannot create enough revenue to pay its bills? Thus, both customers and suppliers want to ensure your business will be operating for the long term before they do business with you.

You will recall from our discussion of community supports in Chapter 2 that we discussed business incubators. A great incubator for personal trainers and other health professionals is to rent gym space by the hour or month from a small or medium-sized local health and fitness facility. This scenario is a small-scale replica of running and owning your own health and fitness facility. Put together your budget and forecast. Can you create, maintain, and grow your business in line with your forecasted revenues and expenses? By testing the waters in this way you have a bit more freedom to learn by trial and error. What marketing works best for you and your business? Can you acquire enough business to lease a building on your own? What are the patterns of the busy and slow times of your business and market?

Regardless of the business location, the small business owner needs to consider the potential means with which to establish the legitimacy of the business in the eyes of the customers and suppliers. Below is a list of classic items that may help establish more legitimacy for your new business:

1. A business checking account with the firm's name printed on the checks; start the check numbering higher than 001, or even 101
2. A business credit card
3. A bank line of credit
4. Professional business cards
5. Professional letterhead, billing slips, envelopes, etc.
6. Professional advertising material such as flyers, brochures, and web-based advertising
7. The prestige of the business address
8. Job titles
9. Telephone answering support
10. A high-quality website
11. A board of advisers/directors with excellent community visibility
12. Endorsements from well-recognized and respected individuals

EXERCISE 3

1. Define legitimacy.
2. Give an example of why a new business must be legitimate to a supplier or customer.
3. Without referring back to the list in this section, name as many ways that a business can legitimize itself as you can, then check your responses to see which ones you might have missed.

You may have noticed that some items in the list above are quite inexpensive, while others are both time-consuming and expensive. For instance, creating job titles for yourself, your partners, and employees can cost nothing but can be a subtle way of adding to your business's legitimacy. We suggest that all new businesses develop a plan to establish and continually enhance their legitimacy. Appearances are not everything, but they are important, especially at the outset of the business.

LO 8.4 Quality

Another important consideration in all aspects of a business venture is the investment in quality. In the recent past, designing quality into your product/service was a means to differentiate a small business from mass-market businesses. Increasingly, however, quality is an assumed standard whether the small business is in manufacturing or is a service business. Individuals have to look no further than fast-food restaurants. For illustration purposes, look at a franchise such as McDonald's. It sells a number of products for $1.00, has playgrounds for kids, maintains clean tables and restrooms, and even puts a toy in a meal for children. The playgrounds are expansive and expensive, while the food quality is guaranteed across the spectrum of all McDonald's restaurants. It is a tremendous value for a very small price, and each store opens with the full complement of offerings. If a new business is to compete against McDonald's, the firm will have to have a similar quality and quantity of offerings to be successful. Therefore, new businesses need to be clear about the expectations for quality in whatever business they pursue.

One of the keys to successfully delivering quality is the monitoring and measuring systems put into place by the founder(s). Dr. W. Edwards Deming is considered the father of the quality movement in the United States. One of his arguments is that quality needs to be constantly and consistently improved. Thus, there needs to be a continuous set of measures for each of the various processes of the organization. Without recorded data, it is impossible to judge the performance of the processes that have been put in place by the owner(s).

Deming went much further and argued that while the organization should set goals for quality, these goals are not to drive every action. If they did, the business might make short-term decisions that were detrimental to the overall direction of the company. To illustrate, a fitness business owner may have a goal to help all his clients meet their individual health and fitness goals according to a forecasted time chart. This is a great way of building credibility and gathering powerful testimonials, but if the business gets too wrapped up in these goals, it may loosen its grip on the quality of its training programs. Being able to meet your original projections for weight loss or muscle gain is great, but some of those goals may need modification to better serve the client. If you stick to the goals single-mindedly, you may gain a reputation as a relentless task master and alienate a good portion of your market.

Deming strongly suggests that businesses be guided by what he calls the "scientific method." In this method, rather than changing many things at the same time, the firm should change only one thing at a time, measuring the impact of that change. It is through this systematic method that a firm knows if it is moving in the right direction and also knows the true impact of each change.

For instance, some fitness clubs have streams of revenue that are ancillary to mainstream membership fees—retail products, group training, classes featuring different modalities, in-home training, etc. It is best to add such ancillary features in a gradual, methodical manner rather than all at once so that you can test each in your market. In this way, you can best manage your time, resources, and space.

EXERCISE 4

1. Explain why, according to Deming's scientific method, it is important for businesses to implement changes one at a time.
2. Create a simple chart for monitoring and measuring a personal trainer's weekly time spent in a facility.

LO 8.5 Technology

Virtually every business in every industry has been transformed by technology, especially in the age of the personal computer. Fitness businesses are no exception. Entrepreneurs seeking to establish a new fitness business must consider at least three general areas of technology in planning their start-up: in the back office, in sales and marketing, and on the training floor.

For many small businesses, a single personal computer may be all that's necessary to run the accounting and management of the business. And because the fitness business is a particularly mobile industry, you are well-advised to make that computer a laptop. Depending on the size of your business, however, it may be necessary for more employees to use computers, and therefore you may need to invest in a server. Depending on your computer skills, a consultant may be needed to set up and administer your network.

Back Office Technology. Much of the work of managing a business will be done on your computer. Aside from the essential time you will spend interacting with your employees and clients in person, you will be working on finances, creating staff and class schedules, and e-mailing correspondence on your computer—and, perhaps, your smartphone or other mobile computer devices, too.

Good computer skills are necessary to run a business, and certain software knowhow can both save cost and add to your company's legitimacy. For instance, your ability to operate your accounting software will allow you to generate accurate and professional-looking invoices and purchase orders, receipts for clients, and financial reports rather than paying a bookkeeper or an accountant to do these tasks. Your ability to use a word processing or page-design program will allow you to create professional-looking letterhead, business cards, and even an e-mail signature rather than paying a graphic designer to do so. At the same time, your ability to recognize your limitations in this area will help you realize that hiring professionals may ultimately be more worthwhile than producing amateurish work in software that you cannot operate well.

Sales and Marketing Technology. It is no secret that the Internet has brought the world into the palm of everyone's hand. Technology gives small business owners the tools to brand and broadcast their company identity to the entire world while sitting in the gym after a workout. Depending on your software skills, you can do any of the following tasks either on your own or using vendors whom you can locate, hire, and interact with strictly on the web:

1. Create a name for your business.

2. Create a logo.

3. Secure a web address.

4. Design and administer your website and even a blog that will help promote your business.

5. Establish and administer your social networking presence on sites such as Facebook, Twitter, Merchant Circle, LinkedIn, MySpace, and Google Ads.

6. Create PowerPoint presentations or simple Picasa slide shows promoting your business to potential clients or investors or for corporate meetings and trade shows.

7. Create e-mail blast marketing campaigns or establish an e-mail newsletter to keep in continual touch with your client base.

And this is just scratching the surface of the marketing potential that exists with current technology, let alone incipient technologies that are just around the corner. Every new technology potentially provides a business owner with a marketing medium. Let's consider just the groundbreaking consumer technologies of recent years from Apple Computer. When the iPod came along, smart entrepreneurs began creating podcasts to promote their products. When the iPhone came along, they created applications (apps) tied to their products—or apps that were the products themselves. When the iPad came along, those apps were adapted to exploit the larger format of the iPad display. Apple iPods used to track a person's workout progress and Nike shoes are prime examples of ever-changing technology. Consider that a dynamic, creative fitness professional could potentially tap into each of the technologies we just mentioned to promote her own business.

On the Training Floor. Gone are the days when a fitness club owner must split his time behind a desk and being on the training floor of his club. With a laptop or a tablet computing device, virtually any business management software can be accessed from any location, allowing a manager to roam freely and maximize the amount of time he spends interacting with clients and employees. So while you are on the training floor, you can, for instance, reference client training programs and make appropriate changes immediately, help clients review food journals and track their weight-loss progress, book appointments into the club's calendar, and send and receive e-mail.

> ## EXERCISE 5
>
> 1. Examine the different types of software listed below. Which types are most important to your business? Which ones would you have to buy and/or learn?
>   - Accounting
>   - Word processing
>   - Design
>   - Fitness-related (exercises, workout plans)
>   - Web design
>   - Video/audio
> 2. What types of technological equipment do you already own? What kinds would you have to purchase for your business?
> 3. Should your lease address technology? Why or why not?

LO 8.6 Equipment

Acquiring the initial equipment for a business can be a daunting task. The basic equipment can easily be the most expensive cost for a new business. For a fitness club owner, it is essential to resist becoming caught up in fads and the need for the biggest, newest equipment on the market. You will be leasing or owning the big equipment in your facility, so it is essential that you consider how the equipment will help you five years down the road, not just for the next few months. You must consider whether you will receive a return on your investment by attracting clients to your club to use the equipment.

It is important that major expenditures on equipment are budgeted strategically, taking a number of factors into consideration, including:

1. Your financial resources

2. Acquiring essential equipment first, followed by ancillary or specialty equipment (i.e., cardiovascular equipment, then resistance training equipment and free weights, then flexibility mats, stability balls, etc.)

3. Your space limitations

4. Your competition (the equipment you need just to compete, as well as any equipment that you think may give you a competitive advantage)

Many fitness club owners advise that it's best to buy the best-quality equipment you can afford because the quality, rather than the quantity, of your equipment will be a reflection of your business.

You may need to purchase smaller, more portable equipment if you plan to take your training mobile. Resistance bands, medicine balls, jump ropes, and a TRX Suspension Cable system can compete with—and outperform—machines. Think of all the things you could do with bands, balls, and body weight and how these activities can be modified for different clients.

It is important that the small business owner accurately evaluate the equipment needs while at the same time recognizing that there is a wide flexibility in the types, ages, methods of acquisition, and availability of all equipment obtained for the new organization. Purchasing new equipment may guarantee that it is the most current available and that it will be delivered directly to the new business; however, it is usually the most expensive method, and delays may be significant if the items are not in stock. Purchasing older equipment has its own risks with quality and availability but should always be investigated. It is relatively common for new equipment to **depreciate** 50 percent or more in the first year.

The ability to lease the equipment is particularly attractive to new companies because it has the lowest initial costs. However, over the long run such leasing can prove expensive. Therefore, the new business owner needs to clearly understand what equipment is needed, how long it will be before it will need to be replaced, and the long-term impacts of the decision. This understanding should also include both what equipment is needed to begin operations and how quickly the company might need more/bigger equipment. The new business owner should then prepare a chart comparing the price and the positives and negatives of buying new, buying used, or leasing that equipment. The positives and negatives should include not only the immediate cost and the ability to overcome the cash flow crunch that impacts all new businesses, but also the impact on the firm's quality, and the long-term impact if the small business grows. Figure 8.1 is a sample chart listing some of the advantages and disadvantages of buying and leasing equipment. Some additional considerations include:

- How long you will need to use the equipment

- What you intend to do with the equipment at the end of your lease

- Your tax situation

[depreciate]

To lose value.

EXERCISE 6

1. Think about the equipment at the fitness facility where you train. What do you think is the relationship between the facility's equipment and its success?

2. What are the "lease or buy" equipment issues you anticipate facing in your business?

3. Prepare a chart comparing the price and the positives and negatives of buying new, buying used, or leasing equipment.

Figure 8.1
Advantages and
Disadvantages of Buying
and Leasing Equipment

Buying New/Used	Leasing
No ability to finance	Ability to finance
Have to buy and will own equipment outright	You "rent" equipment
You are responsible for repair and maintenance	You may not be responsible for repair and maintenance as leasing company will handle.
Equipment may become outdated	Chance to lease updated equipment or upgrade equipment.
May have to save for equipment purchase	Allows businesses to buy equipment "now"
No provision for tax advantage	May be able to deduct lease payments from corporate income

- Your cash flow
- Your company's anticipated future growth needs

LO 8.7 Facility and Equipment Layout

Even before moving into your business space, it is important to spend time planning the layout of your club. The layout will depend on the type of fitness business you plan to operate. Are you doing mostly personal training or will there be a full schedule of group classes? A key to any fitness environment is to create an adequate amount of room so that clients do not feel cramped. Think about a restaurant owner who tries to squeeze in as many seats as possible to maximize his space. But if he doesn't allow enough space for customers to feel comfortable, the business will suffer. The same is true in a fitness club, or even a yoga studio, which should limit class sizes to allow clients to move around and have their own personal space.

So, for example, a small personal training studio or private fitness club of about 1,000–3,000 square feet should plan to have room for the following:

- Dedicated waiting area/reception area
- Office and/or consultation space
- Stretching and body-weight movement area
- Space to run/shuffle, jump, throw, lunge, and use free weights
- Cardio space
- Small spots to sit and rest
- Space around machines for multiplanar movement
- Space to hook resistance bands and suspension cables
- Secure space for clients to store personal items
- Bathrooms and/or dressing rooms

Planning how to arrange all of these dedicated spaces is somewhat of an art. Certain types of space are more important to plan first so you can

shoehorn other areas around them. For instance, here is the order in which a new fitness club owner might plan for space usage:

1. First, plan offices, meeting space, entry, and waiting areas.

2. Next, map out bathrooms, dressing rooms, lockers, and storage.

3. Planning for cardiovascular equipment is the next priority; these machines will reside in a large, fixed spot that eliminates space to do any other training on or near this space.

4. Next, plan the space for storing additional training equipment and the space where clients will use the equipment. For instance, cable functional trainers need up to 8–10 feet in front and 6–7 feet to the sides to be used properly.

5. After you have committed large, fixed equipment to certain areas, you can plan to utilize remaining open space for plyometrics, bands, and stability balls.

6. Other space needs in your plan may include a massage room and Pilates or yoga space.

In planning your space, don't try to copy what the big corporate gyms are doing. They need to accommodate hundreds of unsupervised, novice clients, so their space planning may be motivated by a need to eliminate liability and to maximize choices. Your small club won't need a lot of bulky equipment that allows for limited range in all planes of movement like they do. Versatility should be a top priority in choosing large equipment for purchase or lease. For instance, double-stack functional cable machines that can be operated by clients of any size, age, weight, or ability would be preferable to a Smith machine or leg press machine.

If you are building out a space from scratch, you will need to consult an architect and an electrical engineer to be sure your proposed layout is within building codes and that the flow of business is well considered. Then use chalk to mark off the areas where you want to place equipment. Walk through the space several times and imagine yourself training on the floor. You will find that certain pieces may not fit where you want them or at all. Once you have tried out your layout in this way you will need to consult an architect and lighting engineer to finalize your design. All of this planning must be done before you buy your equipment.

EXERCISE 7

1. Suppose you found a location for your small fitness facility. It is 25 × 50 feet and was previously used as retail space. The space is already set up with two offices side by side in a back corner and a single bathroom with no shower in the other back corner. Modify the space by planning and sketching out the rest of the area. Consider the recommended order of tasks in space planning provided in this section.

2. What limitations did you find?

3. What changes did you have to make with regard to your initial ideas?

LO 8.8 User Space and Safety

As part of the process of planning the space, a fitness business owner must consider issues of liability. For example, space must be planned for equipment such as olympic bars, free weights, medicine balls, and balance balls to be stored out of the flow of traffic. Likewise, you should not place your free weights area next to your stretching area. It would be a liability and a certain lawsuit if a weight happened to drop on someone who is stretching. It is your responsibility to provide the safest possible environment for your clients and employees, and space planning is part of the equation.

To limit your liability, you must also ensure that your equipment is always in its best working order, so you must plan for monthly maintenance of all equipment. This involves everything from service contracts for your machines to a monthly log to check the air pressure in balance balls. You should have an orientation program for trainers and clients that includes introducing them to the facility and instructing them how to use every piece of equipment in your studio, standards on replacing equipment, and cleaning mats and benches. Also included in your orientation for trainers should be a review of standards of conduct to ensure your business is represented the way you want and to avoid

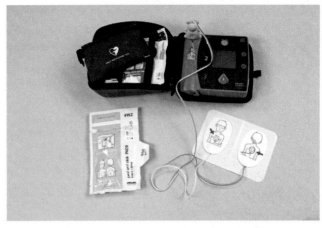

Safety must be taken into consideration when planning a fitness business. For instance, insurance and government regulations may require you to purchase an AED (automatic external defibrillator) for your facility.

injuries due to carelessness. The appendix of this book includes a sample Standards of Conduct form that can be utilized to help establish your standards for your club. As the business owner you are the leading example in your facility. If you establish a standard, be sure to follow it without exception.

As discussed in Chapter 7, every trainer (including you, the owner) should have personal liability insurance and be certified in CPR. In addition, you should have workplace liability insurance to cover any major accidents or mishaps. Everyone that steps onto the training floor should sign an injury waiver form that protects you and your business from accidents.

Personal property is a liability issue you need to protect yourself and your business from. Be sure to have a designated and secure space for clients to put their valuables.

EXERCISE 8

1. Review your sketch from Exercise 7. If necessary, adjust the plan as you consider traffic flow and safety issues.

2. Compile a list of standards you would want to establish in your fitness facility.

3. Devise a simple orientation plan for clients new to your planned space, listing at least five points you would want to cover.

LO 8.9 Timing

It is interesting to note that choosing when to start a business is an important operational element. The temptation for most new businesses is to start their operations as soon as possible. This is rarely an effective strategy. Instead the potential entrepreneur should select the time to enter the market based on when it provides the greatest competitive advantage.[3] The timing of your start is a function of several factors: (1) the general environment, (2) competitor moves, (3) cycles in purchasing and starting health and fitness programs and training, and (4) lifestyle issues.

The general economy moves in cycles of boom, slowdown, recession (or the million other terms that are used as euphemisms for this term), growth, and boom. While the general rule might be that you should open your business during or at the beginning of a boom, the reality is that different businesses depend upon different conditions. A foreclosure business depends upon poor economic times, and storage facilities do best when the economy is heading downward, etc.

Competitor moves may also dictate the opening of a new business. If your business plan is dependent upon having no direct competitors within a specified radius of your operation, a move by another business may accelerate or dramatically alter your plans. Alternatively, the failure of several similar businesses may suggest an alteration of your opening or strategic positioning prior to your actually opening the business.

Some (we might suggest most) businesses have cycles for their purchasing. Your ability to build a strong clientele base in order to establish legitimacy may dictate your lead time and opening time. The busiest time for health and fitness is at the beginning of the calendar year, when people tend to make New Year's resolutions. But opening your business in January will put you behind the competition. Creating a name for yourself and gaining marketing traction in the summer or fall will position you to take advantage of the New Year's boom. Seasoned personal trainers know that December is the time to start signing up new clients by offering special packages to commit clients before the new year. Thus, their schedules will be full by the time January 1 rolls around, meaning that the weeks following January 1 are a difficult time to snare new clients.

The ability of a new business owner to understand these timing issues requires extensive planning and forecasting, without which the new business can fail.

EXERCISE 9

1. Should all new companies open as soon as their physical space is ready? Why or why not?
2. Compose a list of critical timing issues involved in your fitness business. Consider the general economic environment, competitor moves, cycles in purchasing and starting health and fitness programs and training, and lifestyle issues.

LO 8.10 Time Management

The last item is one that is meant to help new business owners as they seek to manage the wide variety of operations covered in this chapter. It is clear from the discussion provided here that business owners will need to manage their own time efficiently if they are to be successful.[4] There are several steps that are helpful in this process.

1. Write down what has to be accomplished in all parts of the business formation.
2. Prioritize which tasks are critical and which would be helpful. Those that are critical must be done and should be the priority.
3. Segment items in terms of the time frame in which they need to be accomplished—short term and long term. The short-term items that are critical have to take priority. The fires

that are burning have to be put out before the longer-term issues approach.

4. Allocate time for dealing with operational issues. The more you become involved in establishing the business and its operations, the more individuals will wish to visit with you about the business. While some of these individuals will be helpful, many simply will wish to sell you something you do not need or to find out what you are doing. As your agenda becomes filled you must ensure that your attention is not diverted to nonproductive activities. This does not mean you should not be flexible when opportunities arise, but it does mean that you must have a clear vision of your work goals.

5. Write tasks down and mark them off when you accomplish them. As your agenda becomes more complex, you will gain satisfaction from seeing things being removed from it. This method also ensures that you will not forget key items. In writing these things down, it is best if you can do this in a systematic, organized manner. Keep a notebook or use a to-do app every day to see what you must accomplish, and take notes about those goals. This approach can also be a valuable resource for keeping notes about meetings, issues that hit you as you think about the business, and issues that others raise with you. From these items and other information, you can keep track of issues to deal with today, this week, this month, etc.

EXERCISE 10

1. Write a list of the tasks that must be accomplished in all areas of your business's formation.
2. Prioritize which tasks would be critical and which would be helpful.
3. Segment the items in terms of the time frame in which they need to be accomplished—short term and long term.
4. Allocate time for dealing solely with operational issues.
5. Develop an agenda based on the tasks you have identified.

---

key terms

depreciate 136
legitimacy 131

review questions

1. Explain how a commercial real estate agent and her reputation can be valuable assets to a new business owner.
2. Is a bank's location the most important feature to a new business owner? Why or why not?
3. Define business incubator.
4. Name all of the types of services you believe your fitness business should offer. Will you offer all of these services upon opening? Will the business be better served by incorporating some of these services gradually over time rather than upon opening? If so, build a prioritized list of the services in the order in which you would like to introduce them. If not, how would it benefit your business to offer them all upon opening?
5. Study the different types of social networking sites available on the Internet. Do you think having a social network on the Internet is important to the fitness business you want to start? Why or why not? If so, which ones do you think would be most beneficial?

6. Formulate justifications for why it is important to involve an architect and an electrical engineer in the design of your facility.
7. Justify why you should have workplace liability insurance at your facility in addition to having all trainers hold professional liability insurance.
8. Suppose you own a personal training studio with three other trainers besides yourself. All of you become completely booked for January through April, but you are getting more and more customers asking to sign up for your four-month New Year's special, which has not yet ended but will in one week. How would you solve the problem of possibly having to turn away business?
9. Recommend some time management techniques for an entrepreneur.

individual exercises

1. Imagine you decide to start your fitness business as an independent contractor rather than the owner of a facility. This may alter any of your plans regarding operational issues of (1) location, (2) initial financial considerations, (3) legitimacy, (4) quality, (5) technology, (6) equipment, (7) space layout, (8) space and safety, (9) timing of opening, and (10) time management.
2. Decide how you would handle each of these issues as an independent contractor. Consider where you will perform your training (your home, customer's home, club, or a combination of these) and where and how you will handle office work (scheduling, accounting, marketing, etc.).

group exercise

1. Break into small groups of two or three.
2. Establish a plan to address each of the critical issues related to the starting of operations for a new organization.
3. Imagine that your team has decided to franchise the business idea. Develop a set of processes/procedures that would allow a third party to become a franchise of your operation.
4. Present your operational plan to the class and ask for feedback.

learning outcomes

After studying this chapter, you will be able to:

9.1 Describe the importance of a solid financial foundation for a small business

9.2 Identify key financial issues involved with starting a business

9.3 Discuss the basics of funding a business

9.4 Explain the importance of proper accounting when starting a business

9.5 Demonstrate knowledge of business and independent contractor taxes

Financing and Accounting

CASE STUDY

Starting a new business takes creative ideas and creative funding. Trish, a very active mother of two, loved to engage in activities with her children and kept them active in sports such as soccer, basketball, and tennis. When it came time for her to work out, she had to take her children with her, only to see them secluded in a room with other children of various ages and little activity. One day, after reading about the removal of physical education in their local school district, Trish began to wonder how much physical activity her children received outside of what she does with them. Then the thought occurred to her. She loved to work out, she wanted her children to be able to work out, and she wanted them to be physically active . . . so why not create a fitness center that would address all of these concerns? Her goal was to design a fitness center that was centered around family so that children and parents could work out together or separately. After researching the idea, Trish found that there were no franchise opportunities out there for such a concept, and to finance such a start-up would be a significant cost, but she believed she could manage it. Trish had recently sold her craft company, so she took those profits and leaped at this new opportunity. Trish knew that to get into the fitness industry usually takes substantial funds, if they are available, or solid financing in order to buy an existing business or start one up. Trish also knew that starting up this type of business was not a small consideration and most likely will take some type of financing. Trish knew that the return can be excellent, but the upfront money needs must be considered from the beginning.

Children and Family Fitness Center opened with just a few families and their children using the center. After a year, Trish was faced with a very expensive rent increase for the building she rented and the first lease payment on the equipment she leased. She began to wonder if she had made the right decision. She cashed out her savings and 401(k) as a last resort before she hit a financial wall.

One afternoon, one of the mothers who frequently visited the center asked Trish if she wanted to make a presentation to the PTA board and its members. Trish hesitated to do this based on the tenuous state of her business, but she decided to approach the idea with her usual zeal. After her presentation, several mothers and fathers approached Trish, claiming that they didn't know such a wonderful facility existed and asking when they could schedule themselves and their families to come in. Trish remembers this simple event as the turning point in her business's success. Within a year Trish would have more than 70 families with about 200 children using her facility on a regular basis.

With a new business up and running, the focus of the business shifts from developmental activities to day-to-day operations. In starting a successful business, good initial development is important, but perhaps as important are the efforts put into the business as it grows. Once in operation, the business exists within the competitive marketplace and is subject to competitive attack, customer response to the services or products offered, collections issues, etc. No operating business ever matches the proposed business exactly. The reality of operations and the ability to adjust to those realities is the key to managing a successful business. Adjusting requires an in-depth analysis of the business's progress.

Financing and establishing the accounting systems are central operational concerns in the start-up of a new business. In Chapter 6 we examined the basic financial analysis (on a pro forma basis) that should be used to evaluate the decision to start a business. Now we must consider the specific financing and accounting issues that impact the operational start-up of the business. Specifically, three questions are examined in this chapter:

1. How will you fund the new business, and what funding level is really needed for the new venture?

2. What accounting records will you maintain, and how will you maintain them?

3. How will you manage the paper/data flow of the new company?

All of these issues are directly related to the establishment of the financial structure and record keeping of the new company. Too often new businesspeople put these issues at the bottom of their priority list (both during and after start-up) and do not devote much time to them. However, it is far easier to establish items such as a sound system to account for the transactions of the business at the beginning of the venture. Some forethought on the process will save frustration after the business is up and running.

LO 9.1 Financial Foundation

The evaluation of a business starts with the mission of the organization and is (as was pointed out in Chapter 4) always relative to the industry in which the business competes. The key measures of the business should focus on the key aspects with which the business hopes to build its competitive advantage. For example, if the mission of the organization is to be a low-cost operation, then rigorous control of expenses would be the focus. This would suggest that very little money should be spent on such activities as research and development or new product introductions. The business's outcomes would be measured at intervals that were relevant to the business, which, in the case of evaluating cost savings, might mean measuring such items very frequently, perhaps even daily.

In this chapter we will examine the development of the various metrics (measures) that should be used to evaluate the business. These analytical techniques are easily available and readily understandable by any business owner.

EXERCISE 1

1. Identify three questions to an entrepreneur that are directly related to the establishment of the financial structure and record keeping of a new company.

2. Fill in the blank: The evaluation of a business starts with _____ and is always relative to the industry in which the business competes.

LO 9.2 Identification of Key Issues

There are a wide range of issues that new businesses need to be aware of that are related to financing of the start-up. The issues we address in this chapter are not ordered by their importance; instead these issues are intertwined with each other. The first is the funding and funding level of the business. The next is the establishment of an accounting system. Finally, the flow of information in the new business needs specific attention. If the new business does not address these issues very early on in the process, then the owners will constantly be putting out fires related to these items rather than focusing on building the business.

Extra expenses, especially early on in a business's life when no (or virtually no) income is coming in, can quickly use up the cash intended to found and grow the business. By the time a new business pays for all start-up and unforeseen expenses, the business could well be out of cash. How much initial funding does a business need in order to survive the first year of operation? What type of financial cushion should be in place to help buffer the business when an unexpected cost arises? Central to a financial cushion is the nature of the business's funding. When considering funding, the business needs to evaluate not only the amount provided but also the sources of that funding. A key aspect of how the funding will be used is found in the information provided by the business, and that comes through the accounting system and the data flow management. Thus, all of these issues are interconnected and will be discussed in turn.

> ## EXERCISE 2
>
> 1. Name the three key issues related to the financing of a new business.
> 2. Are these separate or interconnected issues? Explain.
> 3. Discuss how a business might be out of cash by the end of its first year.

LO 9.3 Funding

Funding for almost any new business starts with the owner/founder(s) and her own resources. However, at some stage (often prior to actual start-up), the business will need to find other sources of funding. These sources may be small and receive no equity (ownership) interest in return for the funding. This funding may be a line of credit, in which a person or a bank agrees to help finance certain functions for the business. This party is paid back with interest as supplies are used and revenue is received from customers. The line of credit can go up and down, therefore, as the need for supplies rises and falls and the account is repaid. In contrast, others will make **equity investments,** in which someone provides funding in return for some ownership in the business. Each of these types of funding will be reviewed in turn.

[equity investment]
Funds received by a business in exchange for a percentage ownership of the business.

Nonequity Funding

There are several principal sources for nonequity capital to start a business. Debt is a major source of such nonequity financing and can come from banks, credit cards, asset leasing, and/or suppliers. Grants are another nonequity funding method that some businesses can access. A grant may come from the government or a nonprofit agency; it is simply money designed to help the new business begin operations.

[debt]

A generic term to describe any type of nonequity funding tied to the business.

Debt. **Debt** comes in many forms, each with positives and negatives for a new business. Debt is any form of dollar infusion that must be paid back with interest. Debt allows the new business to manage its cash flow for various peaks and valleys in the operation of a business or, more important, to handle the disparity between when goods must be purchased and when money will be received from a customer to pay for those goods. The most common forms of debt for small businesses can be classified as follows:

1. loans from
   a. bank or finance company
   b. individuals
   c. founders
2. credit cards
3. supplier credit

[loan]

Contractual agreement whereby the business receives some amount of money that must be repaid over a specified period of time at a specified interest rate.

Loans. A **loan**, regardless of its origin, involves a contractual agreement whereby the business receives some amount of money that must be repaid over a specified period of time at a specified interest rate. Loans are repaid monthly from cash flow and, especially early in the life of a business, are secured by an asset or personal guarantee. In the case of dissolution, debt generally must be paid back prior to any equity investors receiving a distribution.

[asset-based lending]

A loan provided for the purchase of a necessary asset for the business.

Banks have traditionally been a major source of funds for established businesses but are quite restrictive in their lending to start-up businesses, as the risk is perceived to be too high. However, there are some specific ways that banks lend to new businesses. For example, banks will make loans for the purchase of some types of equipment. In this type of lending, the bank will estimate the residual value of the equipment if the bank had to repossess the equipment and then lend the business a percentage of the difference between that number and the sale price. This discount is typically quite significant. This type of lending is referred to as **asset-based lending.** As discussed in Chapter 8, a relationship with a bank is critical to the small business's ability to obtain bank financing.[1]

Banks will also lend money for the establishment and maintenance of inventory by arranging a revolving line of credit. A lender will periodically perform an on-site examination of the inventory to ensure that the inventory is being used properly. A particular problem with lines of credit for inventory is that a business may have old inventory that has not been sold for a period of time. Such inventory needs to be discounted, as its value in the market has shrunk. Too often businesses still reflect that old inventory on their books at full market value.

Individuals are also a wonderful source of funding for the business. For example, loans can come from friends and family. While the conditions may be a bit more relaxed, the small business owner should view the loan as he would one from a bank. One issue to consider in such loans is that if the business fails, the inability to repay such loans can permanently rupture the family relationship or friendship.

The owner/founder(s) of the business may also choose to lend money to the business themselves. While it may strike some as odd to lend money to your own business, debt is a secured investment. Therefore, if you lend your business $1,000, then you, along with the other debt holders, have the right to the business's assets if the business fails to pay off that debt. An equity investor generally receives only those proceeds that are left after paying off all other debts.

Credit Cards. Credit cards are another form of nonequity investment. A **credit card** is another type of credit. However, a credit card is not tied to any particular asset, nor does it have a set repayment schedule (other than a minimum payment), although it is usually tied to a much higher interest rate.

[credit card]
Card entitling one to revolving credit that is not tied to any particular asset, does not have a set repayment schedule, and is usually tied to a much higher interest rate than that of a bank loan.

We have worked with a number of small businesses that decided early on to finance their operations with credit card debt. One small business person running a whole foods store would, when faced with a new bill for the company, go to the center desk drawer to look through more than 60 active credit cards to decide which one should be used to pay the bill. Not only is this a very poor management system that is extremely expensive, but it is also one where the debt is almost always tied personally to the founder(s), thus exposing them to personal bankruptcy. That said, credit cards can be a wonderful short-term method of managing your cash flow, especially during peak times in the early stages of the business. If paid off each month, business-issued credit cards provide the company with an excellent financial tracking system that can be divided up by individuals within the company, and payment can be delayed by up to 25 days, allowing for a unique positive cash flow situation. However, the small business must be able to carefully manage such debt if it is going to be employed.

Supplier Credit. Supplier credit is another form of nonequity funding.[2] Suppliers will generally provide credit on both physical assets (such as gym equipment) and the actual supplies purchased. A business such as IBM Credit LLC is an example of a business that you may be familiar with that exists primarily to fund the acquisition or lease of IBM products. The credit terms offered by such a business can be quite generous, but they are a liability for the company and need to be managed as such. Accepting **supplier credit** ties you to that supplier, limiting your ability to shop around for a cheaper source. The terms can be quite generous and the rates are usually more competitive than those available from traditional bank sources.

[supplier credit]
A form of nonequity funding in which suppliers provide credit on physical assets and supplies.

Grants. The new small business should also explore **grants** from both governmental and private foundation sources. There are special funds that are neither equity nor debt funds that are designed to aid businesses in specific areas. These grants typically target disadvantaged groups, economic areas, or particular industries. There are also grants for target groups such as veterans. The presence of such grants varies widely based on the

[grants]
Special funds, neither equity nor debt, that do not require repayment and are designed to aid businesses in specific areas.

given funding year and where you live. Grants should be explored through groups such as your local Small Business Assistance Center.

Equity Funding

The new business should employ all nonequity funding mechanisms available to it. In the long run (assuming a successful business operation), the cost of such capital is generally less than that of equity investment. However, a growing small business might need to seek equity funding (investors' or founders' capital).

In the founding process, the business generally receives funds from the founder(s) as well as other investors. An evaluation is needed to determine the percentage of ownership each founder will have in the business and the percentage that will be reserved for investors. We will cover valuation of the business in Chapter 13, and we recommend that prior to allowing any nonfounder to invest in your new business, you have a fair and valid estimation of the value of your company. That said, we would like to address several key issues related to equity financing of the new business with outside sources.

Obtaining equity investment from investors has a number of potential operational impacts. Investors can be active or passive, majority or minority, companies that might ultimately wish to buy the whole new venture, and/or suppliers looking to add new volume for their products. Each of these potential sources has characteristics that can have a major impact on your business. Additionally, accepting an equity stake from an outside investor adds a dimension of accountability to the founding of a new business and opens the new venture up to new concerns. Therefore, seeking outside funding is a significant decision for the small business.

To illustrate the impact of outside investors, we worked with an entrepreneur who started a new high-end restaurant. The initial investment needed to make the venture work was substantial and well more than the founder could invest. She sought outside investors for the business from her country club, social friends, and business acquaintances. She ended up with 47 total investors with separate investments that varied from $8,000 to $110,000. The restaurant was built and opened to great fanfare. Thursday, Friday, and Saturday nights were packed, with an average wait for a table of two hours. The founder worked nonstop on those evenings but had continuous problems with her fellow "investors." A number of these investors felt that they deserved preferential treatment at the restaurant because they were "owners." Many of them demanded special favors, such as being placed first in the wait list for a table; walking through the kitchen (not a helpful thing to do on busy nights); talking to the chefs; or even having their meals "comped" (received for free). Some investors similarly felt free to discuss employee performance with the individual employees. These individuals would also call at will to talk to the founder about the restaurant's direction, as well as expecting to be able to meet with the founder at their convenience. The business owner finally had a meeting with all of the investors to lay out the problems involved with their behavior and the disruption to the success of the business. Several of the investors were indignant and demanded their investment be returned. This the business could not afford, and legally the owner did not have to comply with their request. The result was fractious relations with some investors, and an enormous amount of time being taken away from the business to handle "bruised egos." A little care in the initial setup of these relations could have prevented a series of problems later in the operation.

Equity investment involves selling a percentage of the business to an outside party. This should be done in consultation with an attorney who is well versed in this area of the law. The founder(s) must be very clear that in the case of dissolution, each investor is entitled to the percentage of the break-up value equal to his investment percentage of ownership. However, even more critical to the success of the business is to carefully and clearly outline what rights and expectations each investor has as the business grows. Will the new venture divide up all profits at the end of each year? What will be retained in the business for future growth? How can each investor "sell" her shares? Does the company have first right of refusal? Working with an attorney to develop a clear document that details all of the concerns about an equity investor should be completed prior to approaching a potential investor.

As previously mentioned, the sources of equity investment include other businesses, venture capitalists, and business angels.

Businesses as Equity Investors. Many established businesses are willing to make equity investments in other start-up businesses. Large businesses such as Microsoft, Intel, and Cisco have traditionally been among the most active equity investors in new start-up businesses in the technology sector. Of two scenarios that we have dealt with regularly, one type involves a company that will invest in a new venture with the idea of ultimately purchasing the operation. The second type is a large supplier that is willing to invest in a new operation as an additional outlet for its products.

The company that invests with the idea of an ultimate purchase does so because it is one of the least expensive means for trying out new ideas/products/methods. For the established company to try to develop every idea in-house, it would have to redirect significant resources away from the core focus of its business. Instead, the large business invests in a series of businesses that are trying new things within its industry, and in effect, it has taken out a series of strategic options without having to detract from its core business.[3] Those options that turn out to be successes are then purchased and brought into the core organization. This can be a wonderful harvest strategy for a newly founded business; however, the founder(s) may not wish to sell the business at the exact point in time that the larger company wishes to close the sale. Depending on the nature of the investment, the founder(s) may not have the option to decide when the business is sold.

Having a supplier invest in your new business is somewhat simpler, in that the supplier is generally not trying to run your business, nor is it looking to take the business over if it does particularly well. Instead, the issue with this type of equity investment is one of restriction. The deal usually involves an exclusivity agreement to use only that supplier's products. This can be a significant (and in some cases a business-killing) proposition.

The founder(s) must be careful not to trap themselves into an agreement that prevents flexibility that may be needed in the future.

Venture Capital (VC). A form of equity investment that seems to garner considerable press is venture capital. A **venture capital fund** is a fund that is usually organized as a limited partnership.[4] Limited partners in the fund, which may include very wealthy individuals, insurance companies, other businesses, and retirement funds, invest in such funds seeking high returns. The general partner in the fund is the venture capitalist, who then investigates and invests in each new business. Venture capitalists might invest in less than one out of the thousand business plans they see in a year. They are seeking extremely high-growth businesses that have an opportunity to "cash out" with an IPO or sale to a larger company within a relatively short period of time. The result is that it is extremely rare for a VC to invest in a small business. Additionally, VCs are looking to make a significant investment, generally something greater than $1 million. As such, they are not a source of funding for very many small businesses, and we spend very little time in this text on venture capital.*

Business Angels. Business angels are a form of equity investor that is more widely available to small businesses. **Business angels** are high-net-worth individuals who invest widely in businesses.[5] These individuals may include entrepreneurs who have built one or more businesses and have cashed out (i.e., sold their businesses and have the excess cash in hand), executives with large organizations that have high incomes, professionals such as doctors and lawyers, and individuals with significant inheritances. These individuals can be very helpful sources of expertise and contacts in the area. However, the small business owner should seek individuals who have relevant knowledge (not just money) to add to the business. When seeking investment from such individuals, we suggest that you evaluate the nature of their advice, how intrusive they will be, the nature of their business experience, and what other contacts and relationships the angels may have that can help the new business.

[venture capital fund]
A fund that is organized to make significant equity investments in high-growth new ventures.

[business angels]
High-net-worth individuals that invest in businesses not as a business, but as an individual.

ethical *challenge*

You have seen in this chapter that there are different types of investors and there can be different levels of investment. These investors come into the business facing potentially different types of risk and return.

QUESTIONS

1. Think about and discuss the ethical obligations you have to early-stage investors versus later-stage investors. Do you promise more returns to someone that shows faith in you at an earlier stage?

2. What are the ethical obligations if some investors are family members and some are not? Do family members deserve different investor treatment?

---

* If the student wishes to locate more information on venture capital and venture capitalists in his or her area, the National Venture Capital Association is an excellent source of information.

Other Financing Tools

There are several other financing tools that are available to the new business as it starts. These mechanisms include asset leasing and factoring.

Asset Leasing. A possible source of funding for a new organization is an **asset lease** arrangement. Similar to leasing a car, many of the assets needed by the new business can be leased from the manufacturer or from a third-party reseller. Instead of owning the assets, the company simply leases what it needs. In fact, there are companies (third-party resellers) that have a significant part of their inventory in equipment that they lease to other companies. The advantages are relatively straightforward. The new business is able to acquire the assets that it needs to begin operations with a minimal cash outlay. The company pays the lease from production that is a direct result of using the equipment that it has leased. Furthermore, it is not stuck with an aging asset. As newer, higher-quality machines become available, the small business is able to trade up.

[asset lease]

A form of lease tied to a particular asset used by a business to conserve cash and maintain the latest versions of whatever equipment is available.

The big disadvantage to leasing is that over time the small business may spend more money for equipment maintenance than if it had bought the unit outright. However, the net present value of the lease may actually work out to a net positive because the small business owner does not have to put as much cash initially into the lease as in a purchase. Therefore, the decision should evaluate two areas: (1) How much cash does the new business have to invest in equipment up front? and (2) Given the pace of equipment obsolescence in that industry, would it be more advantageous to lease or own the equipment needed to operate the business?

Initial Funding

The new businessperson needs to calculate how much money she will need to acquire prior to start-up. Although it would appear that more initial funding would be somewhat better than less, it must be tempered by what the founder has to give up to obtain the money. In Chapter 6 we examined the financial issues associated with break-even and basic cash flow analysis. The complexity of capital funding increases substantially as the new business requires external investment in order to begin operations.

To calculate the maximum amount that you may wish to obtain in outside financing, recall from Chapter 6 that we recommend that the small business founder calculate his entire cash flow projection without adding in any equity investment and look for the point where the ending cash balance is at its lowest point. A safe rule of thumb suggests taking that number and multiplying it by 150 percent. The resulting amount is what we recommend for the initial equity or equity-plus-debt investment. The new businessperson then connects this amount with the percentage of the business that he previously determined would be made available to other investors. The two points frame the new businessperson's investment parameters. Consider the following example:

Value of the Business Prior to Beginning Operations	$100,000
Lowest Point in Projected Cash Flow	20,000
Required Investment	30,000
Amount Invested by Founder	10,000
Amount Needed from Outside Investors	20,000
Potential Percentage of the Business to Be Expected by Investors (20,000/100,000)	20%

EXERCISE 3

1. How could you best use a credit card as a form of nonequity funding for your business?
2. Report a benefit and a disadvantage of obtaining a loan from a family member.
3. Report a benefit and a disadvantage of obtaining supplier credit.
4. What type of funding is neither equity nor nonequity funding? If you were going to apply for this type of funding, what about your business would make it eligible?
5. Why is it better to use all nonequity sources of funding before turning to equity sources of funding?

It is important to remember that negotiations between the founder(s) and your investor are just that, negotiations. It takes two willing parties to reach an agreement. You may see the investment in your business as worth X, while an investor sees it as worth Y. It will take negotiation to determine the ultimate value. A review of Chapter 12's discussion of valuation and negotiation should be helpful in conceptualizing these issues.

LO 9.4 Accounting

We do not presume in the next few pages to show you how to do all of the accounting that you will ever need to know to manage your business. There are many fine texts and courses available that focus tightly on this huge and complicated area of business. Furthermore, we covered the basics regarding the balance sheet and income statement in Chapter 6. That said, we would like to suggest that the needs of most small business owners are very straightforward and can best be met with one of the numerous computer software programs available.

The new businessperson will need to quickly decide whether she will use a cash- or accrual-basis accounting system. In its simplest form, cash-based accounting recognizes expenses as they are paid and recognizes revenue as it is generated. Accrual-based accounting is the more typical form of accounting utilized, with expenses and revenues being recorded when they apply, regardless of when the cash is received. This type of accounting must be used if

- you have inventory;
- you have gross sales over $5 million per year; and
- your business is a Subchapter C corporation, partnership, or trust.

The end result is that only the smallest businesses use cash-basis accounting.

The small business owner will need to carefully evaluate which accounting program would be the best for his business. We believe that the key to evaluating these programs is knowing what you want to accomplish and what you really need and do not need. All of the major programs have vast capabilities to enter, track, and produce financial information. Following is information about some of the top accounting programs for small businesses. This information will ground you in the major programs that are available.

Simply Accounting Accounting Software

Simply Accounting is the full-featured, entry-level accounting solution for small businesses, providing quick setup, ease of use, and payroll functionality. www.simplyaccounting.com

MYOB Premier Accounting Software

Premier Accounting's complete feature set includes sales, purchases, banking, inventory, payroll, and more. www.myob.com

QuickBooks Accounting Software

QuickBooks is a popular, full-featured accounting and payroll program designed for small businesses. QuickBooks is available in a suite of packages, from a quick start version to editions for accountants. http://quickbooks.intuit.com

Peachtree Complete Accounting Software

Similar to QuickBooks, the Peachtree offerings run the gamut from simple online systems all the way to professional systems used by accountants. www.peachtree.com/

ABC Financial

This is a comprehensive and well-supported club management program that allows business owners to do electronic funds transferring (EFT) and marketing.

EZ Facility + eFit Financial

This software promotes full-service billing, collections, scheduling, and marketing support.

These are just some of the numerous accounting programs that are available to small fitness businesses. Choosing a package that will be useful for your business is a process of understanding your new business first and then finding a package that will accommodate your needs with the least impact on the business. Most of the packages will provide any report that could be demanded by the owner(s), potential investors, auditors, or loan officers. These are some of the key reports that the new businessperson should be prepared to generate: (1) chart of accounts, (2) petty cash register, (3) check register, (4) expense accounts, (5) inventory accounts, (6) accounts payable, and (7) payroll.

Chart of Accounts

The chart of accounts is the master system for tracking the activity of the business. It requires a bit of care up front in its establishment and will need updating as the business grows. This chart is not complex; however, the new businessperson

Table 9.1
Chart of Accounts—Personal Training Studio

ACCOUNT NUMBER	CATEGORY	ACCOUNT NUMBER	CATEGORY
100	Basic Membership	150	Internet Service Provider
101	Premium Membership	160	Equipment Leases
102	PT Package—Basic	170	Insurance
103	PT Package—Deluxe	180	Advertising
104	PT Package Premium	200	Payroll
105	PT Package Unlimited	201	Benefits
106	Group X—Basic	210	Telephone (Cell and Office)
107	Group X—Deluxe	220	Licenses
108	Group X—Unlimited	300	Copy Machine
120	Utilities	310	Tools
130	Security System	400	Building Mortgage
140	Paper	500	Payroll Taxes
141	Letterhead/Business Cards	510	State Taxes
142	Office Supplies—Other	520	Federal Taxes

needs to ensure that the system designed provides the information necessary to analyze the business and its performance. This topic will be discussed more in Chapter 12.

A chart of accounts is simply a listing of each type of activity (income and expense) and each type of asset within the company. The account number used is completely at your discretion, but income categories are usually first, expense categories next, and asset categories last. You may use two-digit or three-digit numbers as you wish and in accordance with the level of detail you anticipate in the future. There are usually far more expense categories than there are income categories. Table 9.1 shows the chart of accounts of a fitness company.

The new businessperson will want to leave room for new account detail to be put into the chart of accounts. As the business develops, you will find that you want to obtain additional detail, as new income/expense categories will appear. Notice that the chart tracks not only income and expense accounts but also asset accounts as well.

Petty Cash Register

There are numerous expenses that are simply too small to write a check for, and there are times when a check is simply inappropriate (for example, if you had pizza delivered for everyone because the whole group was working late to meet a deadline). A petty cash fund operates much like a bank savings account. The founder purchases a small lockbox and writes a check to "Petty Cash" for whatever amount she would like to keep on hand (this is not the same as cash register money, which should be handled as a separate deposit/expense account). A register is maintained to track the amount of money in the box, much like a savings account register. For example, if you decide that $100 is the amount that you would like to have on hand, you would start the box off with $100. As withdrawals are made, each is recorded and all change is put back in the box. The founder should be able to glance at the register and know exactly how much money is in the petty cash fund at any point in time, as well as know how the money has been spent. As it depletes, a new check should be written to "Petty Cash" to fill the box back up to the $100 level.

Check Register

As simple as it sounds, it is important to create a listing of all checks that have been written and all that have cleared through the bank. Today, with online banking and the ability to transfer data directly, this process has become quite easy. Regardless of how the entrepreneur might maintain his personal checking account, it is very important to record and balance the company account on at least a monthly basis.

Expense Accounts

Depending upon the volume of business that your venture processes, you will have either a daily or a weekly listing of expenses. These will allow you to perform a monthly tracking of expenses and ultimately form an annual record of all expenses. The process requires you to have both your check register and your petty cash register available to record all outflow of funds. Credit card payments should be handled by recording the interest as an interest expense, recording the payment made to the account, and then recording each line item with a notation of "Visa," "MC," "Am. Ex.," etc., next to the expense. The only other expenses that are truly handled in a different manner are those related to travel. The IRS has very specific requirements related to the record keeping necessary in order to deduct these expenses.

Inventory Account

Any business that has even a small inventory should maintain an inventory record that lists a description of the item, the quantity, an item number, a unit cost, and a total cost. Inventory should be taken at scheduled times during the year and an exact match should be completed between starting inventory, units sold, and ending inventory. A second record should be kept to track inventory ordered and inventory received. It is a fact of business that **shrinkage** will occur. This reduction in inventory can come from poor record keeping on any of the fronts mentioned previously, but can also result from either employee or customer theft.

[shrinkage]
The difference between what is sold and what was brought into the business.

Accounts Payable

A separate accounts payable record should be maintained for each creditor. All invoices received should be recorded and a record of payment toward each invoice should be included (Date Paid, Amount Paid, and Check Number/Transfer Tracking Number).

Payroll

A payroll record should be maintained for every independent contractor and employee, tracking time for hourly employees and attendance for exempt (salaried) employees. As we discussed in Chapter 7, an independent contractor is a person or firm that performs services for another. It is important to distinguish between employees and independent contractors because independent contractors are not bound by the same laws and standards as employees. Additionally, contractor and employee records that track every payroll check issued to the contractor or employee should be maintained. This record will list all of the items that make up the check:

- Date
- Check number
- Number of hours worked (or 40, for exempt employees)
- Base pay
- Overtime hours worked
- Overtime pay rate
- Gross pay
- Taxes (federal, state, local, Social Security, and Medicare)
- Benefit deductions (if appropriate)
- Net pay

The software packages mentioned earlier have the ability to produce all of these documents plus many more. These become both the control documents and the input documents to produce your financial statements (Cash Flow, Balance Sheet, and Income Statement).

One additional statement is a must-have for most small businesses and directly results from the effective collection of all this information: the **Profit and Loss Statement (P&L Statement).** This statement represents your business performance over time. It is a quick, easily understood document that should be prepared monthly. An example is shown in Table 9.2.

Developing and maintaining effective records is essential in the operation of a business, and some forethought to the process and needs of the business will pay off in the knowledge and understanding developed by the founder(s). We will examine a number of analysis tools in Chapter 12, but for analysis to have any value, good records must be kept.

[profit and loss statement (P&L statement)]

A financial statement that summarizes the revenues, costs, and expenses incurred during a specific period of time.

EXERCISE 4

1. What type of accounting system do you plan to use, cash-basis or accrual-basis? Why?
2. Predict which accounting software will work best for your start-up. Why do you think so?
3. Create a chart of accounts for your business start-up.

Managing Data Flow

The new businessperson needs to recognize that small businesses will differ in the time frame that they need to obtain data. The founder(s) should visit with other similar businesses and find out what reasonable time frames might be for the monitoring of data. The experience of other businesses can be very helpful in the start-up phase of your business.

LO 9.5 Taxes

Taxes come in many forms—from federal, state, and local to payroll and property taxes. The entrepreneur must be aware of and fully compliant in all these forms of taxation. Sound tax advice is key in maintaining a financially successful business. A certified public accountant can become a

Table 9.2
Profit and Loss Statement

PROFIT & LOSS STATEMENT

Period:	Month			
Income	Gross Sales	$114,560.00		
	Less COGS	34,900.00		
	Net Sales		$79,660.00	
	Other Income		13,400.00	
	Total Income		**$93,060.00**	
Expenses	Acct # 120 (Utilities)	$1,084.00		
	Acct # 130 (Security System)	35.00		
	Acct # 140 (Paper)	110.00		
	Acct # 141 (Letterhead/Business Cards)	320.00		
	Acct # 142 (Office Supplies)	45.00		
	Acct # 150 (Internet Service Provider)	79.00		
	Acct # 160 (Equipment Leases)	1,340.00		
	Acct # 170 (Insurance)	367.00		
	Acct # 180 (Advertising)	1,100.00		
	Acct # 200 (Payroll)	47,900.00		
	Acct # 400 (Building Mortgage)	14,370.00		
	Total		$66,750.00	
	Misc. Expenses		1,780.00	
	Total Expenses		**$68,530.00**	
	Profit (Pretax)			**$24,530.00**

great asset to both the new entrepreneur and the well-established business owner.

Federal taxes are federal income tax, Social Security tax, and Medicare tax. You generally must withhold federal income tax from your employees' wages. You withhold part of Social Security and Medicare taxes from your employees' wages, and you pay a matching amount yourself. Federal unemployment tax (FUTA) must be reported and paid separately from federal income and Social Security taxes.

Self-Employment (SE) tax is a Social Security and Medicare tax primarily for individuals who work for themselves. Independent contractors fall into this category and must be reminded of their tax obligations. The general rule is that an individual is an independent contractor if you, the person for whom the services are performed, have the right to control or direct only the result of the work and not the means and methods of accomplishing the result. Taxes on the payment for these services are not paid by the person who receives the services. The independent contractor is responsible for paying the taxes. Form 1099-MISC is most commonly used by payers to report payments made in the course of purchasing services from independent contractors. It is important to note that independent contractors may have their own employees or may hire other independent contractors (subcontractors). In either case, all parties should be aware of their tax responsibilities, including filing and reporting requirements. Forms and more information can be found at the IRS website (www.irs.gov).

Other taxes include various state and local taxes specific to the health and wellness industry such as food, retail, and amusement/entertainment taxes. Property or real estate tax, only applicable if you own the building in which you house your business, and personal property taxes can become quite a headache for the business owner. As a business owner you are responsible for paying property taxes on the land and building, if you own them, as well as on other property used in the business. While in your personal life you do not pay taxes on such purchases as furniture or computer equipment (besides sales tax), as a business owner, some of these purchases are taxable as property tax. Most people know that property tax applies to real property; however, some may not know that property tax also applies to personal property. Most personal property owned by individuals is exempt. For example, household goods and personal effects are not subject to property tax. However, if you buy these items to be used in your business, property tax may apply. For example, if you buy a couch for your home, you only pay sales tax. If you were to purchase the same couch for use in your business, you still pay sales tax but you may also have to pay property tax. (Regulations on property taxes vary by state.)

Inventories of goods or intangible property such as copyrights and trademarks are not taxable. Personal property is subject to the same levy rate as real property. The characteristic that distinguishes real and personal property is mobility. Real property includes land, structures, improvements to land, and certain equipment affixed to land or structures. Personal property includes equipment (such as treadmills and strength equipment), furniture, and supplies. The responsibility for knowing about these taxes lies with the business owner. The savvy entrepreneur must remember that taxes are complex, and gaining a full understanding of this area of business could take a long time.

EXERCISE 5

1. Suppose you have one full-time employee and one part-time independent contractor working for you. Assess what types of payroll taxes you would deduct from each of their paychecks.
2. Determine if you would need to pay self-employment tax if you are a shareholder-employee of the company you founded as a Subchapter S corporation.
3. Verify whether or not your state requires payment of property tax on fitness or office equipment/furniture purchased for your planned business.

key terms

asset-based lending 148
asset lease 153
business angels 152
credit card 149
debt 148

equity investment 147
grants 149
loan 148
profit and loss statement
   (P&L statement) 158

shrinkage 157
supplier credit 149
venture capital fund 152

review questions

1. True or false? The key measures of a business should focus on the key aspects with which the business hopes to build its competitive advantage.
2. True or false? A business's outcomes should be measured during slow periods when there is time to focus.
3. Summarize the three key issues related to the financing of a start-up. Use your own words.
4. Predict a potential hazard of not establishing an accounting system. Why is it important to keep track of finances?
5. Report on the two ways in which large businesses invest in small businesses, describing how it works for both types of business.
6. If you were starting a small fitness club, would you use asset leasing for your equipment? Why or why not?
7. Propose how you would track transactions involving your petty cash fund.
8. Formulate a time frame for monitoring the financial data for your business. Consider the petty cash register, check register, expense accounts, inventory accounts, accounts payable, and payroll. Include when you expect to use the data from these records to produce your cash flow statement, balance sheet, and income statement.
9. Suppose you are a personal trainer who works as a full-time independent contractor. When must you pay federal taxes?
10. Compile a list of taxes for which your proposed business will be responsible. Consider whether you will have employees or contractors, whether or not you will own the building that houses the business, and other such critical matters.

individual exercises

Select one of the two exercises below to complete.

1. Create a report based on your answers to the following questions.
   - How will you fund your proposed new business, and what funding level is really needed for the new venture?
   - What accounting records will you maintain, and how will you maintain them?
   - How will you manage the paper/data flow of the new company?

2. Many of the software applications mentioned in this chapter offer free trial downloads on the Internet. Try downloading one or more that appeals to you and investigate the features. Does your hands-on trial alter your choice of program that you made earlier? Why or why not?

group exercise

Break into groups of three. Suppose you are going to start a small, franchised fitness business together. The required initial investment is $100,000, which includes all needed office and fitness equipment, maintenance of the equipment for one year, and an advertising budget for one year. The franchise requires a 5 percent royalty fee payable monthly. You each have $20,000 to invest and need to rent space to house the business. Determine how best to keep your expenses low. Discuss your funding options. Consider expenses you might have (e.g., labor, insurance, rent, utilities) in the first year and beyond. Debate and determine the best type of accounting system to use for your business. Also determine a time frame for managing and monitoring your business's finances.

part four

Building the Business

Human Resource Management

After studying this chapter, you will be able to:

10.1 Explain the elements of human resources

10.2 Discuss the process of hiring employees

10.3 Analyze the means for retaining employees

10.4 Determine the pertinent aspects of employee probation and firing

10.5 Distinguish the unique aspects of human resources within a family business

CASE STUDY
Extreme Fitness

Kylie opened Extreme Fitness in a Midwestern suburban community. Originally, the staff consisted of herself and two other trainers. The small studio of 1,100 square feet was the perfect size for a three-trainer business. From the beginning, one of Kylie's key values was that her studio must exude a friendly, welcoming atmosphere. She wanted all her employees to bring a positive and energetic persona to their work. She insisted that everyone who worked at Extreme Fitness say "Hello" to everyone that walked through the door, including employees.

Kylie's instincts proved correct. Her clients were overly enthusiastic about Extreme Fitness, and mostly through word of mouth, Kylie's business took flight. In two years, the client base grew from 50 to 200. Kylie also expanded her staff, hiring five new trainers.

Every employee brings her own special skills and personality, but Kylie also noticed that some employees were better equipped to get on board with the attitude she wanted her trainers to exhibit. Within a couple months of hiring a trainer named Valerie, Kylie started getting bad vibes about Valerie's ability to work in the Extreme Fitness atmosphere. She noticed that while the other trainers were developing friendly relationships in and out of

work, Valerie seemed more like a loner and rarely spoke to her colleagues. She was a good trainer and knew her stuff, but her interactions with clients were all business and not especially friendly. Kylie also noticed that Valerie was her only employee who did not follow the guideline about greeting everyone who entered the studio. Kylie didn't mention any of this to Valerie, feeling uncomfortable with the thought of confronting her. She had never had to discipline an employee before, and after all, Valerie was a good trainer.

Eight months after Valerie was hired, Kylie was doing her month-end books and checking each trainer's client counts. She noticed that three of Valerie's regular clients had switched to different trainers on the staff and one client had stopped coming to Extreme Fitness altogether. Kylie was surprised by this because her business had been growing so steadily that she could not recall a trainer ever losing clients. She dug deeper into the records and found that this was a growing pattern: new clients would be assigned to Valerie, but after several weeks they would switch to other trainers.

The next day, two of her other trainers came to see Kylie. They wanted to talk about Valerie. They said that they felt terrible about going behind someone's back, but they felt they could no longer work with Valerie. She never helped out in the studio, never agreed to substitute for colleagues if they were sick or out of town, and was pretty abrupt in their dealings with each other. The previous day, Valerie had confronted one of these trainers in front of clients because her aerobics class was running five minutes long and Valerie was scheduled to use the studio.

Kylie decided there was no way to fix the situation—a person's personality cannot be changed, and Valerie simply did not have the personality for this job. So Kylie gathered her courage and called Valerie into a meeting. Kylie told Valerie that she was disappointed with the attitude Valerie exhibited in the club, that she wasn't behaving as an equal team member, and that she was not enthusiastic or friendly enough toward her clients and colleagues. She reminded Valerie that when she was hired, she was told that this was a key value of her club. She concluded by telling Valerie, "I'm really sorry to tell you this, but I've decided that your attitude is standing in the way of our business, so I'm going to have to let you go." Valerie grew very upset and started crying. She told Kylie she was upset to be receiving feedback like this out of the blue. She told Kylie that she loved her work at the studio and wished there were a way she could be given a second chance. But as she was saying this, Valerie interrupted herself and blurted out, "Oh, this is just too humiliating. Forget it." She picked up her things and walked out.

Human resource management includes the hiring, inspiring, and managing of personnel, which is one of the toughest and yet most important functions for a new company to develop. For example, hiring personnel who are consistent with your business strategy and style is critical to business success, since without them it is unlikely that you will be able to implement your strategy. Similarly, managing the company's personnel so that you increase their skill development allows your operation to develop a key resource. This type of resource is one that other businesses cannot easily copy and one that may in turn lead to better overall performance in your facility.[1] The business of simply meeting the basic legal requirements of your human resource function can be daunting—yet is insufficient for the company to be successful. This chapter will explore the rich set of issues, both legal and nonlegal, that a start-up business must consider.

LO 10.1 What Is Human Resources?

[human resources]

As defined in economics, the quantity and quality of human effort directed toward producing goods and services.

Human resources has been defined in economics as the quantity and quality of human effort directed toward producing goods and services. What this means to a small business owner is far more than simply having the right number of people with the right skills for a particular job. An organization is fundamentally its own small society that exists within a community or city. Why one person works at one particular company or another is often because of the quality of the society that the small business represents. The establishment of this small society requires a number of deliberate actions by the business founder.

The elements that this chapter will explore include hiring employees (job descriptions, job advertisements, discrimination, job interviews, testing, job offers); retaining employees (compensation and benefit systems, wages and hours requirements, performance reviews); and dealing with difficult employees (probation, firing). After dealing with these issues, the chapter will also examine several other issues specifically relevant to dealing with family in a business.

EXERCISE 1

1. Define human resources in terms of economics.
2. Describe a frequent reason why an employee chooses to work for a particular company.

LO 10.2 Hiring Employees

To visualize how important hiring is to a small business, compare the impact of one person in a large organization to that of one person in a small organization. If a large organization has 1,000 employees, one problem employee represents only 0.1 percent of its workforce. In a small company with five employees, one employee causing problems represents 20 percent of the workforce. An unhappy person not working at full capacity will result in the small business owner spending an inordinate amount of time dealing with the problems caused by the troublesome employee. Thus, a poor employee has a triple impact on the small company: (1) the owner's time is lost; (2) the organization does not fully benefit from the employee; and (3) the problems may bleed over to other employees. In the case of Kylie's Extreme Fitness business, the one "bad apple"

employee had a negative impact on her clients. Where larger firms can absorb the resulting difficulties due to their built-in slack (excess resources), a small company can be devastated by a bad hiring decision. The process of finding and hiring new employees is critical and should involve a series of deliberate steps.

Job Description

A **job description** does as it sounds: It describes the job that is to be filled. In a small business, this document is not meant to be a formal, highly structured document as it might be in a large corporation.[2] Nonetheless, we highly recommend that all positions that are hired into the business—even for independent contractors—have a written job description. Too often small business owners say they "know" what they want in an employee, but they never write it down. The reason is probably multifold, including a lack of time, an unclear picture of the new position, or a desire to remain flexible for the right individual. However, the process of generating a job description will assist the founder immensely as he carefully considers the skills, background, and ability of a potential new hire. All too often, the small business owner who fails to develop a job description ends up hiring someone because he "likes" the person.

Taking the time to write down those skills and capabilities will go a long way toward ensuring that all dimensions of the job are considered. For instance, a fitness club owner may be looking to hire a personal trainer, but on occasion that trainer may have to fill in and teach a group exercise class. If the club owner has not written out this job description, he may forget this aspect of the job when interviewing applicants. He may be unpleasantly surprised after hiring the person.

He may even need to be more specific than simply listing general skills. For example, a club owner may have a large segment of senior citizen clients, so he may need someone who has experience with geriatric clients, specifically dealing with osteoporosis, arthritis, and other conditions related to aging. You will need to determine what skills are critical at the

[job description]

Document that describes the job that is to be filled.

stage of hiring and those that you are willing to help develop after you hire someone.

In a similar vein, there is information you need to share with the potential employee. For example, do employees wear company clothing or do they wear their own workout clothes, and is there a dress code if they do wear their own clothes? This kind of information may be seen by the business owner as a small matter, but it may be enough to impact whether or not an employee will be happy in the job. Imagine the impact if an employee arrived on the first day only to be told that she is dressed inappropriately when she was expecting to receive a club outfit.

When making a hiring decision, the new businessperson also needs to consider whether there are skills not required today, but which may be needed in the near future. Putting the job description in writing helps in this process by ensuring that all the elements of the job are considered, as well as forcing the business owner to consider changes as the company grows. Following are brief examples of job descriptions for an independent contractor and for an in-house employee.

Job Title:	Independent Personal Trainer
Description:	Lead, instruct, and motivate individuals or groups in exercise activities including cardiovascular exercise, muscular endurance training, muscular strength training, and flexibility. Work one-on-one or with two or three clients, either in a fitness facility or in the clients' homes. Assess clients' physical fitness levels and help clients set and reach fitness goals. Demonstrate various exercises to help clients improve their exercise techniques. Keep records of clients' exercise sessions to monitor the clients' progress toward physical fitness. Advise clients on how to modify their lifestyles outside the gym to improve their physical fitness.
Qualifications:	Experience as a personal trainer or experience in a personal training setting; a related fitness or health degree; certification from a nationally recognized organization.
Hours:	Varies; dependent on trainer.
Pay Rate:	Varies; $15-$50 dependent on trainer's experience.
Benefits:	None.
Vacation:	None, dependent on trainer.
Sick Days:	None, dependent on trainer.
Job Title:	Personal Trainer
Description:	Lead, instruct, and motivate individuals or groups in exercise activities including cardiovascular exercise, muscular endurance training, muscular strength training, and flexibility. Work one-on-one or with two or three clients, either in a fitness facility or in the clients' homes. Assess clients' physical fitness levels and help clients set and reach fitness goals. Demonstrate various exercises to help clients improve their exercise techniques. Keep records of clients' exercise sessions to monitor the clients'

progress toward physical fitness. Advise clients on how to modify their lifestyles outside the gym to improve their physical fitness.

Qualifications: Experience as a personal trainer or experience in a personal training setting; a related fitness or health degree; certification from a nationally recognized organization.

Hours: May work 40+ hours per week.

Pay Rate: Varies; salary or hourly.

- Annual salary range: $19,610–$44,420 dependent on experience.

- Hourly pay range: $15–$50 dependent on experience.

Benefits: Medical insurance may be provided at no or of little cost to the employee.

Vacation: One week of paid vacation will be earned after one year of employment. Two weeks of vacation will be earned after two years of employment.

Sick Days: Employees may accrue one paid sick day for every six months of employment.

Job Advertising

Once the small business owners have generated the job description, they need to try to attract the largest pool of applicants possible for the job. Word of mouth may be a great way to find new trainers. If you have a current trainer whom you trust, ask that person to spread the word or recommend people to you. Every industry has its own network, but the fitness industry has a particularly broad network, partly because of its vast independent contractor pool (many of whom work for multiple clubs) and also because fitness clients come from all walks of life and develop close relationships with trainers and club owners whom they are enthusiastic about recommending.

While word of mouth is certainly a key means to advertise for a job, we suggest that it is but one of many possible methods for attracting a wider audience. There are a variety of ways to advertise and a large number of organizations that can help promote information on your job opening at little or no cost. These include the following:

- College placement offices
- Trade associations
- Employment agencies
- Facebook and other social network sites

Similarly, if the business is in a very visible location, a sign can be posted outside the office.

A more expensive means to locate potential employees is a traditional help wanted ad, placed either in a newspaper or via an Internet employment site. These advertisements vary widely in cost and ability to reach the audience that you desire. Information from the advertising location on readership/viewership, statistics on reply rates, and rates charged are all-important pieces of information for the small business owner seeking to place an advertisement.

Finally, for unique skill requirements, there are companies that do an extremely good job recruiting and placing people. These companies traditionally charge the company seeking to hire the employee, and that fee can range from a set fee to a significant percentage of the placed employee's first-year salary. As you can see, this can be very expensive, so the new business needs to clearly think through the benefits of casting a more professional net.

In writing the advertisement for the new hire, the small business owner should keep it concise and oriented toward the basic information needed for a potential applicant to evaluate his qualifications for the position. However, there are thousands of generic advertisements placed every week that look identical to one another. You will want your advertisement to be distinct enough to stand apart so it will draw the attention of potential applicants. If possible, your ad should communicate the culture of the company and your desire to have the right person join your organization. The advertisement should also express excitement about the business. Overall, remember to write the ad to sell the job and the business honestly to the potential employee. Even though many people who read the advertisement may decide that they are not qualified, you would like them to walk away with a positive view of the business from their reading of the advertisement.

The advertisement should ask applicants to submit a resume and a short list of references. Virtually all potential candidates will have resumes unless they are applying for the jobs at the very lowest skill levels. A deadline should be established for applying in order to fairly evaluate the applicants in comparison to each other. A typical wording might state, "The application deadline is January 15, 201X, or until the position is filled." This allows a comparison across candidates after January 15, but also allows for the possibility that no one will meet all of your requirements by the deadline.

Discrimination. It is important in designing the advertisement that the company be nondiscriminatory. Title VII of the Civil Rights Act prohibits **discrimination** in hiring, dismissal, level of pay, or promotions on the basis of race, color, gender, religious beliefs, or national origin. This law currently applies to all companies with more than 15 employees. However, there are also state laws that may apply to companies with fewer than 15 employees, plus other federal laws that put the small business owner at risk even if the company has fewer than 15 employees. Therefore, the small business should avoid any discrimination or even the appearance of discrimination. The adherence to a nondiscrimination posture takes effort by the small business.[3]

The small business should write job descriptions and advertisements in a nondiscriminatory manner. Terms like "salesman," "handyman," "young," or "counter girl" should be avoided. Antidiscrimination laws do not require that you hire any one particular person; however, you must give everyone

[discrimination]

In the workplace, hiring, dismissal, level of pay, or promotions based on race, color, gender, religious beliefs, or national origin of the employee. Such actions are prohibited by federal and state laws.

an equal opportunity to be considered. The wide advertising of a job and the establishment of a job description will help the small business owner establish that he acted in a nondiscriminatory manner. If you advertise widely, you have not prevented anyone from applying. The job description helps to ensure that all individuals are judged on the same basis.

Interviewing and Testing

Regardless of whether the candidate has or does not have a resume, you should ask each one to fill out an application for employment. It is important to establish set criteria for every applicant and to have the ability to track exactly who applied for each position. There are a variety of generic forms available at any office supply store or via any one of several software packages. We believe that, at a minimum, the following information should be obtained in the application/interview process:

- Name, address, telephone numbers (home, cell), e-mail address (if applicable)
- Other addresses for the past three years
- Social security number (SSN)
- Driver's license number and state of issue
- Work history
- Date available for work
- Position for which the candidate is applying
- How the candidate heard about the job
- Education, certification, and training
- Professional organization memberships
- Any record of conviction and, if so, details of that conviction
- If not a U.S. citizen, the appropriate documentation authorizing the candidate to work. (Note that sometimes very good people will come and apply for a job and ask you to sponsor them. This typically requires several thousand dollars, which the applicant may be willing to pay. You as a business owner will have to be willing to take the time to act as a sponsor. You will also have to verify that this job requires some unique set of skills that only this person has.)
- References

Once the candidate pool has been set, the founder must winnow the candidate list down to a group to be interviewed. We recommend that you sit with the applications and the job description at one set time period, so that a direct comparison of the applications and job needs can be completed. Those candidates who do not have the minimum requirements for the position should be rejected immediately. Those who closely match your job description should be the ones where you focus your next effort. Those that appear to be the best fit in that group should be considered for an interview.

During the interview process (whether it is in person or on the phone), it is important that the small business owner not discriminate against any

Roger is the manager of a mid-sized fitness club located in a trendy, urban area. Most of the clients are in their 20s and 30s and live in the immediate area; other nearby businesses include upscale bars, restaurants, and galleries. Roger placed an ad seeking a group exercise trainer and received several dozen applicants. After reviewing their qualifications, he decided to bring in eight applicants for interviews. Of those interviewees, several simply did not make a good impression. He narrowed his choices to three finalists. One of the three was Sue, who was clearly older than the rest of the applicants, and older than the club's client base. Although he did not ask her age, Roger estimated she was in her mid-60s. Sue had impeccable credentials. She had been a fitness trainer for more than 20 years and was only looking for a job now because her husband had recently retired, and they had just moved to the city. Roger enjoyed his interview with Sue, and he was convinced she was a top-notch trainer with better credentials than the two other finalists. But Roger was hesitant to hire Sue because she did not fit in with the demographic of his client base or the rest of his staff. Moreover, the group exercise studio was a street-front studio with a wall of windows, so the passing public could see the trainer at work. Roger worried that although clients might love Sue once they got to know her and work with her, she might turn off potential clients who happened to glimpse her from the street. Is it unfair of Roger to allow Sue's age to be a factor in his decision to hire her? If Roger can legitimately prove that Sue's age would create an impediment to the club's business, is he justified in not hiring her? How is Sue's age any different from other personality qualities that can disqualify a candidate from being hired?

given individual. There is a short list of topics that should not be asked about in any interview. You should not ask questions about, nor can you consider in the hiring decision, any of the following:

- Age
- Race
- Disability
- Gender
- National origin
- Religion or creed

Note that you can ask about prior convictions but may not ask about the candidate's arrest record. An arrest is not the same as a conviction. In summary, the discussion during the interview should be based on the needs of the job.

The manager should also use the interview to provide a realistic preview of the job and the company to the interviewee. You should not overpromise what the job will be or the relevant job security present in the company. Too often companies try to sell the employee on the job by overpromising what the job is or underselling the expectations the company has of the employee. Instead, you should provide a valid and realistic perspective that promotes the company but also sets appropriate expectations for the potential employee.

Although it is a tedious process, the founder needs to check as many references as possible, even for potential employees found through personal contacts. However, the small business owner should balance the checking of references with the nature of the job. If the job requires very low skills, then perhaps the need for references might be a bit less important. However, if the job is more central to the organization and has higher required skill levels and client interaction, then the importance of the references increases. The small business owner should also closely check references if the employee might be in a position to put either the business or its customers at risk. Independent contractors' references should also be checked, even though they will not be actual employees. The references proposed by the interviewee and any others that the founder believes would have knowledge of the person should be contacted. If the job happens to require driving, then the manager should inform the job candidate that he will be checking the candidate's driving records. In order to make these contacts and receive information, the person hiring must have signed permission from the candidate.

The interview process and the checking of references are time-consuming processes. It is for this reason that the screening of resumes or applications prior to beginning this course of action is important. However, the small business owner does not want to shortchange the interview and reference process. As a result, should you still be unsure about which candidate to hire after an initial interview and background check, then a second round of interviews should be employed.

Some managers will go even further in making sure that the person is right for the business. For example, some gyms require candidates to train other trainers as part of the interviewing process. This allows the owner to observe the applicant in a controlled setting (so that clients will not be exposed to a potentially poor trainer). It also helps to familiarize the applicant and the staff with each other. Many clubs are team oriented, so it's important to get a sense of how an applicant will mesh with the existing staff.

Additional, formal testing can be a part of the decision process, and testing comes in many forms and in response to many concerns. Some business owners wish to assure a drug-free workplace, and the owner has the right to insist on testing.[4] In fact, some states, such as Florida, offer a reduction in the rates of workers' compensation insurance if the business has a drug-free workplace program. This can be encouraged by requiring all new employees to submit to a drug test as well as requiring all employees to periodically submit to random drug testing. Most small businesses choose not to have drug testing, and they face risks in conducting such tests. The privacy rights of employees can come into conflict with the desire to have a drug-free workplace. Small business owners are encouraged to consult a local lawyer before beginning such programs.

Some businesses require potential employees to complete a personality profile to see if their particular personality is a good fit with the business. Personality tests may reveal aspects of an applicant's potential interpersonal skills that might elude the owner in the interview process. Tests can predict if people are introverted or outgoing, for instance. Or they may identify applicants who work better independently or as part of a team. In a fitness-club setting, it's important to remember that all types of personalities walk through the door as clients, so the personality traits of employees are particularly important to understand prior to making a hire.

The Offer

Once you have selected your top candidate, an offer needs to be extended. We suggest that all of the details of the offer be developed prior to any conversation with the candidate. Consideration should be given to the possibility that the candidate might wish to negotiate the deal. You should decide upon your negotiation position and how much you are willing to offer for this particular candidate. While this is primarily an art, we do recommend that once an offer is made, you allow the candidate the opportunity to accept the offer or return to you very quickly with a counter position (establish the amount of time that the offer will remain in effect before you withdraw it and offer the position to another candidate). At that point, you can make whatever concessions you feel are appropriate and then respond to the candidate. Once an offer is agreed upon between the parties, it should be put in writing by the founder, signed, and sent to the candidate. Only when the candidate returns a signed original of the offer letter should you consider the position closed. We don't wish to be too formal with this process, but we have watched many small business owners become frustrated by employees who thought their agreement differed from that actually offered by the company.

EXERCISE 2

1. Explain what a job description is and what kinds of information it should include.

2. Summarize the ways in which discrimination is prohibited in a work environment, listing a minimum of ten types of illegal discrimination. Resources: This section, http://www.archives.gov/education/lessons/civil-rights-act/, and http://www.eeoc.gov/laws/types/index.cfm.

3. State at least four actions that an employer might take after setting up an interview.

4. Create a sample offer letter for a particular position with your company. Be sure to include leeway for negotiation.

LO 10.3 Retaining Employees

Once you actually hire each employee, you obviously will want to retain those employees who perform well. The process described above takes a lot of time and effort. If it is done poorly and you don't retain the employee, then this process can simply be a waste of valuable time and money, not to mention the loss of productivity as each new employee has to be brought up to an acceptable level of performance. Therefore, the small company needs to retain those employees who add value. The key issues here are the compensation and benefits offered as well as the method and means of reviewing performance.

Compensation

The compensation system chosen by the company is the aspect that is often highest in the minds of employees. In building the compensation system, the small business owner needs to maintain a fair and equitable system for all employees, both now and as the company progresses into the future. Salary and benefits may appear to be a private matter between you and your employees; however, history suggests that this type of information eventually becomes public knowledge among employees.

Equity theory is helpful to understanding how to avoid problems with compensation. This theory argues that we all judge how we are treated

[equity theory]
The theory that we all judge how we are treated relative to how we see others being treated.

relative to how we see others being treated. Thus, employees have a powerful need to feel that their compensation given their level/performance is equitable relative to that of other employees in their company or other individuals in similar situations. As a result, all employees need a clear rationale for how their compensation stacks up against that of others in the organization. Employees can accept that someone who has been in the organization longer has a better overall package; however, they would have difficulty accepting it if they were hired at the same time as another employee and did the same job but received less pay. The owner might have a reason for that difference, but the presence of the difference would be difficult for the employee to understand.

Due to the level of complication within the workforce of most large companies, these companies require a systematic program that evaluates comparable employees both in the region and around the country. This systematic review of the employees will often include the following: (1) how they performed relative to their objectives; (2) plans for future employee growth through experience and training; (3) defined objectives for the next year; and (4) pay raise being awarded.

A small business needs a significantly less-developed system. The small business founder should decide on a basic form of compensation. The options might include the following:

- Hourly wage
- Salary
- Commission
- Hybrid/profit-sharing system

An **hourly wage** is simply the amount paid per hour for work performed. A **salary** is similarly straightforward, as it is a set amount of money for a given time period. A **commission** is involved when the small business owner pays an individual a percentage of sales. The small business owner can also build a **hybrid compensation system,** with a sales commission paid in addition to a basic salary. **Profit sharing** is another example of a hybrid system. The company may set some relatively low level of salary but offer to share a percentage of the profits at the end of the year or some other period of time with the employees. A **bonus** system is similar to profit sharing; a bonus is offered to the employees based on their performance. Typically, bonus systems are not as well defined as profit sharing; instead, the level of reward is left to the discretion of the small business owner. The time period for which such profit sharing or bonuses are given should be relevant to the individuals in the company and within the realities and constraints of the business. It is important that the small business owner provide bonuses in a timely manner. A small business owner may visualize a year as a relevant time frame, whereas workers may be looking for monthly or quarterly feedback on their performance through a bonus.

It is essential for the fitness businessperson to consider the industry standards in developing her compensation system. Those in the industry who have developed a compensation system that works have the potential

[hourly wage]

The amount paid per hour for work performed.

[salary]

A set amount of compensation for a given time period.

[commission]

Payment by the small business owner of some percentage of sales, typically associated with the compensation of trainers.

[hybrid compensation system]

A compensation system that includes a salary along with commission.

[profit sharing]

An example of a hybrid compensation system. The company may set some relatively low level of salary but offer to share a percentage of the profits at the end of the year or some other period of time with the employees.

[bonus]

Similar to profit sharing, a reward offered to the employees based on their performance. Typically, bonus systems are not as well defined as profit sharing; instead, the level of reward is left to the discretion of the small business owner.

to provide information not only on the level of total compensation but also on how to structure it. Some options include the following:

- Some fitness instructors are paid hourly wages. The hourly rates may differ depending on the type of work they are doing. For instance, an instructor may make one hourly rate for individual training, a different rate for group exercise, and yet another rate for small-group training (which may be based on the number of clients enrolled in the class).

- Some fitness instructors are not employees but are independent contractors. Their pay rates may be the same as or different from that of employees.

- Employees or independent contractors may also be paid on a commission or hybrid commission basis. This means they earn commission on an agreed portion of the revenue they bring into the club. In addition to the commission earnings, they may also make a small base salary.

- Other employees of a fitness club who are not trainers (such as support staff, cleaning and maintenance staff) may be paid on an hourly or annual salary basis.

[Fair Labor Standards Act (FLSA)]

The act that established a minimum wage for workers.

Legal Issues with Pay. The **Fair Labor Standards Act (FLSA)** establishes a minimum wage for workers. Virtually all workers (other than workers on small farms and administrative employees) are covered by the act. This federal law requires that employees be paid a minimum wage, which in 2009 was $7.25 per hour. However, states may have higher minimum wages. For example, in 2009 the minimum wage in California was $8.00 per hour. It is even possible for local governments to pass their own minimum wage requirements as long as they exceed the federal requirement. Many major cities have what they call "living wages." A living wage is an index wage that requires the minimum wage to be at least what someone who works 40 hours a week needs to stay out of poverty. As a result, in 2009 the minimum wage in San Francisco was $9.36 per hour. If your business is covered by the FLSA, it is also covered by the Equal Pay Act, which requires that an employer not discriminate in pay to men and women who do the same job.

The FLSA requires that all nonexempt employees who work more than 40 hours a week be paid at the rate of time and a half. Compensatory time is not typically allowed from one pay period to the next. Therefore, if the pay period is only one week and you have employees working overtime this week, then you must pay the overtime rate for those hours. You cannot give them time off next week as compensation. If, however, the pay period is two weeks, then time off in one week can be used as compensation for time worked in the previous week. Thus, the company needs to be very clear on its time frame for issues such as pay. Another legal issue related to pay is child labor. The government closely regulates the employment of children under age 16. The small business owner would be well advised to seek out legal advice if he plans to employ children, even his own, in the business if they are younger than 16 years of age.

Benefits

There are a wide variety of benefits that any business can choose to offer. For example, benefits can include the following:

- Paid vacations
- Paid holidays
- Paid sick or personal days
- Sick leave
- Paid maternity leave
- Medical care (can include vision and/or dental insurance
- 401(k) plan
- Retirement plans
- Life insurance

The package of benefits the company chooses to offer can have as much impact on the success of the small business's human resource efforts as the compensation offered.[5]

Some benefits represent costs to the small business, but they are relatively easy for the small business to provide. For example, a paid two-week vacation after an individual has worked at a company for a specified amount of time is a benefit provided by most companies. There is an expense, as you are paying an employee who is not working while on vacation. If the employee is a fitness trainer, you will either need to pay a substitute trainer to cover the employee's clients while the employee is on vacation, or those clients may choose not to come for their sessions and you will lose that revenue. This cost can be relatively minimal, and could be deemed a worthwhile expense, considering the good will

and employee satisfaction that is generated by paid vacation time, as with many benefits. Tracking and calculating vacation time is relatively easy, especially for a small staff. The same may be said of paid holidays and sick days; the sick days build up over time as the employee is working with the small business. It should be emphasized that all methods of accruing time should be explained up-front to new employees, and business owners should establish a system for regular communication of paid-time-off earned. For instance, if you do not allow unused vacation time to be carried over to the next year, it is essential for employees to know this up-front and to receive reminders of their vacation time usage.

Benefits that are more costly and more difficult to effectively manage include medical care and retirement plans. Medical care is one of the most expensive costs for any business, and yet it is also one of the most desired benefits by employees. On average, private businesses spend in excess of $4,000 per person per year providing health care for their employees.[6] However, the plans most small businesses provide are not the full-coverage plans provided by large businesses. Large businesses are paying in excess of $9,000 per person per year providing for health care costs.[7] The impact of such costs to the small business compared to the large business cannot be overestimated. For the small business, the cost of health insurance per employee will be more than that for a large company. Large companies have the advantage of spreading losses across a large number of people, whereas the small business can be dramatically impacted by a single significant claim. To illustrate, out of 100,000 employees you may expect 23 heart bypass operations and can budget for that with insurance. In a small company, you may have only 10 employees—but what if one employee needs a bypass? The insurance company has likely not charged you enough to cover the costs of the bypass, no matter what it has charged you in the past. The result is that the small company is a much greater risk than the large company. This leads to higher deductibles, user copayments, and out-of-pocket costs for employees of a small business. The small business owner will need to investigate the costs and packages offered by a variety of insurance companies. The sources for such insurance can be located through other small businesses in the area, the chamber of commerce, national trade associations, and the Internet. The small business owner would be well served to investigate and compare various medical programs closely before choosing one.

[performance review]
Review by the small business owner of the employee's goals and outcomes on those goals over some given period.

While traditional retirement plans have fallen out of favor, some types of personal retirement plans have become quite popular. Referred to generally as 401(k) and Roth 401(k) programs, they are usually offered by an employer so that employees can contribute to their retirement on a tax-free basis. Most small companies do not provide any matching, while many larger companies offer matching funds for these accounts.

Performance Reviews

No matter what the size of an organization is, performance reviews should be a part of the management system.[8] In a **performance review,** the small business owner reviews the employee's goals and outcomes on those goals over some given period. Workers are motivated by more than salary. The formal conversation with a worker who is doing a good job, showing that her work is appreciated, is another form of compensation. If the worker is not performing as expected, then the employer should also be very clear about that fact and should offer specific suggestions for improvement. While we recommend that all performance reviews be documented in writing, we do not suggest that a complex form need be utilized. Providing effective feedback can be handled in a number of ways but should cover each of the areas of the employee's responsibility.

For example, a company may establish a simple scoring system for rating employees in different areas of performance, such as timeliness, client interaction, knowledge of fitness routines, effectiveness of training methods, client satisfaction, etc. The rating system could be a scale of 1 to 3 or 1 to 5. The system should not be too complex, and should be well-defined so the employee understands the criteria upon being hired. The review form should also include an area for other comments, including positive feedback. A sample review form is included on Appendix page XXX of this book.

The review system, if handled properly, should not be a negative or disciplinary experience. Rather, it should provide an open forum between employer and employee so that employees can receive direct and constructive feedback, understand methods for improvement, and feel that there is an incentive to improve performance. During this feedback, the business owner is well advised to provide praise where it is warranted and detail any deficiencies and areas that need to be developed. Even the "perfect employee" should have goals for improvement.

Some companies also choose to facilitate the employee's review of the manager. It should be simple and should allow the trainer to give feedback on what he feels is going well and what the trainer feels needs improvement.

Reviews should be performed regularly, either every 6 or 12 months. Some companies have 90-day reviews for new employees. These systems are not mere formalities—they keep the employer and the employee on the same page. As will be discussed in the next section, it is critical that the employee know exactly how his performance is compared to expectations. Consider the example of Kylie and Extreme Fitness at the beginning of this chapter. She allowed a poor employee to continue unchecked for eight months before addressing the situation. Too often small business owners do not want the confrontation, so they will give no feedback or only positive feedback, but then later fire the person. The result is a surprised employee who may seek legal representation to get compensation for unfairly being fired. As will be discussed in the next section of this chapter, if you have not provided accurate performance reviews, the individual may win if the parties do go to court.

Central to being able to do any review is the setting of goals for the employee. The setting of such goals allows the small business owner to judge how well the employee is performing. These goals should be realistic, tied to the performance of the company, based upon some measurable outcome, and periodically adjusted. Again, the time frame for these goals should be one that is relevant for the employee. Thus, for some jobs it may be weekly or biweekly, a time period that relates to the pay period. For most jobs, the relevant time frame will be quarterly or perhaps longer.

EXERCISE 3

1. Use the definitions in this section to report briefly (no more than half a page) on the various options an employer has for compensating employees.

2. Distinguish between profit sharing and bonuses.

3. Suppose you are the owner of a small personal training studio. Make a chart that briefly describes (1) details of four benefits you offer to your trainers (for example, how many vacation days after how many years of service) and (2) your reasoning for offering each benefit.

Benefit	Reason

4. How often should you do a performance review with your employees?

LO 10.4 Probation and Firing

Despite your best efforts, you will at some point hire the wrong person. At times you may find it necessary to fire that person. As a business owner you have the right to hire and fire employees. However, you still must have legitimate, well-documented reasons for the firing. If you do not, you are opening yourself up to a lawsuit by the dismissed employee. Furthermore, you should provide all employees (short of their having done something illegal) the opportunity to rectify their performance.

Thus, you must develop a paper trail regarding all employees and must be particularly diligent in your efforts to assist a poorly performing employee. Recall that in discussing reviews, we argued that an employer needs to be honest about an employee's performance and document those times when she is not performing as desired. You specify over time what is expected of the employee and then document how she is or is not performing to expectations. It is a good practice to follow up any conversations about performance issues with a written summary. It does not have to be a formal "report," but may just be an e-mail recapping the conversation. This is a key part of your paper trail for potentially problematic employees. You cannot wait for an annual review to provide the only written documentation of performance issues.

Firing someone for poor performance that has been documented over a time and in which you have offered a means to correct the problem will go a long way toward providing a defense in any legal proceeding and a proper justification for the employee.

[at-will employment]

A common-law rule that an employment contract of indefinite duration can be terminated by the employer or the employee at any time for any reason.

Many employees—including a large percentage of personal trainers—will be an at-will employee. **At-will employment** is a common-law rule that an employment contract of indefinite duration can be terminated by either the employer or the employee at any time for any reason. It is also known as "terminable at will." If someone is employed at will, her employer does not need good cause to fire her. In every state but Montana, employers are free to adopt at-will employment policies, and many of them have. In fact, unless an employer gives some clear indication that it will fire employees only for good cause, the law presumes that employees are employed at will.

Even if someone is an at-will employee, she still cannot be fired for reasons that are illegal under state and federal law. In these situations, the government has decided to make an exception to the general rule of at-will employment. If an employer is subject to federal and state laws prohibiting job discrimination, its employees cannot be fired because of certain characteristics, such as race, religion, or gender. Similarly, employees cannot be fired because they have complained about illegal activity, about discrimination or harassment, or about health and safety violations in the workplace. Employees also cannot be fired for exercising a variety of legal rights, including the right to take family and medical leave, to take leave to serve in the military, or to take time off of work to vote or serve on a jury.

Placing an employee on **probation** is a formal way of starting the process of firing an employee—or of correcting the performance issues so that the employee can remain a productive member of your team. It is important to remember that in managing employees, it is crucial to provide goal-oriented feedback on ways to improve performance. Even when an employee is failing to perform adequately, the feedback should include ways to improve as well as areas of failure. When placing an employee on probation, a manager sets a specific set of measurable goals for improvement within a limited span of time, such as 30 or 60 days. For instance, if a trainer is chronically late to work, a sign-in time sheet can be established to show when the employee arrives each day. If the employee does not exhibit measurable improvement in the stated amount of time, she is then fired. Or you can choose to end the probation period early and terminate the employee immediately.

Of course, some employee performance demands more immediate and drastic action. If, for instance, a fitness trainer behaves inappropriately toward clients, this is a serious offense that could affect the very existence of your business. Depending on the nature of the behavior and the number of people who witness it, you may choose to fire the employee immediately—not only to remove the employee from your environment but also to mend fences with your clients.

If there are concerns about firing an employee, the small business owner should not hesitate to contact a lawyer for advice.

When hiring an employee, a small business owner typically does not consider issues such as a noncompete agreement or a confidentiality agreement (one designed to protect the competitive advantage of the business). However, when you dismiss an employee these issues may become critical. For instance, a restaurant owner may have secret recipes that are central to her success; she does not want a disgruntled kitchen worker to post that information on the Internet. In a fitness business, there may not be "secret recipes," but you should consider all internal procedures, marketing strategies, future program plans, and especially client lists and contact information to be confidential. Therefore, at the initial hiring, you can limit later problems if you consider having your employees sign the appropriate documents. These documents are available via many software packages and are relatively easy to understand.

There are a series of issues related to employees that all small business owners must be concerned about, although not all companies may be directly impacted by each in the same way.

Workers' Compensation.

Workers' compensation laws are designed so that employees who are disabled or injured while on the job are provided with some type of compensation. Workers' compensation insurance is regulated by each state, with some states running their own insurance funds and others using private firms. The rates of the insurance can differ widely in the various states, depending upon the regulations and generosity of the state legislature. However, the rates for individual companies within that state are fairly standard and are generally based on the industry and size of the company. The payments are typically given to the employee if he qualifies, whether or not the small business owner was at fault for the injury from an unsafe workplace. However, the payments to the employee are limited to partial wage replacement and medical bills.

[probation]
A formal way of starting the process of firing an employee—or of providing a process for correcting performance issues.

[workers' compensation]
Laws designed so that employees who are disabled or injured while on the job are provided with some type of compensation.

The employee cannot receive workers' compensation for pain and suffering. The employee usually cannot sue the small business owner for his injury if he accepts workers' compensation payments.

The Occupational Safety and Health Administration (OSHA). The Occupational Safety and Health Administration (**OSHA**) is charged with protecting the health of workers. OSHA has attempted to shape its regulations to be more lenient toward small business. For example, companies with fewer than 10 employees do not have the record-keeping regulations that apply to larger businesses. Additionally, any fines are lower for small businesses with fewer than 25 employees than they are for large businesses. Effectively, OSHA will not impact many new small businesses that are office-based. However, other businesses that involve physical labor, construction, or handling of heavy equipment need to pay specific attention to OSHA requirements regardless of their size. We would advise a small business owner to consult with industry associations and your local chamber of commerce to judge the potential impact on your company. If the impact looks to be significant, then a visit with your attorney is merited.

Unemployment Compensation. Every state has an **unemployment compensation** law that was put into place in order to provide financial assistance for some period of time to those people who lose their jobs through no fault of their own. Unemployment compensation pays to the former employee some set amount of money for a given period after she loses her job. During the time she receives these payments, she is required to look for a job. The small business owner is required to pay an unemployment tax to help fund this system. That tax will vary by state depending on the unemployment benefits that state provides, as well as the experience rating (the history of unemployment) of the company.

EXERCISE 4

1. You are willing to let a problem employee go if his/her performance does not improve, but you would prefer to see improvement. Develop a simple probationary plan for this problem employee, whose annual performance review is seven months away. Should you wait for the review to address your concerns?

2. As a fitness entrepreneur, how might you protect the health of an employee? What might you do if an employee is injured on the job?

The Americans with Disabilities Act (ADA). The Americans with Disabilities Act (ADA) generally covers those companies with 15 or more employees and provides that each and every business must provide unfettered access to all disabled people. This means at a minimum that ramps or elevators and Braille signs must be provided in the business. The small business may also be required to offer special accommodation to employees who need physical adaptations to work at the company. Some states and cities have additional requirements beyond the ADA that may impact the small business in this regard.

LO 10.5 Family Business

A special category of human resource management applies in family businesses. A family business is one that is generally run by and for a particular family. Human resources in such businesses are still critical, but because family members make up many of the significant employees in the company, everything becomes more delicate.[9] The combination of father, mother, uncles, aunts, and children all in the business has impacts well beyond the standard human resources practice. Small business owners should recognize that this does not eliminate issues of discrimination for a large company; placement of family members because they are family members into positions in a large business can still result in charges of discrimination. The key issue in discrimination is that everyone is not given a fair chance at a job.

Managing family members can be difficult, as these individuals know all of the "hot buttons" that make a fellow family member angry. However, there is no effective way to fire or truly discipline the person without causing major ruptures in the family structure. The result is that family businesses and the human resources in them have more in common with family counseling than they do with the legalistic methods described in the earlier part of this chapter.

One especially tricky human resource issue that occurs in family businesses is succession. The business may have been founded by the father or mother. He or she is ready to retire and has a son and a daughter in the business. Who in the next generation becomes the leader of the business? Too often the parent will put off the tough choices. The parent dies and a battle results in the family. To avoid this situation, the parent needs to choose a successor and prepare that person for the position by ensuring that he or she has all the contacts and understanding necessary to be successful. If the parent then decides to leave the business early, that parent needs to step back and let the son or daughter lead the business as he or she sees fit. Companies struggle to survive with two leaders of the business. The fact that the other child is not selected can result in difficulties in the family. Again, part of the means to overcome these difficulties is to work with professionals who act almost as family counselors to help the family see the rationales for the choices and how to deal with them positively.

EXERCISE 5

1. Debate some of the pros and cons of working with family members.

2. Suppose you are about to leave the family fitness business. Your daughter has been a professional trainer in the business for 10 years but has not helped out much with the business end, except to brainstorm marketing ideas. Your son has a business degree and has been working in the business for four years, but he has no fitness background. Justify how you would choose your successor.

key terms

at-will employment 180
bonus 175
commission 175
discrimination 170
equity theory 174
Fair Labor Standards Act (FLSA) 176

hourly wage 175
human resources 166
hybrid compensation system 175
job description 167
OSHA 182
performance review 178

probation 181
profit sharing 175
salary 175
unemployment compensation 182
workers' compensation 181

review questions

1. Name three elements of human resources, and describe what each element entails.
2. Restate the types of information that should appear on a job application.
3. Identify three steps involved in a job offer.
4. Name five ways to advertise about a job opening. Include types of organizations that might have a job board (online or in-office).
5. Suppose you are a fitness entrepreneur who employs two full-time personal trainers, one part-time personal trainer, two part-time group instructors, two part-time cleaning staff members, and one full-time administrative staff member. How would you compensate each type of employee, based on the information and guidelines provided in this chapter?
6. How would you change the following sentence so that it would be appropriate to appear in a job posting? Young, well-built personal trainer needed for studio catering to young male clientele.
7. Formulate a plan of action for an employee who is nearly always late for client appointments.
8. What are at least two recommendations you might have for the owner of a family fitness business who employs both family and nonfamily staff?

individual exercises

Suppose you own a small family fitness center in a rural area. All of your employees are employed part time and are family members. You plan to be involved with the business for many years to come.

1. Develop a small "blueprint" for how you would handle each of the three elements of human resource management.
2. Do you need to create a succession plan? Why or why not?

group exercise

Find a partner. One of you will role-play an employer, and one of you will role-play a problem employee. Spend about 15 minutes discussing and documenting both of your concerns and an action plan for performance improvement.

learning outcomes

After studying this chapter, you will be able to:

11.1 Discuss the basics of a marketing plan

11.2 Explain how to develop a pricing model

11.3 Differentiate between the various types of promotion available to a new business

11.4 Explain how to use effective communication skills to enhance marketing efforts

11.5 Identify the tools necessary for expanding and keeping existing clientele

11.6 Identify the methods for sales management

Marketing

CASE STUDY

Flora is a Pilates instructor who lives in a densely populated suburban area near Phoenix, Arizona. For five years, Flora worked in two area Pilates studios and then was hired by a healthcare company to teach a Pilates class for patients who suffer from muscle-control disorders—primarily Parkinson's disease. Flora quickly discovered that this work was the most rewarding of her career. She deeply enjoyed helping clients who appreciated even the slightest improvements in their mobility and strength. However, Flora was also frustrated with this class because attendance was sporadic. Many of these clients were elderly and relied on elderly spouses or friends to drive them to the class, so there were frequent absences. Flora spoke to her employer about providing these clients with in-home services, but the provider was not interested in going down that path. The provider would only support the on-site classes Flora was teaching.

Flora seized this as a business opportunity. She started marketing her services to this niche population and began to visit Parkinson's clients in their homes. Her first impulse was to start a website to market herself, but she decided to wait on this. Because most of her potential clientele were elderly people who did not spend a lot of time online, a website was not the most time-sensitive marketing tool. Instead, she budgeted $3,000 to create a high-quality brochure that would use simple terms and clear visuals to introduce people to Pilates. She asked a friend who was in marketing to help her design and write the brochure, and hired a photography graduate student to take some pictures of one of her sessions. Flora thought it would be important for potential clients to see that Pilates involved easy, ordinary exercises that can be done on the floor of a living room and without special equipment. Once she printed her brochure, Flora visited hospitals, healthcare providers, and senior citizens centers to make them aware of her services. It took only a few weeks for calls to start coming in, and before she knew it, Flora's client list was growing. In some homes that Flora visited, a healthcare worker or volunteer was present. Flora always encouraged these people to observe her sessions and always gave these healthcare workers her brochure with a few business cards clipped to the front cover. After just two months of marketing her new business, Flora had more than 20 clients and decided it was safe to give notice at the two Pilates studios where she was still employed. She knew that she had enough continuing business that she could devote herself fully to her new business.

At this point in the process of building a small business, the founders should have developed a unique product or service to offer, and established its business operations so that it is physically able to offer that product or service to the public. However, if the public does not know about the product or service, regardless of how much effort has been put into the small business to date, all of that prior work will accomplish very little. The old axiom "if you build it they will come" works fine in the movies, but the reality of business is that you must do quite a bit to make potential customers aware of your business. People are creatures of habit and in order to get some form of change in their behavior, we must stir the target customers to action.[1] Thus, a new business must aggressively seek to make its target customers aware that they have a product or service that offers a solution to a problem of those customers. A central part of this is that the small business needs to build a credible case as to why individuals need to use its product/service. Is it better, cheaper, higher quality, or reparable, or does it have some other characteristic that other existing products/services do not offer?

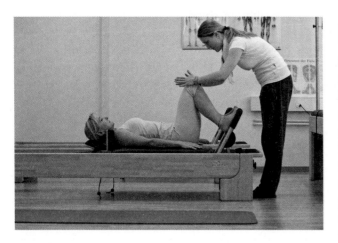

LO 11.1 Marketing Plan

Creating the business and the means to operate it is a necessary but not sufficient condition for business success. An underlying theme throughout this book is that planning and preparation are critical to the success of a small business. Plans may change, but rather than shifting direction with every change that may appear, a business that has a plan will be able to evaluate its past actions, note changes in the environment, and determine what changes need to occur in the future. The same is true of marketing. There is little to manage, record, or evaluate without customers. Therefore, to be successful the small business also needs a plan for its marketing effort. Then, when faced with changes, the company can adapt that plan rather than beginning anew with each small problem faced.

[marketing plan]

The plan developed by the small business to specify who the customers are and how they will be attracted to the company.

The **marketing plan** is developed by the business to specify who the best customers are and how they might be attracted to the company. Developing a marketing plan can be a complex undertaking. Furthermore, marketing is a complete discipline whose level of complexity can be daunting. There are many consulting companies and business courses available to aid you in developing your marketing plan. As the new business grows, it may be advantageous to employ an outside firm to help focus its marketing efforts. However, hiring experts or consulting firms will cost you resources at a time when it would seem that the business could least afford the expenditure. Because such expenses can be very high in some cases, they can be hard to justify when you have limited cash despite the additional knowledge gained. The information garnered in the process of researching and evaluating the market that you are operating within will return substantial benefits to the owners.

The focus of this chapter is the establishment of a workable marketing plan that can be developed by any entrepreneur. This plan should, at a minimum, include identifying your market, specifying the ideal and general target customer, determining a pricing policy that is in line with the strategy of the firm, developing promotion, determining sales management procedures, and, finally, forecasting sales. After developing each of these areas for a marketing plan, we will spend some time discussing unique distribution channels.

Identifying Your Market

In Chapter 4, we outlined a means for the entrepreneur to identify her target market and identify the "industry" in which she will be competing. This was done in the context of developing the idea for the business. The small business now needs to use that information as a foundation to develop a practical and actionable plan for attracting those customers.

An initial point needs to be made about the marketing effort for a small business. These marketing efforts need to be as clearly stated as the business's mission statement.[2] The use of such a mission/strategy statement helps to ensure that the firm is focused and will not seek to be all things to all people. The same focused approach needs to be used by the small business to market the firm's products to those customers that are most likely to buy its products at the price desired. As appealing as it may sound, a small business owner is not trying to get every person in the city to his business in the hope that they all buy the company's product or service. Instead, he is trying to reach those individuals most likely to actually buy from the business.

You will recall from our prior discussions that customers will travel only a given distance to buy from a business. This distance grows shorter as the number of competitors in the area increases. Therefore, a sandwich shop, hair stylist, dry cleaner, fitness studio, or similar service provider could reasonably expect to have large numbers of competitors and should expect customers to drive only a very short distance to shop at their location.

Hiring an experienced trainer with an established client base may attract clients who are dedicated to that individual. Satisfied clients may follow the trainer to a new location even if it is a bit farther to drive. If you market to too broad an area, the costs can be financially draining. A newspaper advertisement in a paper that serves a large city has virtually no targeting to specific consumers—it is a shotgun trying to hit a small target for the entrepreneur. A small business would simply hope that someone who had a need for its product/service would happen to see the advertisement, live close by, and respond to the advertisement. An analogy would be hoping to win the lottery.

Therefore, recall from Chapter 4 the exercise where we asked you to develop a reasonable geographic estimate of the radius your small business might draw customers from. As we stated in that earlier chapter, if you open a sandwich shop in the downtown area of a city, the shop most likely competes with other sandwich/fast food shops in a one- to two-mile radius, and perhaps less, if walking is the primary means of transportation for downtown lunching workers. There are limits to how far someone will travel for a sandwich. Drawing a practical radius around your potential new business location will help the business target the customers that are most likely to patronize your business. (If your business involves traveling to your clients, then you need to consider the reverse issue: how large a radius are you able to serve without becoming so stretched that you are spending too much valuable time in your car?)

In considering the geographic area, the small business owner should also consider how he would reach the potential customers in the area. Every contact outside his market area is wasted money. There is a wide variety of potential marketing activities that can be pursued, including flyers, sponsoring events within the area, and affiliating with complementary businesses. As you look to define your geographic area, there will be several methods that fit naturally with part of your geographic area, but which may not be consistent with another geographic region. Thus, to be successful, the small business must target the right geographic area and do so with the right marketing tool.

To illustrate, consider a small business that plans to use direct mail to contact potential customers. You may find that a given Zip Code covers 85 percent of the market you planned to target. The other 15 percent of your target geographic area is split between two other Zip Codes. The cost of addressing those two Zip Codes, due to the smaller size and special attention, may exceed the addressing costs for the other 85 percent of your market. Therefore, the reasonable thing to do at this stage would be to limit your target market to the one Zip Code. Defining a geographic market served should be a more complex analysis than simply drawing a circle around your potential business. The drawing of a circle is only a start. Building on that, the entrepreneur should make a reasonable estimate of what she can do with the least resources to reach the most people as efficiently as possible. Once the geographic area is defined, then the small business owner should remember that the money invested in her marketing effort should be primarily, if not exclusively, aimed at her target market area.

Target Customer

Once the geographic area is defined, the entrepreneur needs to define the particular segment of the market she is seeking to serve. As part of the basic market/customer identification performed in Chapter 4, you identified broad customer groups that the new business would serve. Now your operational marketing plan needs to go deeper and specifically identify potential customers. Most small businesses have restricted resources, and this is one of the things that differentiates a small business from a large business.

This lack of funds pushes the small firm to direct all of its marketing resources toward reaching the ideal customer. Therefore, once the entrepreneur has identified the target market, she needs to identify the specific customers who meet those criteria in the market area chosen.[3]

To illustrate, consider a new athletic club that was opening in an upper-income area of a large city. Most gyms in the region charged $100 to $150 per month for a club membership. That represents a cost of $1,200 to $1,800 per year, not including any initial membership fees. An individual would need a reasonable income to support that expense. The owners of the gym also felt that the distance that individuals would drive to a gym was slightly farther than the distance they would drive to a sandwich shop. The founders conducted a brief survey of members enrolled at a friend's gym in a nearby city and found that most customers drove approximately two and a half miles or less.

The owners drew a circle of two and a half miles around their location and found that a relatively high population lived in the area. However, this region of the city had a mixture of individual homes and apartments. The newer apartments typically had their own small gyms. Additionally, many of the older apartment complexes were relatively inexpensive and populated by individuals who worked at service jobs in the restaurants and retail outlets in the area. The result was that the owners came to realize that they should target their customers very specifically: homeowners in their area who had a high enough income to join the gym and renters who did not already have gyms in their apartment complexes. Advertising could now be targeted using real estate records. The methods used could be direct mail or phone calls (to those not on the national do-not-call list).

This is not to suggest that the gym would turn away potential customers who did not meet their ideal profile. There might be some customers who joined the gym because they heard about it from another source. There might be others who would join with a friend. However, these customers would not be a direct result of the firm's marketing, so the cost of obtaining those customers would be much lower.

Once the target population is identified, the small business should try to answer questions such as these:

1. How many of these individuals exist within your market area?
2. What percentage of these individuals do you believe is reasonable for you to attract as customers?
3. What percentage of the general population belongs to a gym?
4. Do these numbers match your cash flow projections?
5. What do you need to change if they do not?

> ## EXERCISE 1
>
> 1. Should a small business owner market to as many people as possible in the hope that many of them will buy from the business? Explain your answer.
> 2. Name three marketing activities that you can use to reach people in your target geographical area.
> 3. Explain why marketing to everyone in your target geographical area is insufficient to reach your ideal target customers, and name one additional way you could reach them.

LO 11.2 Pricing

Pricing of services is a critical consideration for the small business. One approach is to value your services for what you believe they are worth to the market. Most small businesses charge a premium for their products or services. However, the higher the profit appears to be, the faster competitors will challenge the small business.

One method for a small business with specific products that are comparable to other products in the market is a **cost-plus pricing** method, in which the company determines its cost and then adds onto that cost some level of profit it determines to be appropriate. This method can be difficult to implement effectively.[4] It requires that the small business initially determine what the total cost is for a particular product. This break-even point is referred to as the **pricing floor,** as the small business owner will not want to price a product at a loss. In calculating the floor cost of your service, you will need to include your estimated cost of marketing and an administrative overhead allocation. The cost of your estimated marketing might change as you develop your marketing plan. As a result, you may need to go through the pricing process several times as you refine the marketing plan.

[cost-plus pricing]

Pricing in which the small business owner initially determines her cost structure and then determines what profit margin she desires and adds that to the cost.

[pricing floor]

The break-even point; the lowest amount that can be charged for a product or service while still making a minimal profit.

Occasionally, the small business owner may choose to have a product that is referred to as a **loss leader.** In other words, a small business may sell something at a nonoperating loss (that is, the price only accounts for the actual cost of the product) to simply get customers to patronize the business. This strategy is related to the thinking behind online discount services like Groupon.com. Businesses use such services just to get new customers in the door, even though they are doing so by offering services at a steep discount, perhaps even at a loss. The hope is that the customer's first experience will be so good that they will become repeat (and full-paying) customers.

Our advice is that the small business owner not employ loss leaders until the business has developed some substantial momentum. The small business owner needs to get the firm on solid ground before employing such

actions, which take considerable skill and have high risk associated with them. A loss leader can become quite a burden if customers buy the leader without buying the other services/products of the company.

In determining the cost of a product/service, we also suggest that the small business owner avoid the time-consuming process of making detailed calculations for every product, especially if there is a wide product selection. Instead, the small business owner should place products in reasonable categories that balance the need for detailed pricing against the need to manage an ever-expanding database of information. The major airlines are large enough to have the resources and the technological ability to manage a system in which every person on the plane may pay a different price, depending on when the ticket was bought, and on predicted occupancy of the plane when it takes off. As a small business owner, you will not have that level of sophistication, nor is it necessary for an effective pricing policy. Therefore, having a data system that generates information that is useful and manageable should be the focus.

Information on the costs of the business is the foundation for determining cost-plus pricing, with the small business owner adding the percentage profit she desires to that cost. Small businesses can seek a profit of 10 percent, 15 percent, 20 percent, 25 percent, or 100 percent or more on product categories. Part of the desired profit margin will be determined by how competitors price their products and how much overhead the business has. There will be a comparison effect as consumers evaluate different firms' products and make decisions based on an internal cost/benefit calculation. For example, a fitness club may have a small retail clothing area. The club's retail prices may be higher than those at a large chain sporting goods store or a discounter like Target or Walmart, but the club offers the convenience of purchasing workout clothing at the very site where workouts take place, and presumably the club's staff can offer expert advice on such clothing. Customers may be willing to pay a premium for this convenience.

Alternatively, you may be able to charge a premium for your services if you have established a reputation that clients believe to be extraordinary or valuable. A fitness trainer who has established long-term relationships with clients can likely institute gradual periodic price increases to the point where clients are paying more to stay with the trainer than if they went to a competitor. However, the clients are willing to pay the premium because they have formed an intense, trusted relationship with the instructor and they do not wish to abandon that to save a relatively small amount of money. In addition, those same clients can bring in new clients at the same rates through word of mouth. However, if there is a significant deviation between your prices and those of your competitors, you must be confident in justifying this pricing difference if your perceived value is to have merit with clients. The small business owner needs to keep abreast of his competitors and their pricing to be able to make such judgments.

It is important to remember that pricing a service such as fitness instruction is more complex than pricing a material product. With a product, a business has a potential price floor based on the cost of manufacturing the goods, whereas a service has only time as the base operational cost. There will still be overhead expenses (rent, utilities, etc.); however, the principal value inputs are your education and experience, which are difficult to establish as a cost. In the case of services, we encourage the entrepreneur to more closely examine the pricing of competitors. These prices can be critical information in determining how to value your service. We would suggest that you not underestimate the value of experience. A trainer with many years of experience and deep client references will be able to charge far more than a trainer who has just received her certification.

The small business owner providing a service should also recognize that pricing is a valuable tool to balance customer flow with the time he has available. There are price-sensitive customers who will make decisions based solely upon price. For those customers, as the price goes down, customer flow goes up, and vice versa. Small business owners who have been in business for a while may find they have too many low-margin customers and cannot provide the level of service they would like to provide. Thus, as their customer base increases, they might need to raise prices to limit the customers coming in at an unprofitable level and profit from their business adequately.

In establishing pricing, there are several caveats that the small business owner should remember. Typically, a small business starting out will need to offer an even greater value for the money charged in order to build a customer base. Once the business has developed a positive reputation, the value offered to the consumer can be changed to provide a bit more financial benefit to the company. Recall that individual consumers are generally unwilling to change the suppliers of their goods and services. As the business grows, the small business owner can shift from a cost-plus type of pricing to one that is based more upon what the market will allow.

A second caveat applies to the actual price charged. Small increments of money should be avoided regardless of the exact percentage of margin desired. This is why retailers would rather charge $0.99 for an item than $1.01. In the customer's mind, $0.99 is far more appealing and represents a greater bargain than the 2-cent discount actually involves. Similarly, when prices are over $1,000.00, the small business owner should avoid using cents in the price.

A third caveat applies to the actual price for services rendered. Both large and small price changes can hurt the bottom line profit. Charging $99 for three sessions of training and then $199 for five sessions of training does not seem fair if your baseline price for training is $35 per hour. However, charging $99 for three sessions and $149 for five may be a good price point for both the business and the customer.

Finally, the small business owner will have to determine if she wants to offer a quantity discount. Much of this decision is based on the nature of the business that the businessperson establishes. For example, a retailer typically does not sell in large enough quantity to be concerned with such issues; however, a fitness instructor may be willing to give a discount to a client who will pay up-front for ten sessions.

EXERCISE 2

1. Summarize the cost-plus pricing method of setting a value to your products or services. Include a description of the pricing floor and a discussion of why cost-plus pricing is difficult to implement.
2. Identify how you can determine an appropriate profit margin. Give some reasons why a business might be able to charge a premium.

LO 11.3 Promotion

[promotion]

The means by which a small business advances its product or service.

Although it is only one part of marketing, people often think of marketing solely as the promotion of the product or service. **Promotion** is the means by which we make our product or service known to potential customers. The most readily seen versions of such promotion are the advertisements seen in a newspaper, viewed on the Internet, heard on a radio station, or seen on television. However, there are many means of promoting a business and each has varying costs and impacts. Promotion must be targeted to the market and customer groups within the industry, as we discussed earlier in this chapter. Furthermore, you will want your promotional efforts to reach the specific target consumers in the most efficient manner possible.

[pure promotions]

Promotions that are strictly financial arrangements in which a business pays for some outputs, such as radio advertisements.

While most promotional efforts involve some type of financial commitment, there are some promotions that are strictly financial arrangements in which you pay for some outputs, such as radio advertisements. These are referred to as **pure promotions.** There are other promotions that cost something but also have an element of community support, and are referred to as **mixed-model promotions.** Lastly, there are promotions that have a very limited financial cost but have a time commitment requirement from someone in the company; these are referred to as **virtually free promotions.** We will briefly discuss each of these ways to promote a business.

[mixed-model promotions]

Promotions that cost something but also have an element of community support.

Pure Promotions

This category encompasses the majority of promotional efforts targeted by the firm. Any form of advertising that is purely designed to promote the products/services of the company falls into this category. This includes signs, flyers, websites, newspapers, radio, trade shows, and television. Each of these will be reviewed briefly.

[virtually free promotions]

Promotions that have very limited financial cost but have time commitment requirements from individuals in the firm.

Signs. An oft-overlooked means of advertising the company comes in the form of a sign on the building or on the street, and on the letterhead/checks/business cards of the firm. A catchy name, a well-designed logo, and some substantial efforts to get the logo/name out can pay significant benefits in recognition and impression management. For most customers,

In promoting any fitness business, it is important to convince potential customers that by using your services they will see benefits in their health. A fitness business must be able to provide its clients with the opportunity to cover all areas of wellness, which may include losing weight, building muscle, toning their bodies, or achieving a variety of other personal health goals. Yet how far can a fitness business go in *guaranteeing* certain results? After all, part of the equation is the behavior of the client when he is not at the fitness club. Most trainers see their clients an average of three hours a week. There are actually 168 hours in a week that the trainer is not with her clients. What kind of language do you think is appropriate in promising health-benefit results from a fitness program, and what kind of language do you think crosses the line of promising results that cannot necessarily be delivered? Do you think it is ethical for a fitness business to use extreme examples of clients who experienced complete body transformation as a way of enticing new clients?

there are myriad businesses where they can spend their money. Why a customer spends that money with your business is at least partially a result of what that customer thinks of your business when that purchase decision comes about. Most sign firms will be willing to aid you in the development of whatever signage you purchase, although the quality of that advice may vary widely. The key thing to remember as you design your signage is that "simple but distinctive" is the goal.

Flyers and Brochures. As we mentioned earlier in this chapter, if you can target a very specific geographic area and perhaps identify a likely customer profile, then using something as simple as flyers might be very effective. They can be delivered directly to the customer's business or home, or posted at appropriately visible spots. Flyers can be changed frequently, printed cheaply, and delivered with low-cost labor. Unfortunately, these very characteristics mean that they have a smaller impact upon customers. Unlike a flyer, a brochure will include more detailed information about a business and tend to be less time sensitive. A brochure may be designed more professionally than a flyer, as well.

Website. In recent years, it has become apparent that almost every business establishes an effective promotional website. While an online presence was considered a truly unorthodox competitive advantage just a dozen or so years ago, today it is an expectation. Customers look to websites for basic corporate information, information about products and services, and the ability to purchase online. The sophistication of your website should be dependent upon the goals of your organization; but particularly for a small business that sells a unique product with a wider target market, this may be one of the primary means to reach clients that live outside your region. The first step, acquiring a domain name, is now an easy process available from a number of third-party providers on the Internet. The second and third steps include purchasing time on a server (usually a service provided by the same acquisition provider, as well as a number of Internet design firms) and having a company design a website for your business. For any design beyond the most basic, we suggest that you have a professional develop your website.

Newspapers. A standard method for promoting your business is through a newspaper advertisement. The process involves two steps: One is designing the ad and the second is placing it in the newspaper. Your local paper will work with you on both parts, or you can hire an advertising agency to design and place the ad for you. Either method is effective; however, newspaper advertisements mean that you will be paying for "views" by many individuals who will never be your customers. This is a broad-based "shotgun" type of advertising. It is no secret that in the digital age, major city newspapers have contracted or vanished. At the same time, other smaller local papers have thrived, to varying degrees. Larger urban markets also have small, targeted publications that focus on arts and nightlife, religious affiliations, parent networks, etc. All of these print media still present viable advertising opportunities for small businesses, and fitness businesses are frequent advertisers in many.

Radio and Television. As with newspapers, a radio/television advertisement can be designed and aired by the station, or you can employ an advertising agency to develop and place an ad. While there may be only one major newspaper in a market, it is likely that you will have a number of radio and television stations reaching your target group. This fact encourages us to recommend the use of an advertising agency that is loyal to you and will place the ads regardless of the desires of a particular station. Radio and television advertisements are qualitatively more difficult and financially more draining than the other approaches. A radio or television advertisement must be designed to make your points, while not upsetting anyone, and be sufficiently creative to draw customers to your business.

Trade Shows. Trade shows are events established around a particular theme where individuals are allowed to set up booths in order to promote their goods or services. For service businesses, there are often trade shows in which a small business owner may wish to participate. Trade shows such as IHRSA's International Convention and Trade Show, IDEA's World Fitness Convention, and the Club Industry Conference and Exposition for Fitness Business Professionals, among others, can be expensive to participate in. However, a small business can successfully participate by strategically focusing its efforts and ensuring that promotion prior to a trade show makes potential customers aware of the presence of the small firm at the trade show.[5]

Mixed-Model Promotions/ Community Support

There are a number of opportunities to promote your business and help the community in a way that targets your customer base. Schools are in constant need of sponsors. Angling your sponsorship to those activities that will provide maximum exposure to your potential client base is an effective and relatively inexpensive means of keeping your name in front of them. Depending upon the business, sponsoring sports activities, clubs in the school, events (dances and fund raising activities), etc., allows you to put your stamp on positive activities and reach the parents/children in your

Local businesses commonly sponsor youth sports leagues as a marketing effort—a perfect fit for a fitness-oriented business.

target customer group. For example, a fitness-related business could be the perfect sponsor for a Little League team, and your business would receive repeated name exposure to the members of those teams, their families, their opponents, and their opponents' families.

A second group of mixed-model promotions/community support is churches within your target area. Church groups look for sponsors to help in various activities for the community or for their youth. Carefully targeted efforts can help the new small business reach an audience that is not normally as targetable.

Virtually Free Promotion

Virtually free promotions are also widely referred to as **bootstrap marketing,** since they require little capital. There are many opportunities to speak with groups about your business or even a specific area of expertise. To illustrate, the individuals that started the athletic club we discussed earlier in this chapter sought out speaking opportunities with groups in their area. The age of the typical Lions, Optimist, or Kiwanis Club member was within the range of the target market for the club. Additionally, those individuals that have time to commit to such organizations typically have sufficient income to belong to a health club. Therefore, the owners actively sought out opportunities to talk to a variety of groups about health programs and how to start exercising. To arrange such talks they contacted leaders of the groups and offered their services, particularly at the beginning of a new year, since many people start off each year with fresh resolutions about their weight. Incidentally, that is when gyms have their greatest increase in membership.

There are speaking opportunities with schools, clubs, and religious groups throughout the year. If the group is relevant to your small business, you should take advantage of talking to it. The presentation should be more generic than a simple promotion for your business. To illustrate, the individuals that started the athletic club we discussed earlier in this chapter sought out speaking opportunities with groups in their areas. There are speaking opportunities with schools, clubs, and religious groups throughout the year. If the group is relevant to your small business, you should take advantage of talking to it. After you make these presentations, it will be your business that the consumer considers when she seeks out a business in your field. There are other free opportunities that the small business owner should seek out—for example, if an opening arises with the local news to comment on current events. There are also many local morning talk shows for which you could put together something interesting for a show spot. For example, these shows often run spots whenever seasons change; a fitness instructor could do a spot on ways of modifying exercise routines when the weather changes.

In any case, it is important to remember that no single advertisement will be sufficient for

[bootstrap marketing]
Marketing efforts that require little capital.

EXERCISE 3

1. Make a chart that describes the three types of promotions, and give at least three examples of each.

Type of Promotion	Description	Examples

2. Plan a website for your start-up business. Visit other fitness-related sites for ideas. Research your options for acquiring a domain name. Outline the sections that you want to include (About, Contact, Blog, etc.) and what information you want to appear (text, graphics, audio, video). Consider costs.

3. Design a brochure for your potential business. Begin by writing what you want to include in the copy and by describing or locating graphical elements. Your brochure does not need to be a completed version but should include a description of the text and graphics you want to use. You may use a template in a word processing or publishing program for assistance in creating a draft version. Investigate professional design services and printing costs.

the business. The attention of your target market is pulled in many different directions. It can take numerous "impressions" for an individual consumer to take notice of your firm or product.[6] Developing a promotional program requires a systematic effort aimed at making sure that the firm obtains the recognition of the consumers.

LO 11.4 Communication in Marketing

When any entrepreneur is marketing a business, she is communicating a message to the public about her business, so it is obvious that clear and professional communication skills and techniques are essential. In a service industry such as fitness training, communication is especially crucial because the businessperson communicates directly with current and poten-

tial clients every day. Even when you are not explicitly marketing or advertising your services, you should maintain the attitude that all communication is a form of marketing.

PEEC

The crucial aspects of client communication can be easily remembered as PEEC—Professionalism, Enthusiasm, Encouragement, and Clarity.

- Professionalism is the most important attribute to exude as a trainer and businessperson. Professionalism includes such important habits as arriving on time for appointments ready to go, but professionalism should also be the earmark of how a trainer communicates with potential and current clients.

- Enthusiasm is exhibited in the ability to have and maintain excitement and positive energy in everything you say to clients.

- Encouragement is a key tool that trainers must use to keep clients going forward in their training regimens.

- Clarity requires that you provide clear, direct, and succinct information to existing or potential clients.

As a business owner and manager, you must communicate clearly, and you must also train your staff to understand the importance of PEEC.

Sales and Marketing Team

In your small fitness business, it's important to think of every interaction you have with clients or potential clients as a sales and marketing effort. Likewise, almost every employee you hire will, in effect, be part of your sales and marketing team. In a service business such as fitness—in which interpersonal contact with clients is an essential part of the product—every client's perception of satisfaction is extremely powerful. And those perceptions can tip from positive to negative from simple misunderstandings or incidental conflicts. This is why we cannot emphasize enough that clear, professional communication is just as vital a resource to your business as are weight machines, knowledgeable trainers, or a clean, modern facility.

Of course, when an entrepreneur starts a small business, his staff may just be one: himself. He is not only the founder and owner, he is sales manager, sales rep, receptionist, and a litany of other jobs all rolled into one. As the business grows, the founder must remain aware that each new hire is an addition to the sales and marketing staff as well as to the administrative, training, or maintenance staff.

Staffing in fitness businesses has changed dramatically over the last decade. For example, it is no longer financially viable for most businesses to have a front-desk person whose sole responsibility is to answer the phone and greet the members. Today, such a person's sales and marketing responsibility must be considered. To many potential clients, this person provides the first impression of your business, so this team member must be capable of and well-trained in appropriate communications. Indeed, every employee who has client contact carries the responsibility of projecting your message to the clients: through their words, attitude, behavior, skills, and personal appearance. Depending on the size of your business, your staff may eventually become more important "marketers" of the business than you.

First Contact with Potential Clients

From the first phone call, e-mail, or personal interaction with a potential client, it is essential that you and your staff utilize PEEC qualities in your communication. First impressions count for everything, and potential clients can be lost literally within minutes if you do not communicate well.

When a client contacts you with questions about personal training or your services, return their e-mail/phone call as soon as possible—the same day or early the following day. If you do not, you may lose these prospects.

Keep in mind the relatively fragile and fleeting state of a potential client's attitude toward fitness. Different people have different reasons for searching for a fitness trainer. Many clients are motivated by body image— they don't like the way their clothes are fitting, they dislike the way they look in pictures, or they are told by a doctor that their cholesterol or blood pressure is too high. Whatever the reason, you must realize that the motivation is often charged with emotion and urgency, yet the urge can also pass quickly.

The path every individual takes toward starting an exercise routine is unique. However, we can safely generalize that most people follow a path such as this:

1. Pre-contemplation: not exercising and not intending to start

2. Contemplation: not exercising but intending to start; gathering information

3. Preparation: beginning to exercise a bit but not regularly; gathering information

4. Action: recently started exercising regularly

5. Maintenance: exercising regularly and long term

In the early stages of this process, there will be countless reasons for people to lose their nerve, lose interest, become distracted, and abandon the path.

Fitness trainers must recognize this fact. When a potential client reaches out, she could be in one of the early, fragile stages and could seize on any excuse to back out. One such excuse could be, "Well, I called this trainer three days ago, and he never called me back, so forget it!" It's important to act quickly and respond right away with a positive, encouraging reply.

One of the first things to discuss with potential clients is their goals. Some clients may have simple goals ("I want to lose 20 pounds") and others may have more complex or ambitious goals ("I want to improve my cardio-vascular endurance so I can run a marathon in three months"). It's your role to validate their goals and make them feel special. Potential clients should quickly understand that you are interested in working with them because you understand and support their goals, and that achieving their goals is the sole reason to begin the relationship. In other words: it's all about them, not about you.

Whether your first contact is on the phone or the client walks in off the street, be sure to greet him with energy and a smile. It can be hard to muster genuine enthusiasm every hour of every day, but remember that clients come to you for motivation. If you are not upbeat, your client's motivation will vanish.

First Meeting with a New Client

When transitioning a person from potential client to actual client, your approach to communication should remain just as consistent, professional, and upbeat. You must exude a sense of enthusiasm and professionalism, and you must be committed to providing the ultimate in customer service. The following points are important tips for a first orientation session with a new client (but could also be applied to *any* sessions with clients).

- **Arrive early.** Arrive 10–15 minutes before your scheduled client's appointment. You will need this time to prepare your client's work-out, to make sure you have all needed equipment, and to get your head wrapped around work in general.

- **Have a plan.** Based on your initial conversation, it is important to map out clients' first fitness routines that are suited to their experience and needs. However, you must be flexible enough to alter the plan if a client shows up and provides new information such as a physical condition he did not reveal in the initial meeting.

- **Look polished.** Although you may wear athletic shoes and shorts to work, you still need to look professional. So you should stay fit, fix your hair, wear clean clothes (not clothes you just wore for a workout), and project the attitude that a fitness club is a place of business. As with verbal communication, the way you present yourself physically carries meaning in a marketing sense. Think of yourself as a sales rep for your business. When you meet with sales reps for any other kind of business, what would you think if they arrived at a sales call looking unkempt?

- **Greet your client by name.** In fact, you should greet *everyone* who comes through your door—say hello and make them feel welcome. Always try to use people's names because people simply love to be called by their names. Some club owners insist that all employees learn the names of every client so that anyone who enters the club can be greeted by name.

- **Find connections.** Although your conversations should focus on fitness, also find comfortable opportunities for casual conversation so you can make connections that you can carry over to subsequent sessions. If you discover that your new client is proud of his flower garden, you have something to ask him about during his next session. As the conversations continue over the weeks, your relationship deepens, and the client becomes more connected to you. So ask questions about clients' lives—their jobs, their spouses' jobs, their families, their travels, their hobbies. But remember that the focus must remain on the client, and not on you.

- **Explain.** Every client has a different amount of experience with fitness training. Some may have never set foot in a gym before; others may be fitness pros. Most fall somewhere between these extremes. At the beginning of your relationship with new clients, be sure to explain exactly what they should do for each exercise routine, as well as some background on why they are doing these specific routines. It's important to strike a balance: provide enough information but not so much as to overwhelm them. It's important that a new client infers that you have listened to him, assimilated the information he has provided, and that you have designed a workout that will benefit his specific needs.

- **Provide positive feedback.** Throughout the first session and at its conclusion, give your new client positive feedback. Even if your client is struggling, you must find positive aspects to point out. Your communication skills must be honed so that your feedback is useful and genuine; don't appear to be condescending or insincere. Again, think of every interaction with a client as a marketing opportunity. Your positive reinforcement is as powerful as a discount coupon in motivating your client to return to your business.

- **Set goals.** No matter how positive or discouraged a new client may be at the end of his first session, it is crucial that he does not leave your facility without a set of goals. Leave time at the end of the session to sit down and schedule his next few sessions. You can also begin providing the client with some exercises he can do on his own.

- **Follow up.** If you do your job well in an orientation session, clients will come back wanting more. But clients do not necessarily return automatically. Even after a successful first session with a goal-oriented plan in place, new clients may need another dose of encouragement to commit to their exercise routine. Or they may need a reminder of what an effective, insightful, and motivating trainer you are. A follow-up call or e-mail a couple days after the orientation session can accomplish this. For some clients, additional follow-up techniques can be useful. Sending thank-you notes or news of discounts or promotions can be useful tools to lure new clients back through your door and on their way to their ultimate health.

Keys to Effective Communication

Many personal trainers focus their education solely on the sciences of the body, not of the mind. You can earn a master's degree in exercise physiology or biomechanics, but if you don't learn how to communicate effectively, you will not be able to convey all that knowledge you have worked so hard to learn.

Rapport. The effort to teach and communicate with someone does not always work out as planned. Rapport-building in the opening rounds of your relationship with a client will pave the path to a successful, long-term relationship. Before a client chooses to open her mind and ears to what a trainer might have to say, that client must let down her guard and have a reason to listen. Rapport-building is all about creating a common ground on which both parties can find a level of comfort that will facilitate open communication. Trying to force your opinion or thoughts on someone is an exercise in futility and works against building rapport.

One technique in building rapport involves some simple things that the trainer can "mirror and match" in the client:

- Verbiage
- Tone
- Tempo
- Volume
- Physiology
- Eye contact
- Proximity

The goal of the trainer should be to observe each of these aspects in the client and attempt to mirror and match them. An example would be if the client is sitting with arms crossed and using a lot of slang, then the trainer might also cross his arms and use slang in the conversation (without going to extremes, of course). It would be a mistake to try to counter such a client's personality with an extremely proper, formal tone and attitude. So by becoming a bit more like the client, the trainer has proven to be on the same page as the client, and subconsciously the client opens up, becoming more receptive to communication, and rapport builds.

Teaching. One of the main functions of all great personal trainers is that of a teacher. A trainer is a teacher of such subjects as how to perform particular exercises, how to stay motivated, how to lose weight, how to manage stress, how to improve nutrition, etc. Viewing one's role this way is another important, although subtle, marketing technique. Being seen as a teacher only adds to the aura of professionalism and legitimacy that a service entrepreneur needs to establish for his business to flourish.

Do you know what kind of teacher you are? Most often people model their teaching styles on teachers they have had in the past. A math teacher, an English professor, and a football coach all used different mannerisms in their attempt to teach their respective students on the given topic. Considering these experiences, a personal trainer should develop a teaching style with which she is comfortable. A style might include bits and pieces taken from the various teachers in that personal trainer's background, but ultimately the style must be genuine and one's own.

There are three basic requirements for effective teaching: a passion for the subject, a strong desire to share it, and a modicum of authority in that subject. The first two requirements are essential, and although the third point is important, it oddly pales in comparison to the first two. You may be a world-class authority on weight training, but unless you can transmit an innate passion for the subject and exhibit a true enjoyment of training, your knowledge will fall on deaf ears. Regardless of the information the teacher is trying to share, the secret of teaching it successfully lies in how the teacher communicates.

Image. What can a trainer do to project a professional image? Arguably the most important thing to remember is that your posture is your biography. Every time you walk onto the gym floor, you communicate with everyone in sight and earshot. Physical appearance is the trainer's first statement. You could be the best trainer in your town, but if you are 25 pounds overweight, your first statement is not a positive one. Your conditioning, clothes, and hair are all part of the image you communicate. Within the club setting, although uniforms are not a necessity, they do help communicate that personal trainers see themselves as professionals. Although none of us wants to be judged, the truth is that it is happening everywhere we go. So if this is just how the world works, why not improve your chances of creating a great first and continuing impression by looking the part of a fitness professional?

Approachability. Another factor that both precedes and facilitates contact with prospective clients is approachability. A beaming smile, positive attitude, healthy self-confidence, and general good health are all evaluated quickly by anyone who sees you. If clients perceive that you are shy or introverted (for example, if you have trouble making eye contact), you will have difficulty in gaining clients' trust and building rapport with them. Probably the most powerful and realistic assessment of a trainer is made when others observe you while you are working with a client. Your mannerisms, your

EXERCISE 4

1. Analyze the information you developed for your website and brochure in Exercise 3. Update them as necessary to reflect the PEEC aspects of communication.

2. Think of some trainers or teachers you have had in the past. What about their teaching style did you like and would want to emulate? How do you think you could incorporate these characteristics into your own training style? What communication skills do you have that will support you in being a trainer? What communication skills do you think you need to improve?

attentiveness to the client, your sense of humor, and your level of competency can all be plainly observed.

LO 11.5 Retaining Clients

Once a client launches his workout routine with you, do not assume that the relationship will automatically last forever. A successful service business is, of course, built on a steady base of continuing clients, not on a series of one-time sessions with prospective clients. Obtaining new clients can cost, on average, six times the money and three times the marketing effort that is required to retain existing clients. Fitness businesspeople should be well-prepared to employ many communications and marketing techniques aimed at retaining clients.

A major part of client retention is the continuing need to motivate clients to want to stick with their workout program. And assuming that the client's motivation is sustained, the businessperson must be aware that a client's satisfaction will be based only partly on his success in training sessions. Good communication and customer service play important roles as well. Such factors as club policies, billing and payment information, and referral benefits could be just as important as the number of pounds or inches off the waistline.

Deepening the Relationship

Once a new client has started working with a fitness trainer, and once goals have been set, a deep and long-term relationship may have begun. The benefits for both parties are many, and one of the keys to achieving those benefits is a consistent, rigorous commitment to top-quality customer service, and there are many ways of creating satisfied customers beyond the obvious good health benefits they will gain from training with you.

Revisiting Goals. Revisiting and revising goals is just as important as setting them. Clients who meet their goals or perceive that they have reached a plateau may lose their motivation to continue working out. Trainers will need to develop devices that will enable clients to see the value in pursing another goal or maintaining the course to break through the plateau.

Communicating Promptly and Clearly. Just as it is important to respond quickly to potential clients, it is important to respond to active clients within 24 hours. Returning client calls immediately exhibits your respect for that person. Clients want to know—and need reminders—that you care about them and respect them. They must not perceive that they become a low priority to you once they have signed up.

Scheduling. Setting a consistent schedule is important to maintaining client relationships. It's a reality that certain clients have hectic schedules and frequently need to reschedule sessions. But *you* should not be the cause of chaotic scheduling. If you are constantly shifting session times, your clients will become quickly frustrated. If you are consistent with your schedule, your clients will be more consistent. Remember that you must set the tone for the client/trainer relationship. If a client knows you are dedicated to her, she will be dedicated to you.

Most fitness clubs have a 24-hour cancellation policy. The purpose is to let the client know you are serious about your job and that you want the client to take her workout seriously. Communicate this policy up-front, and enforce it consistently. When a client calls to cancel a session within 24 hours, inform her (politely) that she will be charged per the policy so there is no misunderstanding.

Providing Incentives to Try Other Services. After a client has been with you for a while, you can start encouraging him to try out other services you offer, such as yoga, Pilates, and Zumba. If you have a nutrition specialist associated with your business, you can connect your client to this person. But your personal advice might not be enough to push a client to try something new. A financial incentive can yield outstanding results. If a loyal client is offered a new service at a 20 percent discount for a limited time, he will be much more likely to try the service. And because he is already an existing client, your risk of losing him if he doesn't like the service is low.

Discounts do not just apply to new services. Discounted rate plans on basic services for long-time, loyal customers can help in securing the customer's continued patronage, good will, and commitment to your business. Such long-time customers are likely to become an ongoing source of referrals (see below) and positive word of mouth in the community. The benefits these customers bring to your business can outweigh the marginal revenue you give up through discounts.

Encouraging Referrals. You can also establish a bonus program to encourage client referrals. The benefit of client referrals is twofold: not only do you gain new clients, but the referring client is that much more committed to your business because she has recommended her friends and family to you.

LO 11.6 Sales Management

Sales management refers to the individuals who build and maintain relationships with customers, as well as to the methods and means by which they do this. As discussed in this chapter, everyone in your fitness business is involved in sales; however, sales management refers to how that sales process is managed. Issues that need to be considered include the following:

1. How many contact points will the business have with each client?

2. How will each client be greeted?

3. What is the process for managing a customer once the relationship has begun?

EXERCISE 5

1. Imagine you are an independent personal trainer with a studio in your home. You have five regular clients whose 10-session (twice per week), introductory-rate packages will be ending in two weeks. They have not yet told you that they plan to return after the introductory sessions are over. Compose a marketing plan to retain those clients. Consider whether or not initial goals will have been met in 10 sessions. Will you offer the same introductory rate? What incentives might you provide?

2. Create a detailed customer referral bonus program. Research how a program like this might work, both inside and outside of your industry, and devise a plan that you think will work best for your business.

[sales management]
The individuals who build and maintain relationships with customers and their methods for doing so.

4. What controls are in place to ensure the quality of services?

5. How much information will be collected on each client?

6. What will the business do with the information collected?

Designing and maintaining a sales management system is certainly part art and part tedious coding; however, a consistent approach and image that is designed around your mission statement will pay off tremendously as your business develops.

Forecasting Sales

Estimating sales without any history is an act of guesswork that is dependent upon the founder's ability to narrowly focus a customer group as well as to attract that customer group to purchase. There are many ways to estimate sales, all of which should be modified as real sales data become available. The two methods we will examine are market potential and customer demand.

Market potential methods take a macro look at the market and estimate potential sales for the firm based upon the number of potential consumers in the target area. These data are then modified by a likely percentage of those potential consumers that will be attracted to the specific business. This can be estimated by looking at the direct competitors in the area or looking at close competitors in another, similar area. As we pointed out in Chapter 4, your direct knowledge of the market and your competitors will be essential to your sales forecast. To illustrate, the founders of the gym we have been discussing believed that their customer base would exist within a two-and-a-half-mile radius of the business and that those customers would own houses. Data from the census bureau and the local government helped identify the number of homes that met the criteria. The individuals starting the gym estimated there were one and a half potential consumers per house and limited their analysis to those individuals who had full-time employment. The result was a potential population of almost 50,000 customers in their geographic area of interest.

The small business start-up owners must then estimate what percentage of their total market potential might use a business in a given area. For some companies, there will be industry information from industry associations. However, even without this it is relatively easy to estimate. For example, several of the fitness websites estimate the number of people who are members of a gym. Armed with that information and a quick search to find out how many gyms there are in the United States, our founders estimated the size of their likely customer base. They then talked to a gym owner in another state to find out how long it took that gym to ramp up to its current level of customer traffic. They made a logical estimate of monthly growth and then modified it as customers actually signed up for memberships.

The second method is customer demand. This method takes a micro look at the market and estimates how many customers the business can handle given its location, staffing, etc. The founder then estimates how many individuals it will take to break even, make X profit, etc. For example, a fitness club owner could make the following estimate:

1. The club has parking for no more than 10 cars at one time.

2. It is estimated that each client would be in the club for an average of 60 minutes.

3. Staffing meant that most of the time they could handle only six clients simultaneously.

4. The average sale was expected to be $75 per hour.

5. It was estimated that during a typical day, the club would be full of customers only three times.

With this information, the business was able to establish a sales forecast and staff the business appropriately. The owners modified their forecasts based upon the experience of the firm once it was actually in business.

Of course, creating a sales forecast is an impossible task without a clear marketing strategy. Considerations of sales and marketing should be taken hand-in-hand if either strategy is to succeed. To successfully forecast sales, the small business must know the customers who would be ideal targets for its services—that is, to whom the services will be marketed.

As we have discussed in this chapter, marketing is a complex endeavor, particularly for a service-oriented business. The small business must utilize its developed mission/strategy to narrowly target the perfect customers and how to market to them. If the small business owner does not understand these issues, it is easy to spend the firm's scarce resources in a manner that produces no tangible benefit.

EXERCISE 6

1. Write a sales forecast for your business start-up using either the market potential method or the customer demand method.

2. Suppose you are a personal trainer who just started working part time as an independent contractor at a small exercise club that currently has no other personal trainers. The club owner requires that you do your own sales forecasting for the next six months, as he has no experience in that area and is offering personal training as a service for the first time. Provide an argument for why the owner should bear some of the responsibility of developing the sales forecast. Decide what questions you would ask the owner to arrive at a sales forecast that aligns with the business goals.

key terms

bootstrap marketing 197
cost-plus pricing 191
loss leader 192
marketing plan 188

mixed-model promotions 194
pricing floor 191
promotion 194
pure promotions 194

sales management 205
virtually free promotions 194

review questions

1. Name the six basic steps that should be included in a marketing plan.
2. State why a business develops a marketing plan.
3. Restate in your own words the four caveats to remember when establishing pricing.
4. Report why a major city newspaper is not the best promotional tool for advertising but why small, targeted publications may be.
5. Provide some ways in which you plan to use bootstrap marketing to promote your start-up business.

6. Do you have the three basic requirements for effective teaching? Why or why not? If not, what can you do to meet the appropriate requirement(s)?
7. Do you agree that having a modicum of authority in your subject is not as important as having a passion for the subject and a desire to share that passion? Why or why not?
8. Create a basic script for meeting with a new client. Include lines for how you will make connections and build rapport, how

you will extract information from the client about goals and where he or she is on the general path regarding exercising, how to provide positive feedback, and other important issues that need to be covered in a first session. The script, of course, cannot be used verbatim in an actual setting, but it can provide you with a general outline for the questioning and information sharing that need to occur.

9. Think of some ways by which you can determine the level of satisfaction that your customers have with your services, and create the necessary tool(s). For example, create a customer satisfaction survey, or develop a script to gather informal feedback in meetings with clients.

10. Do you think a fitness professional or a sales professional would make the best sales manager at a large fitness facility? Justify your answer.

11. At a small fitness facility or an independently owned studio, the sales manager and trainer roles may overlap. Justify why a fitness professional with strong sales skills could perform well as a sales manager in such a business.

individual exercise

Develop a general marketing plan for your potential business. Use the six basic steps that you learned in this chapter (below), and also include any other information that you believe is relevant. For forecasting sales, use the method you did NOT use in Exercise 6.

1. Identify the market.
2. Specify the ideal and general target customer.
3. Determine a pricing policy that is in line with the strategy of the firm.
4. Develop promotion.
5. Determine sales management procedures.
6. Forecast sales.

group exercise

Break into groups of two. You and your partner are going to role-play a first session between a new client and a personal trainer. Take 5 minutes to prepare for each role. As a new client, choose a reason for visiting the trainer (what is your fitness goal) and a basic personality (you do not need to behave as yourself but may choose a personality that might challenge the trainer somewhat). As a trainer, consider how to build rapport, your teaching style, where the client may be on the general path of exercising, PEEC, approachability, and other points covered in this chapter about a first session, such as follow-up. After 5 minutes of preparation, decide who will play which role first. After 10 minutes of role-playing, switch roles and begin a new role-play.

Other Issues

The Future of Your Business

CASE STUDY

Ever since Leo was a teenager, he loved basketball shoes. When he was a kid he idolized Michael Jordan, and Leo lost count of the number of Jordan's signature basketball sneakers he had owned. Leo was a good enough basketball player to play on his high school varsity team, but once he got to college he played just for exercise and fun as he concentrated on earning his business degree. He worked his way through college at a national-chain sporting goods store—in the shoe department, of course.

Immediately after graduating from college, Leo and one of his fraternity brothers successfully launched a small store called Campus Sneakers. The store was Leo's dream come true: a chance to sell the latest in basketball, running, and other athletic shoes to a college-age market. The store also carried licensed sports paraphernalia. Leo was in charge of procuring inventory from suppliers, sales, and marketing. His partner, Rahul, also worked sales but was mainly in charge of finance and operations. Rahul was lucky enough to find a perfect location for Campus Sneakers: just a few blocks from the university's football and basketball stadiums.

The business opened the fall after their graduation, and it built a rapid, loyal following. Leo worked hard to procure the most cutting-edge sneakers—shoes that kids could not buy at the other local sporting goods stores. As the years passed, about 40 percent of their sales came from shoes, with the majority of sales coming from university sports gear.

In their fifth year in business, their landlord informed Leo and Rahul that when their current lease expired in four months, their rent would have to increase dramatically. The partners knew they would be challenged to pay the new rent, so Rahul immediately went to work trying to find a new location. The only affordable storefronts he could find were more than a mile away from campus. Rahul thought they should move the business, but Leo was worried. Most of their sales came from university-related merchandise, and he worried that changing locations would eliminate their significant game-day business. As much as he loved selling shoes, Leo knew in his gut that shoe sales alone could not sustain Campus Sneakers.

Just when time was starting to run out on their decision, Leo and Rahul attended a local chamber of commerce event and met an entrepreneur who owned several specialty clothing boutiques in the city. She was looking to expand her group of shops, and she told the partners she would be interested in buying Campus Sneakers. Leo and Rahul had never thought about selling their business, and when their potential buyer asked for a rough idea of what it would cost to buy them out, they realized they had a lot of work to do on an aspect of their business that they had never before considered.

Eventually there will come a time when the owner needs to, or wants to, exit his business. This decision may be based on a variety of factors. One may be that the business has done very well and the owner has decided to cash out of the venture. On paper the owner may appear to be very wealthy, but if all of the assets are in the business, then the individual is not very liquid and is subject to rapid changes in wealth as the value of the business changes. Selling the business turns some of the hard-developed value into cash. The ability to turn some or all of the business value into cash at some point allows the business owner a real flexibility of choice as he goes forward.

Alternatively, it may be that things have not gone well and the owner needs to either turn the venture around or close down the business. There is a wide set of issues that must be addressed in all of these cases, including such issues as a plan for paying off investors, establishing the value of the business, attracting buyers, negotiating a sale, meeting all of the legal requirements for the sale, and consummating the deal. These issues can become even more complex if you have to look at turning a business around that has started badly. While difficult, the ability to turn a business around is a valuable skill, as markets can change dramatically and quickly. This chapter will explore these areas.

LO 12.1 Exit/Harvest

The small business owner benefits from considering several dimensions of what is required to sell the business, both at the founding and when she begins the selling process.

Why Consider Exit/Harvest Now

It may appear odd to consider the topic of exit and harvest while you are only beginning the process of getting the new business up and running. However, this early stage is the best time to develop a well-defined exit plan before personalities clash. A business is an investment of both time and money. Developing a practical exit plan will help validate the business idea and provide some peace of mind to the family and the investors. The key starting point for any decision to exit or harvest the firm is the true valuation of the company. Developing an accurate valuation at, or just prior to, founding helps to

- provide insight for the owner as to the amount of capital and labor she should invest in the effort
- secure loans (either direct or working capital) by demonstrating the value of the firm to potential creditors
- convince outside equity investors of the potential long-term returns associated with the harvesting of the business
- generate potential offers to buy out the business (a relatively common occurrence in the life of a small business)
- benchmark the growth of the firm by establishing a true starting point

Why Consider Exit/Harvest Later

Having at least laid some initial groundwork will help the small business owner if she later decides to exit the business. As discussed in Chapter 2, the small business entrepreneur must determine what she is in business to accomplish. If the business is very successful but no longer interesting or enjoyable, it is probably a good time to exit. A small business takes too much time and personal commitment to be something that is not enjoyable. Similarly, there may be other opportunities available. The small business owner may not have time to run the existing business and pursue these new opportunities at the same time, so it becomes necessary to exit the first business. Alternatively, the founder may sense that while the business is strong now, the future does not hold the same potential for success.

> **EXERCISE 1**
>
> 1. Name three instances when it is a good time to exit a business.
> 2. Provide two reasons why developing an exit plan early, when the business is just beginning, is a good idea.
> 3. Define valuation.

LO 12.2 Steps in Selling a Business

When a business owner decides to sell or harvest the business, there is a series of steps that need to occur. The first is to develop some sense of the true value of the business. The second is to prepare the business to be sold. The last step is the negotiation and actual selling of the business.

Valuation

There are several standard valuation models and rules of thumb for established, publicly traded businesses. For example, public companies have an established market capitalization that is technically the value of the business as it exists at the present time. Following the standard on Wall Street, this market capitalization already accounts for future earnings and all future prospects of the business that are known today. If you wished to acquire one of these organizations, the general assumption would be that the market capitalization is the floor from which all negotiations begin. Calculating the premium that will be offered above the market capitalization is more a matter of art than one of science.* Issues such as how much cash will be paid versus stock transferred and the future investment in the newly combined organization are a matter of negotiation, not to mention the overwhelming concern regarding what will happen to the executives of the acquired firm. These issues are substantially different when we consider the valuation and acquisition of a privately held venture.

Virtually all small businesses are private firms that do not report their earnings to the public. In addition, small businesses often adjust their annual company "earnings" with the payment of large year-end bonuses to the founders in order to limit the profit and therefore the taxes on the business. The small business may also have creative company **perquisites** ("perks") for the owners in order to minimize the tax owed by the organization. The owners of a small business may also have other individual personal expenses paid for by the firm. The result is that the firm pays fewer taxes, but the firm also may appear to be worth less than it really is worth.

For example, a fitness facility that is owned by two individuals allows the owners to use "profits" for the benefit of the facility as well as themselves in a perfectly legal and ethical manner. If sales were particularly good in one year, the owners may decide to provide perks for themselves. This expense

[perquisites]

Benefits paid for by the company. Examples include vacations, vehicles, loans, gifts, financial contributions to retirement plans, etc.

---

* There are a number of other quick methods for calculating a purchase price, including a multiple of sales, discounted future earnings, discounted projected free cash flow, etc. We provide all of this by way of comparison.

dramatically reduces the "profit" of the venture, whereas the reality is that the business is quite profitable. Similar expenses also occur in public companies, but they are required to disclose such items in an audited annual report, whereas a small business venture rarely goes to the expense of having audited financial records. Thus, it should be clear that different methods of valuation are needed when considering the purchase of a private company.

There are a large number of unique systems used for the valuation of a private business. Most accounting groups and many private companies provide business valuation services. We would suggest that you work with these organizations when you are really ready to sell the business. They will use commonly accepted practices to refine the value of the ongoing business. However, in general, we encourage the small business owner to utilize only a few of the most common methods to get a rough estimate of the value of her business as the business begins and grows. Valuing a business is as much art as it is science. Ultimately, the true "value" of the business is the amount of money that a willing seller and a willing buyer agree upon for the sale of the business. Thus, you want to be well prepared for the range of prices that may be offered and understand why you might agree or not agree with those prices. An investor, lender, or potential purchaser may take issue with several of the assumptions in your projections, or might want to reduce the numbers more severely than the founders believe is realistic. In order to maximize the selling price of the firm, the founders must intimately understand the numbers to be able to discuss such issues intelligently with those individuals. These methods include (1) discounted future net cash flow, (2) price/earnings valuation, (3) asset-based valuation, (4) capitalization of earnings valuation, and (5) market estimation valuation.

Discounted Future Net Cash Flow. By far the most widely accepted method of valuation, and the most insightful, discounted future net cash flow involves some form of discounting the estimated future net cash flows of the business. As you might recall from Chapter 6, cash flow tracks the actual cash inflows and outflows of the business. For estimation purposes, a potential buyer can subtract any perks that have affected the net cash position of the venture. The detail available in a well-designed cash flow statement and the understanding that free cash flow, not profit, is the key to entrepreneurial success make this the ideal document to use in the valuation of a business.

The cash flow method of valuation requires that the net cash flow of the business be projected for some period of time into the future. Our experience has suggested that estimating cash flows five years into the future and adding a salvage value for the firm is a good ballpark floor valuation for a small business. The information for this example appears in Figure 12.1.

In this example, the net cash flow for each year is as follows:

Year 1 ($101,885)

Year 2 $30,575

Year 3 $143,725

Year 4 $161,000

Year 5 $446,100

	YEAR 1	YEAR 2	YEAR 3	YEAR 4	YEAR 5	TOTALS
Receipts:						
Sales	$25,000	$325,000	$675,000	$880,000	$1,560,000	$3,465,000
Consulting	20,000	20,000	60,000	80,000	100,000	280,000
Total Receipts	$45,000	$345,000	$735,000	$960,000	$1,660,000	$3,745,000
Disbursements:						
Salaries	$45,000	$95,000	$ 210,000	$305,000	$450,000	$1,105,000
Travel	4,050	31,050	66,150	86,400	149,400	337,050
Equipment Leases	4,000	6,000	7,500	11,000	13,800	42,300
Rent	900	6,900	14,700	19,200	33,200	74,900
Payroll Taxes	2,700	5,700	12,600	18,300	27,000	66,300
Insurance	5,500	6,000	7,500	9,000	13,000	41,000
Fuel/Maint.	960	4,500	8,000	13,000	21,000	47,460
Owners Comp	64,000	72,000	78,000	84,000	89,000	387,000
Benefits	13,500	28,500	63,000	91,500	135,000	331,500
Advertising	2,000	26,000	54,000	70,400	124,800	277,200
Supplies	225	1,725	3,675	4,800	8,300	18,725
Utilities	3,150	24,150	51,450	67,200	116,200	262,150
Misc.	900	6,900	14,700	19,200	33,200	74,900
Total Disbursements	$146,885	$314,425	$591,275	$799,000	$1,213,900	$3,065,485
Beginning Balance	$0	$98,115	$128,690	$272,415	$433,415	
Equity Investment	$200,000					
Net Cash Flow	**($101,885)**	**$30,575**	**$143,725**	**$161,000**	**$446,100**	**$679,515**
Ending Balance	$98,115	$128,690	$272,415	$433,415	$879,515	$1,812,150

Figure 12.1
Example Cash-Flow Statement

Those most interested in a good estimation of firm value (potential buyers, lenders, equity investors, and founders) will recognize that these numbers are simply estimates that are based upon a set of assumptions. In order to understand and accept the cash flow predictions, it is important that each interested party accept the underlying assumptions. Therefore, a critical addition to any business plan, and certainly a necessity for any valuation analysis, is a complete set of assumptions used by the founders. An example from a group of entrepreneurs that were proposing a specialty transport company in the spring of 2009 appears in Figures 12.2 and 12.3. This company would transport people to sports events related to local colleges. The business would start focused on a single school and ultimately expand to other schools. The plan was to sell alcohol and limited food on the bus.

The example above illustrates that to understand a cash flow statement, a small business owner needs to have an in-depth knowledge of the assumptions that went into the statement. Given the nature of predictions and assumptions in general, there is a need for these values to be discounted by some rate that not only represents the return expected by an investor, but

- Liquor sales are not included in the cash flow statement and are determined on a per trip basis, depending on how much alcohol the group orders. We will charge a 10 percent markup rate for each order.

- We applied an 8 percent payroll tax to salaries.

- Championship games for football are not accounted for in the cash flow statement. There will be a price markup that will be determined based on factors such as how big and how important the game is, who the opponent is, etc.

- We assume that the men's and women's basketball teams play a total of 6 out of 12 possible games in the tournament.

- We are assuming that the base school makes it to a bowl game.

- Pricing on the competitive map is based on football season rates.

- We plan to fill the buses during various alumni events during the summer. The base school currently has five major events on its annual calendar. We assume we can fill all four buses for each event because of their high importance. This is accounted for in the cash flow statement. We assume there will be other events we can cater to, whether through alumni associations or directly through the base school. We did not account for these numbers on the cash flow statement because estimating how many events we will book and how big each will be is difficult at this point, but we will stay in close contact with the school and alumni groups and work on making reservations. We are confident our summer sales will be higher.

- Gas costs were based on an assumption that the price is $1.60 per gallon for diesel fuel. According to Energy Information Administration, this has been the average price for the last two years in the Midwest region.

- We assume there will be no significant economic recessions within the next five years.

- We have researched laws pertaining to continuous operation for a commercial driver and will assure that all itineraries are planned accordingly.

Figure 12.2
General Cash Flow Assumptions for Specialty Bus Company

also accounts for the riskiness of the venture. We have seen discount rates range from a ridiculously low 10 percent to an almost absurd 90 percent. However, a rule of thumb for new small businesses being operated by owner/managers is to use 30 percent as a discount factor. This should not only account for a generous annualized rate of return but also build in a reasonable factor for risk. While we are in favor of simplicity in these calculations, we recognize that some interested parties prefer to separate return from risk. There are a variety of sophisticated financial models available to those who wish to be more precise in their analysis.

Using this rule of thumb, the entrepreneur should take the net cash flow figure generated for each year and discount that cash flow back to today's dollars. The discount rate remains the same, while the factor increases as you move further away from today. Thus, in year 2 the discount rate is squared (1.3 * 1.3), in year 3 it is cubed (1.3 * 1.3 * 1.3), etc. To illustrate with our previous example, we calculate the present value of the net cash flow on page 217.

- Sales tax for each state and the surrounding municipality is 7 percent, applicable to the rental price.
- Income will be consistent throughout all of the centers in the different states. This is because we have hand-picked each school and have taken great efforts to make sure that they are all similar in population, athletic activity, demographic makeup, and geographic locations.
- Maintenance overhaul will occur in the first quarter for each bus at a cost of $1,000 per bus.
- All acquisitions and expansions will be financed internally; there will be no need for second- and third-round financing.
- Salaries are set at $30,000 for each officer, with an increase to $35,000 in year 3.
- Insurance is a once-a-year payment, including $10,000 for base coverage with each additional bus adding $1,000 plus tax, stamping, and processing fees.
- Waste removal is billed by volume plus service fees, estimating $75 to $100 per visit.
- Credit card charges account for 30 percent of all sales with a processing fee of 2.1 percent.
- Transportation costs are associated with moving buses within the state, either to their home stations or to meet customers.
- Accounting/legal fees will occur periodically throughout the year, with a concentration of accounting fees during tax season and legal fees during periods of expansion/acquisition.
- Fees/permits include registration costs, inspection fees, and other associated costs with each bus, as well as the costs of providing CDL licenses and training to officers at the inception of the company.

Figure 12.3
Example of Specific Cash Flow Assumptions

Using the information in Figure 12.1 and assuming a 30 percent discount rate, we can calculate the present value of the net cash flows as follows:

$$(101,885)/1.3 + 30,575/1.3^2 + 143,725/1.3^3 + 161,000/1.3^4 + 446,100/1.3^5 = PV(NCF)$$
$$(101,885)/1.3 + 30,575/1.69 + 143,725/2.19 + 161,000/2.85 + 446,100/3.71 = PV(NCF)$$
$$(78,373) + 18,091 + 65,959 + 56,372 + 120,145 = \textbf{\$182,194}$$

Without accounting for the sale price of the business, this calculation would suggest that the current value of the business is approximately $180,000.

Price/Earnings Valuation. Another method of estimating the value of a business is to use the industry **price/earnings (P/E) ratio.** This is a relatively straightforward system that utilizes the industry in which the start-up operates. The founder should locate the P/E ratio for public companies in the same industry via the many sources of this information (the Internet, *The Wall Street Journal,* the library, etc.). That average should be multiplied by the net cash flow for year 5 and discounted back as a potential sales price in year 6 of the venture. Therefore, use 1 + the discount rate raised to the 6th power. In our example that would be 1.3^6 (4.826).

This example illustrates how to calculate your P/E ratio valuation:

P/E for Industry	10 (obtained from industry sources)
Net Cash Flow for Year 5	$446,100
Discount Rate	30%
Sale/Residual Value	446,100 * 10 = $4,460,000
	$4,460,000/1.3^6$ = Discounted Sales Price
	4,460,000/4.826 = $924,005

[price/earnings (P/E) ratio]

A value derived from public companies that divides the current earnings per share into the price per share.

Utilizing these calculations, we would suggest that the value of the firm today would be the addition of the present value of the future cash flows plus the discounted sales price of the firm. For this example, that would be the following:

$$\text{Discounted Cash Flow} + \text{Discounted Sales Price} = \text{Current Value}$$
$$\$182{,}194 \quad\quad + \$924{,}005 \quad\quad = \$1{,}106{,}199$$

There are two other relatively popular methods for valuing a business: asset-based valuation and earnings valuation.

[asset valuation]

A method of business valuation that simply totals all of the hard assets of the organization and adds in a goodwill value.

Asset-Based Valuation. **Asset valuation** involves accounting for all of the hard assets of the organization: buildings (if owned), equipment (if owned), furniture, cash, and marketable securities held in the name of the company, as well as (in most cases) the value of any signed and executable contracts. Once all of the assets of the organization are tallied, the value of the business is typically calculated by taking that total number and adding an acquisition, or goodwill, value to it. This acquisition/goodwill value is determined by examining similar companies that have been acquired, or more often by simply looking at the percentage premium being offered in general on all new public acquisitions. If the business were performing poorly, there would be virtually no goodwill value. Asset valuation is typically the lowest business valuation number that you will calculate, unless you are an asset-intensive business.

Following is an illustration of asset valuation:

Building (Market Value minus Mortgage)	=	$108,755
Cardiovascular Equipment		
1) 4 Treadmills	=	$18,000
2) 3 Ellipticals	=	10,200
3) 2 Stair climbers	=	9,000
4) 1 Rower	=	1,850
5) 3 Upright bicycles	=	4,600
6) 2 Recumbent bicycles	=	2,600
7) 1 TreadClimber	=	3,500
8) Various fitness equipment	=	3,700
		$53,450
Strength Equipment		
1) 21 Selectorized machines	=	$110,500
2) 10 Olympic platforms	=	15,000
3) 6 Stretching stations	=	10,800
4) 20 Pairs of dumbbells	=	43,500
5) 4 Flat benches	=	11,500
6) 1 Cable crossover machine	=	10,700
		$163,000
Cash/Marketable Securities	=	$26,800
Total Asset Value	=	$243,250

Total Asset Value * Acquisition Premium = Value of the Business
$243,250 * 4.3 = $1,045,975

In this particular instance, a quick analysis of the industry revealed that an average asset acquisition premium for this particular industry was running at approximately 4.3 times assets. Therefore, the business as it currently stands (via this method) would be worth approximately $1,000,000. This method tends to depress the true future value of a growing business, so some investors/lenders will factor in a growth premium to "bulk up" the total valuation. "Art" intrudes once again.

Capitalization of Earnings Valuation. Very similar to asset valuation, **capitalization of earnings valuation** is performed by taking the earnings (net profit) of the organization; subtracting or adding any unusual items that the lender/investor feels are not customary, normal, or usual items; and dividing that figure by a capitalization rate. The capitalization rate is determined (rather loosely) by the nature of the business, including longevity, business risk, consistency of earning, quality of management, and general economic conditions.

This illustrates capitalization of earnings valuation using our example firm:

Net Profit (Earnings) of the Company = $32,900

Capitalization Rate = .2

$32,900/.2 = $164,500

Utilizing this system involves much more than simply accepting a final net profit figure. As was stated in Chapter 6, the net profit of a small business is an easily manipulated figure that is wholly dependent upon the needs/desires of the founders. Therefore, lenders/investors adjust this figure to account for the individual actions of the founders. Would-be buyers readjust the net profit of the company to account for these nuances of small business and then apply a capitalization rate that is a combination of the buyers' risk propensity and the current situation in the business acquisition marketplace.

Market Estimation Valuation. A valuation via **market estimation** is by far the simplest of the techniques. Fundamentally, it involves taking the earnings (or projected earnings) of the small business and multiplying that figure by the market premium of companies in its industry. A popular method is to take the EBITDA (earnings before interest, taxes, depreciation, and amortization), reworking the figure based upon an analysis of the cash flow statement, and multiplying the remaining figure by a market multiple. An examination of the NASDAQ or NYSE provides a group of companies in virtually every industry classification. Taking the group as a whole or attempting to find companies that are similar to your business yields an estimated market premium that can be used to calculate the value of the business. Once again, lenders/investors will attempt to adjust the earnings of the organization to reflect a more balanced picture.

The following illustrates market estimation valuation using our sample firm:

Net Profit (Earnings) of the Company = $32,900

Industry Multiple = 13

$32,900 * 13 = $427,700

Valuation Overview. As can be seen, there are wide variations in the potential valuations of this business, from several hundred thousand dollars to 1.5 million dollars. Every company has unique features that provide it some type of competitive advantage. In Chapter 5, we developed a strong argument for the development of a sustainable competitive advantage that enabled the new business to gain true economic rents relative to the competition. These "art" characteristics of an organization are important considerations in the valuation of a business and should be part of the equation when determining the true value of your business.

Preparing the Business for Sale

When the determination has been made to sell the business, the small business owner must begin a process that is somewhat akin to selling her home. She must make sure the business looks its best in order to obtain the highest premium possible.

One of the key issues for the survival of the business after the sale is the change in leadership that will occur. Recall the example of Leo and Rahul's small business, Campus Sneakers. Leo, one of the founders of the business, had all the key supply-chain contacts in a specialty merchandise area. If he exits the business, the new owner must ensure that she makes a smooth transition and picks up relationships with those suppliers. Indeed, in many small businesses, especially service-oriented fitness businesses, the owner's personality, expertise, and connections are among the business's key assets, which can pose problems for an owner who wishes to sell the business. There could be little value in the business beyond the owner himself. Potential buyers may not want to buy a company whose contacts and relationships walk out the door when the founder sells the business. How will the business run after the founder leaves? How does a business founder transfer his contacts and reputation to new owners? There should be a transition plan in place for this transfer in order for any purchase to be viable.

This difficulty is compounded by the reality that most small businesses run a very tight operation in which every individual has specific functions, and there is little slack available for cross-training. The company founder might handle the marketing/sales functions, execute all contract negotiations, and be the point person for each customer, while the company has another individual handle all of the operational details. Replacing the founder would require him to integrate others into his areas of responsibility. All of this requires a significant investment in the future without obvious payoffs in the present. Most small business owners find this quite difficult. These and other types of human resource issues unique to a small business were covered in Chapter 10.

The company also needs to examine its operations to ensure that the procedures of the business are codified and simplified for easy handover to a new owner. It is a reality in small business that the operational procedures develop as the business grows. The effort to put these procedures in writing will go a long way toward making for a more seamless transition.

Another operational issue is the accounting of the firm. A system in which the owner keeps the books herself is perfectly acceptable and perhaps even desirable when starting up and running the small business. However, a potential buyer wants assurances of the accuracy of the financial information. Our advice for ventures considering a sale is to contract with a CPA firm to have it do the following:

1. Audit last year's financial statements.

2. Put all of the statements into a standardized format.

3. Develop procedures for the accounting of all activities.

4. Provide an audit of this year's financial statements and render an accounting opinion.

This effort provides a level of legitimacy to the business and assures the buyer of the accuracy of the financial statements of the organization.

Maintaining an estimate of the value of a business as it grows and develops is the responsibility of the business owner. However, the small business owner should obtain a professional valuation of the business before attempting to actually sell the business. The valuation may turn out to be much less than the owner feels that the firm is worth, and therefore there would be little need to pursue the attempt to sell the firm.

The methods that will be used by the professional valuation experts will likely be very similar to those detailed earlier in this chapter. The businessperson would be well served to conduct her own estimate and then compare that to what the professional advises. The small business owner should actively challenge the analysis and discuss it with the valuation professional. The knowledge that she develops regarding the valuation of the business will help her as she negotiates the sale of the business.

Another important aspect in preparing the business for sale is the recording of all the informal practices of the organization. Policies and procedures develop in the life of a new venture. When to order certain supplies, what time to begin closing each day, the process of closing each day, the methods for dealing with customers, payment practices, human resource benefits and policies, etc., must all be codified. Anyone wishing to purchase a whole company will want all of these practices to be in writing for ease of analysis and for the understanding that this provides for the inner working of the business.

Small business owners also need to plan for the type of sale that will maximize their returns. The best method to actually exit the firm will very much depend upon the type of business. Businesses that have moved well beyond the founder's personality will be simpler to sell than those that are intimately tied to the active participation of the founder. While there are literally thousands of possible ways to construct a sales agreement, it might take some careful forethought and years of preparation work to make the business valuable to an outside investor.

One of the authors recently worked with an established accounting business where the two founders were both in their early 70s and looking to exit the business but really wanted a continuing revenue stream. One of the founders' sons was also an accountant who wanted to take over the company. Unfortunately, neither partner felt that he had the ability to carry on the work of the business in a managing role. Therefore the two partners began to ponder how they would sell the firm. In the accounting business, as in many other companies, relationships are critical to the success of the business. Rather than a quick sale that would lead to the founders' leaving the firm immediately, they envisioned an opportunity where they would leave gradually. They also had a specialized customer base that consisted primarily of hospitals. Hospital audits are usually completed on a schedule that differs from that of traditional corporate audits, which could allow a larger accounting business to rationalize its accounting work flow. At a conference during the prior year, a larger firm had expressed an interest in an association with the firm. The two partners approached the head of the larger firm and worked out a deal that included the following:

1. A small up-front cash payment.

2. A five-year management agreement with the two founding partners.

3. A gradual handover to executives from the larger firm.

4. An annuity payment to the founders for 10 years, based upon bookings.

The result was a smooth sale of the business in which both the acquiring and the acquired firms' owners were pleased with the results.

Actually Seeking to Sell the Business

Once the decision has been made to sell the business to an outside party, then there are a number of choices available to the owner. The most common would be to sell the business intact to a third party with the aid of a broker, lawyer, etc. A second very common option is to sell the business to a competitor or a larger business interested in your location, your position in the market, your product, etc. A third option is to divest portions of the business that will maximize the value of the business. It is not uncommon for the total value of the firm to be higher if the business is split into separate entities. A fourth option, which is rarely used but certainly the option most idealized by the business press, is an **initial public offering (IPO).** The reality is that only a very small fraction of start-up businesses that end up being very high growth actually seek to conduct an IPO. In fact, for the small business owner, an IPO may not be the most profitable means to exit the business. Given the rarity of this type of event, we only mention IPOs.

Not surprisingly, actually putting a business up for sale is a bit more art than it is science. The process of getting the word out that a business is for sale can occur through a variety of avenues:

1. Hiring a business broker who will market the business for a percentage of the sale price.

2. Contacting competitors or businesses that have expressed an interest in your business.

3. Letting your accountant and your lawyer know that you are interested in selling your business. Individuals in both of these professions

[initial public offering (IPO)]

The initial listing of a firm as a public entity in the public equities market.

In the process of preparing his firm to be sold, one entrepreneur sought to make the business look as attractive as possible to prospective buyers. He had the opportunity to make a large sale right before the business would be inspected. However, the entrepreneur was well aware that the buyer was in bankruptcy proceedings and that he might or might not actually be paid. On the other hand, the price being offered was quite high. He also had a large manufacturing equipment base that could be made to look better with some minor cleaning. The maintenance records were sketchy at best, so the value of the equipment might lie in its appearance.

QUESTIONS

1. What are the entrepreneur's legal requirements in presenting the business to a buyer?
2. Do the ethical requirements differ? Isn't it simply "buyer beware"?
3. How do you as a business owner make sure that the firm looks attractive to purchase but at the same time provide realistic information?

have numerous business contacts and may be aware of individuals seeking to buy a business.

4. Contacting your suppliers and perhaps (if appropriate) your significant clients to let them know about your interest in selling the business.

Negotiation Strategies

While it may be obvious to state this, negotiating a sale is the art of trying to reach an agreed price between a willing buyer and a willing seller. Thus, a sale is based on the needs/wants of both parties. For example, if the buyer has other similar businesses in the city and the acquisition of your firm will provide coverage in the final section of the city where they currently are not located or will provide the buyer an outlet in the fastest-growing part of the city, then perhaps a higher price will be offered. Similarly, if the buyer is only interested in the business if he can get a bargain, he might try to pay less. The small business owner should not believe there is some absolute price that the buyer will not go above or below. Negotiating to sell the business is a process that the small business owner must actively engage in if she is to be successful.

Negotiation is a completely separate field of study, and there are texts that explain the various nuances and techniques. Several important points to keep in mind regarding the negotiation of a sale include the following:

1. Use a professional mediator for anything but the most basic level of discussions. Your lawyer can play this role provided he has the experience. As we discussed in Chapter 7 (on the legal aspects of the small business), you will want all issues to be clear and specific. Do not make assumptions. Your lawyer can make sure that what you think the contract says is what actually ends up in writing.

2. Know the buyer. Ask for as much information about the company that is making an inquiry as they ask from you, or more. If they agree to pay you over a period of years but they default after a year, the result may be that you have a failed business returned to you, with only part of the former value of the firm having actually been paid to you.

3. Retain your own advisers. It is very tempting to save money at this point and allow the buyer to provide the services; however, you are well served by having your own independent advisers.

4. Recognize that there are a myriad of options for selling the business. You may sell the company as a whole or you can break up the business for maximum value. For example, you can sell the equipment to one company, the location to another, the name to yet another, etc. The goal upon exit is to maximize your own value.

5. Get cash for the firm. Frequently buyers may want to combine your firm with their firm to create a new business. As a result, they will offer you part cash and part stock in the new venture. If you take stock in the new venture, you are dependent upon their success and your liquidity is often reduced.

6. Look to the details. For example, frequently new owners want a non-compete agreement from you once you sell. This will prevent you from directly competing with the new owners for X number of years. However, if your buyout is not substantial, how will you make a living? Be sure you know all the details and ramifications of the negotiations.

EXERCISE 2

1. Describe, in your own words, discounted future net cash flow.

2. Identify how capitalization of earnings valuation involves much more than a lender or investor accepting a given final net profit figure.

3. Construct a table that lists, in the first column, all of the hard assets you expect to have in your start-up and, in the second column, the value of each hard asset. Research what the average asset acquisition premium currently is for your industry. At the bottom of your table, include a row that shows the total asset value multiplied by the asset acquisition premium. Refer to the illustration of asset valuation in this chapter for an example to follow.

4. Which method of valuation would you choose for your start-up company? Explain why you would choose this method.

LO 12.3 Turnaround

Another related issue that faces small businesses is turning around a firm that is in a decline. It is possible that you have developed a solid business that prospered for a number of years. However, after some time and for a variety of factors, both internal and external to the firm, the business starts a period of decline. The effort to reverse that decline is referred to as **turnaround.**

[turnaround]

The effort to reverse the decline of a business.

It is very difficult to successfully turn around a small business once it starts into a decline. The fact that the small business has limited slack* or excess resources results in the small business's having a very small leeway to respond to a decline. This is in contrast to large firms with massive resources, which the firms can rely on for years in the face of poor performance.

---

* "Slack" in this case is the time available per individual that is not dedicated to day-to-day work. It includes most time spent in meetings, as well as time spent reading the newspaper, talking in the hallways, getting coffee, taking smoking breaks, answering personal e-mail, making personal calls, etc.

The firm must first seek to retrench. This activity is analogous to medical situations in which doctors must quickly seek to stabilize the patient before they can do more substantive actions. If they do not stabilize the patient first, the patient might die and there will be no value in trying other activities. For a small business, such retrenchment efforts focus on the firm's gaining control of its cash flow quickly, regardless of the impact to the long-term effort. This can be accomplished by bringing in accounts receivable more quickly, delaying the payment of accounts payable, renegotiating with suppliers so that supplies do not have to be paid for in cash, eliminating staff, and working with employees to cut costs. Once the bleeding of cash flow has been slowed, the firm can move on to more substantive actions.

While it is obvious that a huge environmental shift in the economy can cause a serious decline in virtually all businesses, the root internal causes of decline are usually based in either operating or strategic problems. To place it in straightforward terms, operating problems relate to either not selling enough of the product or service, or not being sufficiently efficient in producing the product or providing the service. Strategic problems are most often related to poor positioning choices. Strategic problems often include diversifying into unrelated domains and not being able to successfully manage the business.

Unfortunately, businesspeople tend to focus on the easiest problems to solve first. These are most often simply symptoms that take significant time to correct and yield very little in overall business results. Therefore, we advise businesspeople to choose the one key reason why the business is suffering. Identify it as either operating or strategic and dedicate the resources of the firm to solving that issue immediately.

If it is an operating problem, then the solution should be an operating solution. These solutions include increasing marketing or marketing effectiveness to sell more products if the problem is that sales are down. Alternatively, if the problem is production inefficiency, then the focus should be oriented toward reengineering, simplifying, and measuring. Recall that we discussed quality management in Chapter 8. This is most often the focus of operating solutions and is certainly one of the best places to start the effort to turn around the business.

Strategic solutions rely on exiting those poor strategic choices that have been made over the years. Consider the example of a wonderfully successful fitness equipment company that sells and installs large equipment such as resistance training machines and cable crossovers. The company diversifies into selling smaller equipment such as yoga mats, stability balls, and other small training tools. The business had solid positive cash flow and was looking to find a positive outlet for all the cash it was generating. But within a year the owners realize that not only are they losing money on their new business, they are also installing equipment into fewer facilities because their corporate officers were distracted by trying to get the new business up and running. They quickly exit the new business and redouble their efforts on their core operations. If they succeed at all, their turnaround could take a year or two before they return to the point where they had been before the foray into the seemingly related business. Recall that we discussed in Chapter 2 the need for small business owners to evaluate the skills they personally possess before going into a business. In this situation, the small business owners may be quite good at installing large equipment, but that does not mean they will be successful with businesses that appear on the surface to be related. The key to success is not seeking to learn the small fitness equipment and tools business (one that involves a wide inventory with no need for installation), but instead, focusing exclusively on their large-scale equipment installation business. When bad strategic choices are made, exit them quickly.

The business media suggest that for a large, established business the CEO of the organization and its top management team be changed in a turnaround situation. The argument suggests that these individuals have paradigms, or ways they view the world, that created the decline in the first place. It is therefore supposed to be difficult for such individuals to see the problems and be creative in developing solutions to solve those problems. Small businesses do not have this option. We have found few small business founders who are looking to fire themselves. Therefore, it is necessary that the small business owner in a decline situation actively seek creative solutions. While not easy to do, this means that they must question themselves and others to a much greater extent than they have done before.[1] A well-developed board of advisers, which we have discussed previously, can be a critical aid in this regard. A board of advisers that will provide honest and insightful advice that challenges the small business owner can be very helpful in finding new ways to compete and new ways to overcome the problems faced by the firm.

LO 12.4 Closing the Business

It is unfortunate, but bankruptcy may need to be filed by the small business owner if the turnaround effort does not succeed quickly enough. The procedures for bankruptcy are arduous and have lasting impact upon the owners, and yet there are circumstances in which this is the only viable route. There are several types of bankruptcy that can be filed.[2]

Chapter 11 bankruptcy allows the firm to be reorganized. When you file a Chapter 11 bankruptcy, the firm receives immediate protection against all lawsuits and other efforts to collect from the firm. At this stage the firm has 90 days to propose a reorganization plan. This plan needs to show how the business will pay off its past-due debts and stay current with its other debts. The company's banker and other creditors will commonly refer to your account as a "workout." They will be willing to meet with you and seek a resolution regarding the money that is owed to them. Most creditors will be willing to take less than their full payment with the hope that the strength of the firm will return in the future and they will then be in a position to receive more of their debt repayment. If they do not work with the failing small business, they face the potential of the business simply liquidating and the lender only receiving a small percentage of the proceeds from the sale of the assets. This reduction in the amount of money that the creditors ultimately accept is referred to as a "haircut."

If the firm's debts are less than $2 million, there is a fast-track version of Chapter 11 that gives creditors far less control than in a larger organization Chapter 11 filing. The fast-track plan must show how back taxes will be brought current over a five-year period. It must also show how those creditors who have pledged collateral behind their debt will be brought current. The unsecured creditors are those who do not have collateral pledged behind their debt, and their debt is the lowest priority. It is generally not necessary to show how unsecured creditors will be paid in this type of Chapter 11 reorganization. During the reorganization process it is possible to terminate leases, contracts, and union agreements that are too burdensome. The bankruptcy judge has the ability to force creditors to accept a plan for reorganization if it appears equitable and fair but the creditors are still unwilling to accept it.

Unfortunately, there are instances in which the business must simply be closed. In this case, a Chapter 7 bankruptcy is invoked. In these cases, selling the business consists of selling the "assets" of the business. The assets of the organization include all of the physical assets (equipment, signs, furniture, fixtures, etc.) as well as any valuable intangibles, such as the corporate name or patents held. The process is similar to that of selling the business, but the owner can add a liquidator to the scenario, as well as the possibility of an auction, as a quick means to clear out of the business.

Two other types of bankruptcy are Chapter 12, used by family farming businesses, and Chapter 13, which is used by sole proprietorships. In each of these cases, the individual files for bankruptcy and includes the firm in her personal assets and liabilities. Chapter 13 is intended for small firms with limited debts and assets. The effect of a Chapter 13 filing is similar to that of a Chapter 11. However, because it is for a smaller firm, the process is even easier. For example, the time to approval is typically quicker and no creditor committee is required.

A final point to be made regarding the turnaround or closing of a business is the protection of personal assets. As was discussed in Chapter 7 (on legal matters), the form of business chosen has many impacts upon the operation of the business as well as the ending of the business. One of those is the extent to which the individuals involved in founding a firm are personally liable for its debts. Incorporating a business (using the Subchapter S, Subchapter C, or LLC forms that were discussed in Chapter 7) goes a long way toward providing limited liability to the small business owner. However, many entrepreneurs personally guarantee loans that are made to the company. Doing this negates the limited liability nature of a corporation and exposes

EXERCISE 4

1. Justify incorporating your fitness business based on the information in this chapter.

2. Suppose you know an entrepreneur who has decided to close, not sell, her successful limited liability corporation. The business does not have any debt, and she plans to sell the physical assets. Does she need to file for bankruptcy? Why or why not? If so, what type?

3. Suppose you know an entrepreneur who has decided to close his limited liability corporation. The business has more debt than the sale of all its assets could repay. Does he need to file for bankruptcy? Why or why not? If so, what type?

the entrepreneur to a major loss of personal assets. While no one starts a business with the intent of failure, the reality is that many do fail. Effectively preparing for that possibility at the beginning of the venture can be a great blessing in the event that the business does not develop as the founder(s) had hoped.

key terms

asset valuation 218	initial public offering (IPO) 222	perquisites 213
capitalization of earnings valuation 219	market estimation 219	price/earnings (P/E) ratio 217
		turnaround 224

review questions

1. Name five ways an accurate valuation at, or just prior to, the founding of the business helps a start-up company.
2. Define price/earnings ratio.
3. Report in your own words why a market estimation is the simplest technique of valuation.
4. Suppose you were going to do a market estimation of your start-up business. Determine the industry multiple you would use in your calculation.
5. Compose a list of tasks you would hire a CPA firm to do if you were going to sell your business. In addition, explain why it is a good business practice to hire a CPA firm to perform such tasks.
6. Create a schedule for personally estimating the value of your start-up business. When should you obtain a professional valuation?
7. Propose when it is a good time to start thinking about developing a turnaround plan.
8. Interpret whether or not taking your family on a company-paid vacation to Orlando is a justifiable perquisite.
9. Assess the differences between a Chapter 7 bankruptcy and a Chapter 11 bankruptcy.

individual exercises

1. Determine a valuation for your start-up business using any of the five methods you learned about in this chapter except for asset-based valuation, as you did that in an earlier exercise.
2. In order to make handing over your planned business to a new owner go smoothly, codify your planned business operational procedures as clearly and briefly as possible.

Consider such things as when you might order certain supplies, the process of opening and closing the facility each day, methods for dealing with customers, payment practices, and human resource benefits and policies. Keep this document brief for now; when you open your business, you can revise it as necessary, but you will at least have a good starting point.

group exercise

1. Select a partner to perform this role-play exercise. Determine who will be the business owner and who will be the potential buyer of the business.

2. If you are the business owner, go to step 3 (do not read step 4). If you are the buyer, go to step 4 (do not read step 3).

3. Here is your situation, which you may choose to disclose to your partner or not. You want to sell the business quickly, but you want to sell it for as much as possible, too. You have no other potential buyers. Share your valuation from the Individual Exercise with your potential buyer, and prepare to validate your valuation or negotiate a new one. Go to step 5.

4. Here is your situation, which you may choose to disclose to your partner or not. You have been wanting to start a business similar to this one but have not because you know that the market could not support another business of this kind. You were happy to find out that this business is for sale and want to buy it as soon as possible, as you have been planning and saving for a year. Review your partner's business valuation, and devise a reason for wanting to adjust the valuation. Go to step 5.

5. When you are both ready, negotiate a price on which you both agree to buy/sell. If you cannot reach an agreement, seek the advice of your "lawyers" and "accountants" (fellow students or the instructor).

6. Document the agreement, including the price, when payment(s) will be made, how payment will be made (cash, stock, combination), and whether you will also need a noncompete agreement.

7. If there is time, switch roles and perform this exercise again.

Franchising and Purchasing an Existing Business

After studying this chapter, you will be able to:

13.1 Describe the elements of franchising

13.2 Explain the process for buying a franchise

13.3 Discuss the process for buying an existing business

CASE STUDY

Talia had built a 15-year career as a business analyst for a major investment bank. When her bank suffered major setbacks during the global economic crisis in 2009, Talia was laid off along with many other colleagues at her bank. Although Talia had enjoyed many aspects of her work, the stress had been getting to her for several years. When she lost her job, she decided she needed a fresh start in her career.

Talia's main passion outside of her job was working out. She had run cross-country through high school and college, and was a lifelong exercise fanatic. She had even completed several triathlons and marathons. She was a member of a national-chain health club, and one day while she was working out, overheard the manager of the club mention to an employee that he was not just the manager but also the franchise owner. For the rest of that day, this conversation snippet stuck with Talia. She had never realized her health club was a franchise operation, and as she thought further, she realized that running a health club would be a dream career for her. She could combine her experience in business with her passion for fitness.

Over the next several weeks, Talia did some research about health club companies. She discovered that one of her health club chain's competitors was seeking franchisees. After some digging, she found that the franchisee's minimum investment would be $100,000 plus a franchise fee of $25,000. Talia had more than this amount to invest. It was at this moment that Talia picked up the phone and called the company's home office. It was the first phone call of her new career.

This book has focused principally on the process of starting a new small business from scratch. Two other common options exist for individuals interested in starting their own businesses. The first is purchasing a franchise. The other is purchasing an existing business. Both of these activities have opportunities and drawbacks in comparison to starting a new business, and we will examine these, beginning with the opportunities and drawbacks with franchising.

LO 13.1 Basics of Franchising

The purchase of a well-honed, thoughtfully positioned franchise can dramatically decrease the downside risk inherent in the process of starting a business. Franchising can be viewed as the new business entrepreneur's creation of a business from a well-established formula. Thus, the franchise is essentially a prepackaged business, where there are policies, procedures, and buying patterns in place prior to beginning operations.

The **franchisor** is the firm that originates the idea for the business and develops the operational methods. The entrepreneur is the franchisee. The **franchisee** pays a fee to obtain a franchise from the franchisor. This fee entitles the franchisee to open a branch of the business in a given area, use the franchisor's name, and operate a business within the guidelines of the agreement. The franchisee also receives operational advice on how to run the business and typically some level of marketing support to promote the business. Responsibility for the business location, establishment of the business, and build-out is the franchisee's and must usually be fulfilled in accordance with the specifications of the franchisor.

The franchisor, in turn, establishes minimum standards regarding the operation of the business. For example, the **franchise agreement** is the basic contract generated by the franchisor for all franchisees, and it usually contains clauses requiring the purchase of supplies, the displaying of marketing material, and the payment of fees that are based upon the sales of the branch operation. The requirements, however, may be more extensive. For example, McDonald's requires that its franchisees clean not only their own property but also the block around their franchise unit.

The International Franchise Association estimates that in the year 2005, franchises made up almost 1 million businesses in the United States, providing almost 11 million jobs. The range of franchises you use every day would likely surprise you. For example, most small one-on-one gyms such as Anytime Fitness, Snap Fitness, and Fitness Together are simply locally owned franchise operations.

In part, the reason franchising is so widespread is that the franchisor can offer a standard, well-known product that is produced by a consistent, well-tested process. The success of the franchise is furthered by its group-purchasing power for supplies and its regional and perhaps national brand-building advertising. The franchisee further benefits because the franchisor will typically continue research and development on its products and processes—efforts that a small, single business simply could not afford to pursue. This all occurs with the entrepreneur spending less of her resources than if she had had to found such a business by herself. The franchisor benefits by enabling a rapid expansion while minimizing the funds invested in that expansion.[1] The success of franchising is dependent upon the hard work of the franchisee and the value added by the franchisor.[2]

In a franchise operation, businesspeople work for themselves, not for some large corporation, and as a result, all the decisions that the small

[franchisor]

The firm that originates the idea for the business and develops the operational methods, then sells them to franchisees.

[franchisee]

The entrepreneur who buys the franchise from the franchisor.

[franchise agreement]

The basic contract generated by the franchisor for all franchisees; it usually contains clauses requiring the purchase of supplies, the displaying of marketing material, and the payment of fees that are based upon the sales of the branch operation.

business owner makes are to maximize the value of her own business. The success of franchising is also a result of the fact that the franchisee will act in ways to maximize the profit of the business, while a corporate employee might not do so.[3]

The franchisor makes money in a variety of ways, including

- selling the franchise to the franchisee;
- selling supplies to the franchisee;
- collecting a percentage of sales; and
- in some cases, providing company-specific training courses/materials.

For example, a very successful franchisor like Sonic, which sells hamburgers and related items using a drive-in format in more than 30 states, charges a fee to obtain a franchise, but the significant income comes from royalties and being able to sell the franchisee items that range from Sonic-labeled hamburger wrappers to the peppermints that come with the food. The franchisor typically argues that it can obtain the supplies cheaper through its bulk buying; plus, it wants to ensure that the output continues to be a consistently high-quality, name-enhancing experience, as it is sold under the Sonic brand. A franchisee that has inconsistent quality, service, etc., not only hurts her own business, but impacts the brand image of all franchisees.

The continuing revenue stream to the franchisor from royalties and selling of inputs to the franchisee is a more important revenue source than the initial fees for selling the franchise. Thus, the franchisor and the franchisee are successful by helping each other. The franchisor makes money when the franchisee stays in business, needs lots of inputs, and pays continuing royalties. On the other hand, the franchisee is successful if the franchisor puts a program in place for all of the franchisees to be successful, such as high-quality marketing, good site selection, high-quality products, and continuous research into both product/process development and brand management.

EXERCISE 1

1. Define franchise.
2. Identify at least three items contained in a franchise agreement between a franchisor and franchisee.
3. List at least three fitness- or wellness-related franchises in your geographical area.

LO 13.2 Buying a Franchise

As we have emphasized throughout this text, the entrepreneur who is best prepared will be the most likely to succeed, whether his focus is starting a business from scratch, buying a franchise, or purchasing an existing business. Thus, many of the issues in choosing a franchise are similar to the issues already examined in this text.

General Franchise Questions

Some issues can be viewed as broad, generic issues rather than as issues specific to that particular franchisor. These general issues include the following:

1. The potential franchisee should carefully evaluate his individual interests and skills to determine a potential fit with running a franchise and to identify an industry or multiple industries in which he wishes to attempt to purchase a franchise.

2. When determining the type of franchise to purchase, each potential franchisee should examine the demographics, the potential competitors in that demographic, and his position relative to other new franchisees that are entering the industry.

3. The potential franchisee should carefully examine the competitive strength of various franchises in the industry. For instance, what are their various sustainable competitive advantages in the market?

4. The individual looking to buy a franchise should identify a franchisor that is the best potential match for him in terms of support, history, expansion plans, etc.

5. The person considering a franchise should examine that franchisor as though the potential franchisee were buying the whole business. This includes contacting other franchisees to discuss their experience as well as comparing the franchisor to other franchise opportunities.

Specific Franchise Questions

Each franchisor will have a different package it will try to sell to a franchisee. The franchisee needs to examine the exact package that is offered and

ethical *challenge*

You are a fitness professional with more than 10 years of experience and in recent months you have come to the conclusion that you want to become a business owner, and purchasing a franchise could be an expedient path toward your goal. You found an opportunity to purchase a franchise of a national company. Over the past few weeks you have been reviewing the franchisor's standard franchise agreement. You have met with several current franchisees and talked with the franchisor on more than a few occasions. You have had the opportunity to see them in operation and to look at the books.

After all this effort, you have concluded that you don't need the franchisor to run a business like this one. You've decided to open up your own independent fitness facility and plan to run it in virtually the same way as is done by the franchisees. You have made a significant effort to make some of the operations different, but you also like most of what you saw. What you didn't like was the $44,000 in upfront fees, the $28,000 in training costs, and the fact that you would have to pay the franchisor 8 percent of sales. Do you have any ethical obligations to the original franchisor? No one is required to buy a franchise; therefore, isn't the franchisor opening their books simply their means of trying to make a sale?

balance the cost and the benefits offered. The issues to consider in examining which franchise to purchase include

- what a franchise includes;
- franchisor and franchisee obligations, as stipulated in the United Franchise Offering Circular (UFOC); and
- steps in the process of obtaining a franchise.

Each of the issues to consider in purchasing a specific franchise will be examined in turn.

What Does a Franchise Include? There is an extraordinary range of support that can be provided by a franchisor to the franchisee. This ranges from simply buying into a name and general plan for operation to what almost amounts to a full partner living your business with you. There is no universal standard regarding what is provided by a franchisor; instead, as in any market system, different franchisors offer distinct sets of supports at varying prices. The entrepreneur must choose which package of benefits he wishes to pursue, and at what price. The discussion below lists some of the issues that a new businessperson buying a franchise should consider to ensure the franchise has the right mix of supports and costs for him.

Both the franchisor and the franchisee have an alignment of interest in their mutual desire to produce a quality product and successfully expand the business. However, they can have honest disagreements about what is best for the organization. Franchisors make decisions based upon what is best for the total business; franchisees want to have the ability to cater to their local markets. Thus, can you as a local franchisee of a sandwich shop in Texas add hot peppers to the standard sandwich—or, if you are

in Wisconsin, can you add sauerkraut to the same sandwich? The franchisor may want uniformity and thus consistency, but the franchisee will want the flexibility to meet local needs. The individual buying a franchise needs to determine whether the franchise will have the level of flexibility she feels is necessary for success.

When you purchase a franchise, you typically are buying some consistent items, although the specifics of what you are buying in each individual case should be examined. These include the following:

1. The right to an established name, branded products, and service.

2. The right to operate under that name for a period of time. The time period is usually some standard such as 5, 10, or 20 years.

3. The right to a single store or the right to have multiple units.[4]

4. The right to a commitment from the franchisor to limit the number of franchises within a specific radius of the new franchise. This is one of the most important issues involved in the purchase. One of the key competitive advantages is having the name-brand operation without having to compete against fellow franchisees. In the best situations, franchisees work with each other in local geographic areas.

The franchisor typically provides both the operational systems and the monitoring techniques to run the business in a manner that matches the rest of the organization. The specificity of this operational information varies widely from franchisor to franchisor. You will recall from Chapter 8 that an in-depth understanding of operations is necessary to be successful in a small business. Although most of the operational management systems will have been designed by the experience of the franchisor, the franchisee must intimately understand both why and how these systems work. To illustrate, if you purchase a franchise for a shop that makes fitness clothing, the franchisor will have established procedures for the design of the internal layout of the shop, plus the look and feel of the physical storefront. It will have established processes for virtually every type of service that could be requested by a customer. If you do not have at least a minimal understanding of clothing shops, it will be difficult to judge the operating system the franchisor is providing. Buying a franchise does not eliminate the need for the small business owner to have a deep understanding of the business. If you do not have that understanding, you cannot judge the quality of the operational support provided by the franchisor.

True understanding of those processes comes from experience. In many cases, potential franchisees are required to work in an established operation of the business for some period of time prior to being allowed to purchase a franchise. This time period allows the potential franchisee the opportunity to learn the business from the ground up, learning the procedures not from a manual, but from experience with an established operation. This fact is particularly important because some franchisors have very specific limits on how many changes you can make to their operational systems. The franchisor wants a franchisee in Oklahoma City, Oklahoma, and another in Utica, New York, to operate in essentially the same manner in order to develop and preserve the brand. A careful examination of the amount of regional/local customization available can be an important part of the business acquisition process.

There are a number of specific support areas that the potential franchisee should use to evaluate the franchisor's operations.

1. Accounting Support. As part of the operational aspects of the business, the franchisor will often provide an accounting system that is customized to the dual needs of the franchisor and the franchisee.

2. Marketing Support. This is a broad area that encompasses such things as brochures, signs, logos, television advertisements, newspaper advertisements, sales techniques, and internal business design. The quality, quantity, and overall value of each of these items can vary widely from franchisor to franchisor. There are also some significant downside risks to this apparent positive. First of all, advertising support comes at a price. Most franchisors charge each franchisee a fee that becomes part of a larger common advertising budget. The franchisor develops the advertising and buys the spots/spaces in the newspapers. Doing this centrally allows for volume discounts as well as expertise in ad development/placement. Second, if you are the only franchisee in Colorado while most of the other franchisees are in Minnesota, Iowa, and Wisconsin, you are likely to see a smaller relative share of the advertising budget being targeted to your area. What are the franchisor's development plans for Colorado?

3. Training. Franchisors offer a variety of training opportunities for the new franchisee and his employees. These include providing classroom training, providing training at other locations, having an experienced

manager work at your location for a period of time, or, as we have mentioned, working at a current establishment. The more that is offered as part of the franchise fee, the better it is for the franchisee. In addition, the availability of continued training opportunities should be an important criterion to help ensure franchisee success.

4. Real Estate Services. Some franchisors operate a large and profitable real estate brokering service. Others offer a more basic site selection service, or nothing at all. The assistance in real estate selection, acquisition, building construction, etc., can be invaluable if done professionally.

5. Other Services. Human resources support to develop performance management programs, quality control methods, forecasting, and purchasing of equipment are all very valuable services that act as guidelines rather than mandates in deciding on a franchise.

As this discussion indicates, there is a wide range of potential activities that the franchisor may provide to the franchisee. The range of those activities, the quality of those activities, and the cost should be judged by the small business entrepreneur.

Government Requirements for the Franchisor/Franchisee Relationship. The principal governing mechanism of the franchisor/franchisee relationship is the **Uniform Franchise Offering Circular (UFOC).** As with many business domains, at one time there were excessive abuses in the industry. Individuals thinking they were buying a franchise that gave them an opportunity for success found that they had paid for what amounted to little more than a name, which often had a terrible reputation. The result was the passage of the UFOC, which specifies the information that must be provided to the franchisee prior to his investment.

[Uniform Franchise Offering Circular (UFOC)]

The principal governing mechanism of the franchisor/ franchisee.

This document must be provided to the franchisee early in the process of her buying a franchise. In effect, the UFOC is a franchisor-disclosure document with 23 specified items:

1. **The Franchisor, Its Predecessors, and Affiliates.** Any predecessors to the current business and other businesses affiliated with the business must be disclosed.

2. **Business Experience.** The background of the principals must be detailed. Issues such as how long they have been in the business and their experience in the industry must also be detailed. You want to make sure those running the franchisor have experience in the industry.

3. **Litigation.** Any pending litigation must be noted. Such litigation can destroy the value of your franchise if your franchisor loses the case.

4. **Bankruptcy.** Any prior or current filings by firm or key management must be disclosed.

5. **Initial Franchise Fee.** Under items 5 and 6, the franchisor must disclose all fees that are charged.

6. **Other Fees.** The "other fees" category is an area that entrepreneurs should understand clearly. The cost of the initial purchase of the franchise may appear low, but if there are extensive fees that the franchisor can charge the franchisee for services that are offered, the value of the franchise may be very different than initially thought. The supports provided may appear to be desirable; however, there may be separate costs for those supports that are independent of the initiation fee to buy the franchise.

7. **Initial Investment.** This is more than the initial fee paid by the franchisee; it includes a reasonable estimate of the total investment needed to begin operations.

8. **Restrictions on Sources of Products and Services.** This critical portion of the document details franchisor sourcing. The potential franchisee needs to be clear about what must be purchased directly from the franchisor and what may be sourced independently.

9. **Franchisee's Obligations.** Specific obligations must be listed. For example, the franchisor may require that the product be produced by certain equipment and that equipment be replaced on a certain time schedule. These restrictions can extend into domains that the small business owner may not initially consider to be the purview of the franchisor. Thus, once again, questions such as what flexibility the entrepreneur will have in operating the franchise need to be examined. For example, upon opening, you as the franchisee may be happy with some balloons, having the local mayor cut a ribbon, and a story that goes into the local paper. But the franchisor may have an extensive program that it requires of all new franchise openings. The franchisee may be required to fund these activities through various fees, whether or not he agrees with the program.

10. **Financing.** Many franchisors make significant financing available to potential franchisees. The financing available and terms are outlined in this section of the document.

11. **Franchisor's Obligations.** In this section, all of the ancillary services are detailed. As outlined above, this may include site selection, training, placing experienced managers on-site for a period of time, etc.

12. **Territory.** This section details the amount of exclusivity your franchise will have relative to other operations of the franchisor.

13. **Trademarks.** Items 13 and 14 detail the exact status of all trademarks, patents, copyrights, and trade secrets that are part of the business.

14. **Patents, Copyrights, and Proprietary Information.**

15. **Obligation to Participate in the Actual Operation of the Franchise Business.** The franchisee can be required to take an active role in the daily management of the business, as opposed to simply hiring managers.

16. **Restrictions on What the Franchisee May Sell.** This section lists limits placed on the franchisee by the franchisor. The franchisor may put extensive restrictions on the franchisee as to what she can do with the product and its production.

17. **Renewal, Termination, Transfer, and Dispute Resolution.** The exact method of dispute resolution is detailed, along with which party will have the financial responsibility.

18. **Public Figures.** This details any public figures or celebrities involved in the business and what they are paid.

19. **Earnings Claims.** This section contains a description along with some specific detail regarding the financial performance of typical franchisees.

20. **List of Outlets.**

21. **Financial Statements.**

22. **Contracts.** This section contains sample contracts you will be asked to sign later.

23. **Receipt.** You will be asked to sign a page to acknowledge that you received this information.

The small business owner is well served to study the document carefully to understand all of the details of the business arrangement. It is a long document, and should be read through several times and reviewed with an attorney prior to agreeing to the stipulations. A clear understanding of the document now will prevent significant problems in the future.

Franchise Process. The founding of a franchise is quite similar in form and method to creating a new business from scratch. A significant upfront cash payment is necessary and the ability to leave the venture if the entrepreneur does not enjoy the business is severely limited. Similarly, an assessment of the skills of the individual should be a mandatory beginning of any new business investigation. If the individual has no skills in styling hair and he buys a hairstyling franchise, the odds of success are not particularly good, regardless of what supports are present in the franchise.

Depending upon the franchisor for market analysis is a poor move under any circumstances. The market must also be thoroughly and independently understood by the potential franchisee. As we pointed out earlier, sometimes there is a very good reason that no similar businesses are in a particular area. We knew an individual who was searching out a franchise to buy. She hit upon the idea of buying a franchise that supplies temporary employees to local businesses. Unfortunately, all of the local businesses (and there were only a few) used only full-time employees. The market for temporary workers was severely constrained. We would also caution against purchasing a franchise that is part of a fad. Products such as those you see advertised on TV—such as the Ab Roller, the Shake Weight, and Electric Muscle Stimulation—were a lot of fun for a while, but owning an Ab Roller or Shake Weight franchise was a disaster for the franchisees. Those fads died as quickly as they were born, but the franchise agreements lasted anywhere from 5 to 20 years. It does little good to invest money in a franchise that will see demand for the product disappear quickly. In the case of a fad, we have very simple advice. Get in, make as much money as you can as an independent, and GET OUT!

The International Franchise Association is a good source for quickly locating potential franchisor firms; its website can be found at www.franchise.org. Each of the franchisor firms typically has a website where you can request information from that firm. They will gladly send you a packet of information that details the firm's operations, its business, and the costs of the franchise. At this stage, there will be a very short application form that the entrepreneur must fill out. With this information the franchisor will call the entrepreneur and have a phone interview to ensure that the individual is at least a potential match for the firm. The small business owner needs to note that it is a mutual selection process. The franchisee can select among one of the 10,000 or more franchise opportunities. The franchisor also gets to decide to whom it will sell a franchise. Given the geographic restrictions imposed by many franchisors and encouraged by the franchisees, it is in the best interest of the franchisor to pursue only the most motivated, best capitalized, and most skilled individuals. A poorly performing or disruptive franchisee detracts from the overall operation as well as taking time and effort of the franchisor away from the business of growing the brand. Because of this, it is simply easier to make sure that there is a match between the two parties from the beginning.

Once the potential franchisee has been vetted (a credit and personal background check has been completed), the entrepreneur will be sent the complete UFOC and asked to fill out a more complete application. A series of meetings ensues between the franchisor and other franchisees in the area, between the franchisor and the potential franchisee, and between the potential franchisee and the other franchisees in the area. The ability to meet other franchisees is critical in the evaluation process. While the UFOC does not require that specific information on profitability of individual franchises be provided, it is quite simple to back into such information by calculating the total profits of the group and then dividing by the total number of franchises. Unfortunately, there may be a bimodal distribution, with some great performers and some that perform poorly. The ability to interact with franchisees in your geographic area, with similar profiles to what you can expect from your operation, helps provide great insights into the reality of the franchise life. You will gain tremendous insights from these individuals regarding their relationship with the franchisor. The relationship between franchisor and franchisee is somewhat like a marriage; they are both dependent on each other for success. If the relationship is an unhappy one, there can be nothing quite as miserable. Existing franchisees can also provide you insight regarding the value of the franchisor's staff. Many of the services that the franchisor provides are dependent upon the quality of the people providing the service. Marketing advice is a qualitative area that can be either very helpful or of limited value, depending on who is developing and delivering the research.

Assuming that both parties are pleased with their findings, negotiating the deal is the next step. While the franchise fee tends to be set in stone, most franchisors are willing to negotiate on a wide range of items. For example, if there are few franchises in an area, the franchisor may be willing to finance a greater portion of the start-up expenses, provide additional marketing support, or even pick up some of the initial expenses of a franchise in order to get a foothold in a new geographic area. Similarly, if you have had prior success in business and the franchisor is new, it might negotiate a completely different deal with you in order to get started with a self-sufficient operator. Also, very high-profile individuals frequently can negotiate unique deals. For example, in a region of the country where there is a professional athletic team, high-profile players on that team often obtain preferential opportunities. This allows the franchisor to publicize that that person is one of its franchisees. The small business owner should explore what aspects of the contract are negotiable by making a list of wants and desires.

Some areas that such negotiations should explore include upfront capital requirements, financing arrangements, and continuing fees. Is it possible to purchase other franchises or build out the existing franchise? The time frame of the franchise (5, 10, 20 years) may be negotiable, as well as a first right to renew your franchise. An important consideration is not only the territory of the initial franchise, but also first rights on adjacent or fast-growing territories. Some franchisors will have performance quotas to maintain the franchise; if yours does, ask what those quotas are and what percentage of franchisees meet the quota. If you fail at those quotas, or some other aspects of the franchise, can you negotiate the remedies to solve that problem? Does the franchisor require a personal guarantee? The personal guarantee is something many successful entrepreneurs seek to avoid, since it places their personal assets at risk. Are there operational constraints that you feel would put you at a disadvantage relative to your competition that you wish to have the franchisor waive? The small business owner is well served to take the time to work with a lawyer and develop a solid contract that meets the needs of the franchisor and still gives the franchisee the best opportunity for success.

EXERCISE 2

1. Using the general franchise questions at the beginning of this section, scrutinize whether or not you would be interested in purchasing a franchise. Explain why or why not.

2. Make a table showing the five main support areas that a potential franchisee should use to evaluate a franchisor's operations, and, using short, bullet-point statements, describe each area and points you must consider as a franchisee.

Support Area	Description/Points to Consider

3. Using GoodSearch or Google, search for "sample UFOC document" on the Internet. When you locate a good, free sample, examine the document, and report how many of the 23 items you learned about in this section are specified.

LO 13.3 Buying an Existing Business

We covered the process of obtaining a franchise first because this process is well defined and well regulated, and there is a wealth of information available to anyone who would like assistance. Another very popular means of going into business for oneself is the purchase of an existing business.

How to Buy

Similar to a franchise, an existing business has the benefit of having an established set of processes; although unlike a franchise, a continuing business has an established cash flow that

you are purchasing. As such, the operation has a higher likelihood of success when compared to starting a business from scratch, and that does not mean that buying a business does not take as much planning and thought as starting a business from scratch. There are still significant risks involved in buying a business.[5]

A business you may buy is an ongoing entity, so there is a greater premium attached to the business than if you started it from scratch. The primary exception to this is if you buy a troubled business at a discount. You will need to quickly restructure that business. As we saw in Chapter 12, turnaround is a special topic and requires very specific skills for you to be able to act quickly to reverse that decline.[6] Our typical advice to small business owners is to not attempt such activities unless they have specific skills and a plan to turn around a business that is in significant decline.

For the purchase of a reasonably stable or healthy firm, all of the same processes that have been discussed in this text should be the foundation of your effort. Therefore, you first need to understand your own skills and abilities and the nature of the current market. Assuming that you have completed all of the preliminary analysis effort, there are still several unique aspects to purchasing an existing business. These include (1) locating a business to purchase; (2) developing a plan for the business; (3) negotiating a deal to acquire exactly what you want from the operation; and (4) organizing the process of change within the organization.

Locating a Business to Purchase. Locating a business for sale is a job that takes lots of patience and effort. There are **business brokers** in virtually every city in the United States that specialize in selling businesses. Additionally, businesses are listed for sale in newspapers, in local magazines, and on websites. All of these are fine places to start your search process; however, we recommend several other means for finding a business that meets your needs:

1. Law and accounting firms may have clients who have expressed their desire to sell their business. Contacting local firms and asking about businesses they might know that are for sale usually yields some interesting possibilities.

2. Our personal favorite is to identify a particular business that you believe is not maximizing its opportunity, one to which you believe you could bring unique skills/advantages that could propel the business. We recommend that you put together a short letter to the owner indicating your interest in the business and follow that up with a request to take the owner to lunch to discuss the opportunity. Most (if not all) owners of an ongoing business are willing to listen to an offer to buy their business.

3. The trade association for an industry usually maintains a listing of all member companies and is a wealth of information regarding the status of various organizations within the industry. The two main trade associations in the fitness industry are the International Health, Racquet & Sportsclub Association (IHRSA; www.ihrsa.org) and the IDEA Health and Fitness Association (www.ideafit.com).

4. The local Small Business Administration Office and/or the Small Business Development Center in your area has significant contact

[business brokers]
Businesses that specialize in selling businesses.

with businesspeople and both are geared toward supporting and encouraging the growth of small business.

5. Another favorite of ours is to look at the bankruptcy filings in your local community. Many companies file for bankruptcy due to lack of financial resources or poor management practices. Listings of such bankruptcy filings can easily be found through a web search. The opportunity to contact these individuals and buy the operation before the bankruptcy procedure is completed can be the source of a business at a bargain price. However, remember that this effort would be a turnaround project that would require unique skills and abilities.

Plan of Operation. Once you have located a business for sale, but prior to beginning the negotiations to purchase the business, you as the potential small business owner should develop a plan of operation for the business.

The cost of the business should include any premium for its current performance. What will you do differently from what is currently being done? If you are paying a premium for a business but have no plans to change the business operations, then how do you hope to achieve success?

Will you bring a new mission to the business? Will you position the firm or its product differently? Do you have some unique talent, etc., that will make the business that you are considering buying a success, or make it more successful? An understanding of what you have to offer and what the current business is missing will provide the basis for your negotiations. What is important to the current owner may or may not be important to the potential owner, given the new direction for the company. Adding value to a business is a critical step in the process of deciding to purchase a business. We would recommend that the entrepreneur take the same approach as was outlined in Chapter 5 to develop a new mission for the organization. What are the resource-based advantages of the new organization under the new leadership?

Having developed a new plan for the business, the potential small business owner is prepared to negotiate the deal. In Chapter 12 we outlined procedures that a seller should use to put his business in the best position for sale, as well as negotiation strategies. We would recommend that a potential buyer do the same and demand this from any seller.

Finally, there is the complex issue of organizing the process of change from the former business to the new business. While there are a number of ways in which this can be accomplished, the tasks are relatively similar. We must point out that there is a lot of nuance and "art" in the handling of these processes. Once negotiations are complete and all contracts are signed, there will be a transition period that should be spelled out in the contract for sale. During that transition time period, there are a number of tasks that should be completed. The new owner should do the following:

1. Meet and discuss the transition with every member of the current staff. If there is a layoff plan, then that should be enacted immediately.

2. Spend significant time being visible in the new operation, talking with employees, making suggestions, and doing some of the more menial work.

3. Make all significant changes in one day so as to alleviate any lingering concerns by the employees.

4. Implement new metrics and standards as soon as possible.

5. Ask the former owner(s) not to be at the business for several weeks while the transition is taking place. Loyalties and work processes get confused when the former owner is around every day.

6. If appropriate for the type of business that has been purchased, send out a letter/e-mail to every customer/supplier informing each one of the ownership change. Ideally this letter is signed by both the former owner and the new owner.

If you want to run your own business and are into fitness, then running a fitness franchise might be your best option. A fitness franchise can be a valuable investment and can be personally and professionally fulfilling. It doesn't come without a lot of hard work. Don't focus solely on the quality of the product. Question current franchisees about their business. Are they making a profit? Have they added new customers and new product lines every year? How helpful has the franchisor been? Check to see if litigation is pending against the franchisor. Seek out franchises that offer protected territories—exclusive rights to operate within a geographic area. If territories are not protected, talk to existing franchisees about the impact on their business when another unit opens nearby. Once you have done your initial research and answered these questions, you will be ready to open the doors of your franchise.

* * *

If you read this book then you most likely want to be your own boss. Many individuals leap into entrepreneurship out of frustration with their jobs, or they seize an opportunity to start anew or take over an existing business. No matter what path leads you to this realm, you must make decisions through careful, reasonable examination and consideration of all aspects of your small business. This is a key to your success.

The success of an entrepreneur comes from hard work, thoughtful planning, skilled decision making, and a bit of luck. Small businesses come and go every day, and understanding the components of success and failure is essential to becoming a flourishing and thriving entrepreneur.

EXERCISE 3

1. Suppose you heard from other members at the club where you work out that the owner has been thinking of closing or selling. You know that membership has been steadily declining over the last few months, but you do not know the details of the club's finances. You do have ideas about how to increase membership and perhaps turn the business around if necessary. Propose how you might take steps toward becoming the new owner of the club.

2. Now imagine that you discover during your meeting with the owner that the club owes a large amount of debt. Do you think you have the skills and experience to turn the business around? What would make the buying of another owner's business most attractive to you?

3. In this section you learned six tasks to do as the new owner of an existing business. The tasks do not necessarily have to be done in the order given. Prioritize the steps according to what you think is the most important. Include any other tasks that you think are also important.

key terms

review questions

1. Distinguish a franchisor from a franchisee.
2. Name four ways that a franchisor may make money.
3. List four ways that a franchisee may be successful through a franchisor's program.
4. Why is it a poor idea to purchase a franchise around a fad product or service?
5. Study the franchise process given toward the end of this section. Detect and record the main steps of the process.
6. Create a questionnaire showing the questions you would want to consider during a negotiation with a franchisor.
7. As the new owner of an existing fitness business, you have decided to focus on group classes and remove personal training from your service offerings. Formulate a plan of action for laying off all of your contracted personal trainers.
8. Verify if there is a fitness-related business for sale in your area. What step(s) did you take to get the information?
9. Interpret how developing business plans for an existing business is similar to yet different from developing plans for a new business.

individual exercises

1. Research fitness-related franchises that might do well in your area and that do not already exist in your market.
2. Explain why you think the franchise would do well or why it would not be successful in your market.
3. After appraising how the franchise might fit into the market, consider whether or not you would like to open this franchise in your market. Justify your decision with details from your research.

group exercises

1. Select a partner to perform this role-play exercise. Determine who will be the franchisor and who will be the franchisee. The franchise is a small exercise studio like Curves.
2. If you are the franchisor, develop some of the general terms of your typical franchise agreement.
3. If you are the franchisee, develop a list of negotiation points you want to cover in your franchise agreement.
4. Discuss and negotiate the various points with your partner.

NOTE: This exercise is not so much about your negotiation skills as it is about debating the many points of consideration you learned about in this chapter. Therefore, be sure to discuss some areas of support, such as marketing and training, and some of the items that appear in a UFOC document, such as renewal/termination/transfer/dispute resolution. The more points you can cover in the time allotted, the better you will learn the material. However, in an actual negotiation, you want to ensure you devote enough time and thought to every point.

Sample Forms for a Fitness Business

1. Waiver, Release, and Assumption of Risk Form

2. Waiver and Assumption of Risk (Home Workouts)

3. Letter of Agreement

4. Health History Questionnaire

5. Medical Clearance and Physician's Consent to Participate in Fitness Assessment and Exercise Program

6. Injury Report

7. Goal Inventory

8. Lifestyle Questionnaire

9. Staff Performance Evaluation Form

1. Waiver, Release, and Assumption of Risk Form

Waiver, Release, and Assumption of Risk Form

This form is an important legal document. It explains the risks you are assuming by beginning an exercise program. It is critical that you read and understand it completely. After you have done so, please print your name legibly and sign in the spaces provided at the bottom.

Waiver, Informed Consent, and Covenant Not to Sue

I, _____, have volunteered to participate in a program of physical exercise under the direction of (Your business's name), which will include, but may not be limited to, weight and/or resistance training. In consideration of (Your business's name)'s agreement to instruct, assist, and train me, I do here and forever release and discharge and hereby hold harmless (Your business's name), and their respective agents, heirs, assigns, contractors, and employees, from any and all claims, demands, damages, rights of action or causes of action, present or future, arising out of or connected with my participation in this or any exercise program including any injuries resulting therefrom. THIS WAIVER AND RELEASE OF LIABILITY INCLUDES, WITHOUT LIMITATION, INJURIES WHICH MAY OCCUR AS A RESULT OF (1) EQUIPMENT THAT MAY MALFUNCTION OR BREAK; (2) ANY SLIP, FALL, DROPPING OF EQUIPMENT; AND (3) OUR NEGLIGENT INSTRUCTION OR SUPERVISION.

Assumption of Risk

I, _____, recognize that exercise might be difficult and strenuous and that there could be dangers inherent in exercise for some individuals. I acknowledge that the possibility of certain unusual physical changes during exercise does exist. These changes include abnormal blood pressure; fainting; disorders in heartbeat; heart attack; and, in rare instances, death.

I understand that as a result of my participation in an exercise program, I could suffer an injury or physical disorder that could result in my becoming partially or totally disabled and incapable of performing any gainful employment or having a normal social life.

I recognize that an examination by a physician should be obtained by all participants prior to involvement in any exercise program. If I, _____, have chosen not to obtain a physician's permission prior to beginning this exercise program with (your business's name), I hereby agree that I am doing so at my own risk.

In any event, I acknowledge and agree that I assume the risks associated with any and all activities and/or exercises in which I participate.

I acknowledge and agree that no warranties or representations have been made to me regarding the results I will achieve from this program. I understand that results are individual and may vary.

I ACKNOWLEDGE THAT I HAVE THOROUGHLY READ THIS WAIVER AND RELEASE AND FULLY UNDERSTAND THAT IT IS A RELEASE OF LIABILITY. BY SIGNING THIS DOCUMENT, I AM WAIVING ANY RIGHT I OR MY SUCCESSORS MIGHT HAVE TO BRING A LEGAL ACTION OR ASSERT A CLAIM AGAINST (YOUR BUSINESS NAME) FOR YOUR NEGLIGENCE OR THAT OF YOUR EMPLOYEES, AGENTS, OR CONTRACTORS.

_____   _____

Participant's signature   Date

_____

Please print name

2. Waiver and Assumption of Risk (Home Workouts)

Waiver and Assumption of Risk (Home Workouts)

Please note: This form is to be used in addition to, and not in lieu of, the general Waiver and Informed Consent form.

This Agreement, dated this _____ day of _____, 20_____, by and between _____ ("Client") and (your business's name) ("Consultant").

Recitals

1. I, _____, have requested that Consultant, through its authorized agents or contractors, conduct our training sessions in my home.

2. I will provide the equipment to be used in connection with our workouts, including but not limited to benches, dumbbells, barbells, and similar items (the "Equipment"), and I will have control over the area in which we perform our workouts.

In consideration of Consultant's agreeing to conduct our training sessions in my home, I hereby agree as follows:

1. I acknowledge and agree that (i) Consultant (or, if applicable, any independent contractor employed by Consultant) has not inspected the Equipment, and that (ii) I have sole custody and control of the area in my home in which workouts will be conducted and that I am solely responsible for the condition of the Equipment.

2. I hereby agree to hold Consultant, and their respective agents, assigns, employees, and contractors, harmless from any loss or damage resulting from or connected with any injury that I sustain as a result of any defect, latent or apparent, in the design or condition of the Equipment, and/or the condition of the area in which we work out, and I hereby assume any and all risks connected with the condition or design of the Equipment and the condition of such area.

3. I hereby assume any and all risks arising from or connected with any hazardous condition in my home, in the specific area in which the workouts are conducted or otherwise, that may result in my injury during any workout with Consultant or Consultant's agents, employees, or contractors.

4. This waiver and release of liability includes, without limitation, injuries which may occur as a result of (1) Equipment that may malfunction or break; (2) any slip, fall, dropping of Equipment; (3) any improper maintenance of Equipment or facilities; (4) any hazardous condition that may exist on the premises, including the specific workout area, my home, and the surrounding property; and (5) your negligent instruction or supervision.

5. I acknowledge that I have thoroughly read this waiver and release and fully understand that it is a release of liability. By signing this document, I am waiving any right I or my successors might have to bring a legal action or assert a claim against (your business's name) for your negligence or that of your employees, agents, or contractors.

AGREED AND ACCEPTED THIS _____ DAY OF _____, 20_____.

_____
Client's signature

_____
Please print name

3. Letter of Agreement

Letter of Agreement

This Agreement made and entered into this _____ day of _____, 20_____, by and between _____ ("Client") and _____ ("Trainer").

In consideration of the mutual promises exchanged herein and other good and valuable consideration, the parties agree as follows:

1. Client and Trainer have agreed that Trainer will conduct ___ one-hour workout sessions. Each session will begin at a mutually convenient, agreed-upon time and shall be subject to the policies attached hereto as "Section A."

2. Client will pay Trainer, in advance, the sum of $_____ for these workout sessions. Client acknowledges and agrees that no credit or refund shall be due for sessions canceled by Client, except as provided in the Policies attached hereto as Section A.

3. Concurrently with the execution of this Agreement, Client has executed and delivered to Trainer a Waiver and Assumption of Risk Agreement and a Waiver for Home Workouts Agreement (if applicable) (these agreements herein collectively referred to as the "Waiver Agreements"), in which Client assumes the risk of participating in an exercise program and agrees that Trainer and his or her agents, employees, or contractors, if any, shall have no liability for any injury, illness, or similar difficulty that Client may suffer arising out of or connected with Client's participation in Trainer's program. Client hereby acknowledges and agrees that the execution and delivery of the Waiver Agreements are material inducements to Trainer's permitting Client to participate in Trainer's program and agrees to be bound by same.

4. Client and Trainer may agree to conduct additional sessions at such times and locations as they may agree upon, and in such event (i) the provisions of this Agreement, including the Policies attached hereto as Section A, shall be deemed to apply to such additional sessions and (ii) Client will pay Trainer, in advance, the sum of $_____. Client acknowledges and agrees that no credit or refund shall be due for sessions canceled by Client, except as provided in the Policies attached hereto as Section A.

IN WITNESS WHEREOF, Client and Trainer have caused this Agreement to be executed on the day and year first above written.

by:_____
Trainer's signature

_____
Trainer, please print name

by:_____
Client's signature

_____
Client, please print name

Section A

Policies

1. Sessions last about one hour. Please be ready to begin at your scheduled time.

2. Time slots are available on a "first-come, first-served" basis by appointment. Clients who train on a monthly basis will usually have priority since they can schedule regular standing times (for example, Monday, Wednesday, and Friday at 5:30 p.m.).

3. About cancellations:

   a. During the period of your first _____ sessions ("Initial Training Period"), you will receive no credit for canceled or missed workouts, regardless of the reason, unless we cancel, in which case you'll receive a free workout for each session canceled.

   b. If you continue as a client after your Initial Training Period, you will pay the monthly rate and receive credit for canceled sessions as follows:
   $_____ per session, subject to paragraphs c–g below

   c. You will not receive credit for any workout unless it was canceled with at least 24 hours' advance notification. Cancellations must be given by calling ( ) - to be deemed effective.

   d. You will not receive credit for more than one (1) canceled workout per month unless we cancel, in which case you will receive credit for each canceled workout.

   e. If you receive credit for a missed workout, you must use the credit within 60 days of the missed workout, or it will be waived.

   f. If you are entitled to credit in accordance with this paragraph, such credit will appear on the following month's invoice and shall not be deducted from the current month's invoice.

   g. No credit shall be due if a session is canceled due to any of the following: floods, fires, earthquakes, tornadoes, power failures, or similar severe weather conditions or acts of God making travel extremely difficult or impossible; automobile accidents involving you or resulting in your inability to arrive at your scheduled workout; or any event of similar magnitude, beyond the control of the parties. (You will still get credit if we cancel because we are involved in an accident, illness, or other difficulty.) See the following paragraph for holiday credits.

   _____
   Client's initials

4. Payment is due in advance of the first session. If you are training on a monthly basis, you will receive a statement on or about the first of the month, which is due and payable on or before the fifth of the month. If you want to train on a monthly basis but your start date is on a date other than the first of the month, you will be billed a prorated amount for the month that you start. Then you will receive an invoice on the first of the next month. If a regularly scheduled session occurs on one of the following holidays, no credit is due: President's Day, Memorial Day, the Fourth of July, Labor Day, Thanksgiving Day, Christmas Day, New Year's Day. Sometimes holidays necessitate schedule modifications. For example, the gym may close early on

Christmas Eve or New Year's Eve. If you are unable to modify your schedule to fit in a workout under these circumstances, no credit will be due.

5. You will be required to sign and return the following forms to me before taking a fitness evaluation or beginning any program:

   a. Waiver, Release, and Assumption of Risk Form

   b. Waiver and Assumption of Risk (Home Workouts), if applicable

   c. Health History Questionnaire

   d. Goal Inventory

6. If you have any of the following physical conditions, you will be required to have a Medical Clearance and Physician's Consent Form:

   a. Hypertension (>145/95 mm Hg)

   b. Hyperlipidemia (cholesterol >220 mg/dl or a total cholesterol-to-HDL ratio of >5.0)

   c. Diabetes

   d. Family history of heart disease prior to age 60

   e. Smoking

   f. Abnormal resting EKG

   g. Any other condition that I in my sole discretion may deem to present an unreasonable risk to your health, were you to participate in a fitness evaluation or program.

7. Clients will be required to keep a food diary for 2 weeks at the beginning of the program. After 2 weeks, the diary will be analyzed for nutritional content, and I will make suggestions to help you improve your diet.

8. Clients are required to observe any and all rules of the gym or facility where workouts take place.

9. Shirts and shoes are required at all times during sessions. I suggest that you also bring a towel and a lock, since these are not supplied at the gym.

10. Clients have the right to terminate a particular exercise or workout at any time. You are in control of your workouts! If an exercise is uncomfortable or painful, or if you want to stop for any reason, you may do so. If a particular exercise is painful for you to do or you have an injury or other limitation that makes it difficult for you to do, I can probably substitute another exercise to work that particular muscle group.

11. Clients are encouraged to drink plenty of water during the workout. You do not need my permission to get a drink or go to the bathroom.

12. You will get from your workouts what you put in. I will show you how to work your muscles correctly and encourage you to go to your safe limit, but whether you reach your goal is ultimately up to you. You are the only one who can make sure you work out consistently (missing workouts is a guarantee to get nowhere!), eat properly, rest enough, and live a healthful lifestyle.

_____

Client's signature

4. Health History Questionnaire

Health History Questionnaire

Name _____ Date _____

Street address _____ City _____

Phone (home) _____ (work) _____

E-mail address _____ (cell phone number) _____

Person to contact in case of emergency: Date of birth _____

Name _____ Phone _____

For most people, physical activity should not pose any problem or hazard. The following questions are designed to identify the small number of adults for whom physical activity might be inappropriate or those who should have medical advice concerning the type of activity most suitable for them.

Common sense is your best guide in answering these questions. Please read them carefully and check the "Yes" or "No" response opposite the question if it applies to you.

Yes   No

_____ _____   1. Has your doctor ever said you have heart trouble? If yes, please describe the problem and state when it was diagnosed.

_____

_____

_____ _____   2. Do you frequently have pain in your heart or chest?

_____ _____   3. Do you often feel faint or have spells of severe dizziness?

_____ _____   4. Has a doctor ever told you that your blood pressure was too high?

_____ _____   5. Has your doctor ever told you that you have a bone or joint problem, such as arthritis, that has been aggravated by exercise or might be made worse by exercise?

_____ _____   6. Is there a good physical reason not mentioned here why you should not follow an activity program even if you wanted to do so?

_____ _____   7. Are you over age 65 and/or not accustomed to vigorous exercise?

_____ _____   8. Are you or have you ever been a diabetic?

_____ _____   9. Are you now pregnant, or have you been pregnant within the last 3 months?

_____ _____ 10. Have you had any surgery in the last 3 months?

_____ _____ 11. Have you been hospitalized in the last 2 years? If so, when and why?

_____

_____ _____ 12. Have you ever seen a chiropractor, acupuncturist, or other alternative medicine practitioner? If so, when and why?

_____

Please check the box if you have ever experienced any of the following symptoms:

	When first experienced	Treatment used
☐ Pain or discomfort in the chest	_____	_____
☐ Unaccustomed shortness of breath	_____	_____
☐ Dizziness	_____	_____
☐ Labored or uncomfortable breathing, with or without pain	_____	_____
☐ Swollen ankles	_____	_____
☐ Heart palpitations	_____	_____
☐ Heart murmur	_____	_____
☐ Limping	_____	_____

☐ Yes ☐ No   Do you have high blood pressure? If yes, what is your current blood pressure without medication?

_____

☐ Yes ☐ No   Are you taking any medication for hypertension? If so, what medication?

_____

☐ Yes ☐ No   Is your total serum cholesterol level over 240?

☐ Yes ☐ No   Do you smoke?

☐ Yes ☐ No   Have you ever smoked? If so, when did you quit?

☐ Yes ☐ No   Do you have diabetes?

☐ Yes ☐ No   Do you have a family member who has had coronary or atherosclerotic disease before age 55?

☐ Yes ☐ No   Do you have pain or discomfort in your back?

☐ Yes ☐ No   Do you have pain or discomfort in your knee? If so, ☐ right or ☐ left?

☐ Yes ☐ No   Do you have pain or discomfort in your shoulder? If so, ☐ right or ☐ left?

☐ Yes ☐ No   Do you have pain or discomfort in your elbow? If so, ☐ right or ☐ left?

☐ Yes ☐ No   Do you have pain or discomfort in your wrist? If so, ☐ right or ☐ left?

☐ Yes ☐ No   Do you have pain or discomfort in your ankle? If so, ☐ right or ☐ left?

If you checked "Yes" above, please describe your pain. On a scale of 1 to 10, with 1 being almost nonexistent and 10 being excruciating, how severe is it? Does it get more or less severe as the day goes on? When do you notice it? What really aggravates it?

_____

_____

_____

_____

☐ Yes ☐ No   Have you ever torn ligaments or cartilage in your knee? If so, when?
_____

Did you have surgery on this knee? If so, when?
_____

☐ Yes ☐ No   Have you ever dislocated your shoulder? If so, when?
_____

☐ Yes ☐ No   Have you ever had shoulder surgery? If so, which shoulder? When?
_____

☐ Yes ☐ No   Have you ever had a neck injury, such as whiplash? If so, when?
_____

☐ Yes ☐ No   Have you ever been treated for a spinal disk injury? If so, when?
_____

☐ Yes ☐ No   Do you ever experience tingling or numbness in your elbows or hands?
_____

What is the present state of your general health? _____

What regular physical activities do you do now?_____

How often? _____ For how long each session? _____

I, _____, certify that I understand the foregoing questions and my answers are true and complete. I also understand that this information is being provided as part of my initial consultation and may not be periodically updated.

I, _____, assume the risk for any changes in my medical condition that might affect my ability to exercise.

_____   _____
Signature   Date

If you answered yes to one or more questions and you have not recently consulted with your doctor, do so before beginning an exercise program. Tell your doctor which questions you answered yes to and explain that you plan to undergo an exercise program that may include, but may not be limited to, weight and/or resistance training. After medical evaluation, ask your doctor

1. which activities you may safely participate in, and
2. what specific restrictions, if any, should apply to your condition and which activities and/or exercises you should avoid.

I, _____, acknowledge that I have read the foregoing statements and understand the content thereof.

_____   _____
Signature   Date

5. Medical Clearance and Physician's Consent to Participate in Fitness Assessment and Exercise Program

Medical Clearance and Physician's Consent to Participate in Fitness Assessment and Exercise Program

To: (your name, address, city, state, and zip)

Dear Personal Trainer:

My patient, _____, has advised me that he or she intends to participate in (1) a fitness assessment, including body composition assessment, muscular endurance and flexibility tests, a blood pressure reading, and cardiovascular fitness assessment; and (2) an exercise program, which will include, but not be limited to, resistance training. The sessions will last approximately 1 hour and will begin at a very moderate, submaximal level.

Please be advised that my patient, _____, should be subject to the following restrictions in the fitness assessment and/or in his or her exercise program:

_____

_____

_____

In addition, under no circumstances should he or she do the following:

_____

_____

I have discussed the foregoing restrictions and limitations with my patient, _____, and, with these specific restrictions, he or she has my permission to participate in a fitness assessment and pursue an exercise program under your guidance.

Very truly yours,

_____
(Please sign name here)

_____, M.D.
(Please print name here)

Date: _____

Phone number: _____

6. Injury Report

Injury Report

(This report would be used only for serious injuries. Note day-to-day aches or pains in the client's workout record form, and monitor them. If they don't get better, you'll need to refer to a physician.)

Name of injured person _____

Date _____   Time _____ ☐ a.m. or p.m.

Location

What happened? (describe the event, and the mechanism of injury)

Anatomical area involved (be sure to specify left or right side)

Witnesses

Action taken (first aid administered, EMS involvement if any)

Referral action? ☐ yes or ☐ no

If yes, to whom referred? _____

_____

(Trainer's signature)

7. Goal Inventory

Goal Inventory

Client _____   Date _____

1. What I want to accomplish.
   These are my outcome goals for the next 8 weeks:

2. Why I want to accomplish these goals.
   These goals are very important to me because:

3. I'll do almost anything except this.
   I am willing to do anything within reason to reach these goals, other than (please be as specific as possible):

4. "I think that my exercising at least 4 days a week, every week, is highly likely." Please circle the number of the answer that best describes your response to this statement.
   1 Strongly agree
   2 Agree
   3 Disagree
   4 Strongly disagree
   If you circled 3 or 4, why? (Please be as specific as possible.)

5. When I reach this goal, here's what I will get and how I will feel:

8. Lifestyle Questionnaire

Lifestyle Questionnaire

Your Attitude Toward Food

Diets

Have you ever been on a diet? If so, please answer the following questions:

How many diets have you been on in the last 2 years? _____

Describe any diets you've been on. Did you go to a commercial weight-loss service (Jenny Craig, Diet Center, etc.)? Did you follow a diet from a book or article? If so, which one?

_____

_____

Describe your experience with diets. Did you lose weight? Did you gain any of it back?

_____

_____

Food

☐ Yes ☐ No   Do you eat breakfast?

☐ Yes ☐ No   Typically, do you eat after 8 p.m.? If so, what do you usually eat?

_____

How many times a day do you eat?

_____

☐ Yes ☐ No   Can you recall ever eating to avoid doing something? If so, when was this?

_____

☐ Yes ☐ No   Do you ever eat when you aren't hungry? If so, when?

_____

How often do you read food labels?

_____

☐ Yes ☐ No   Do you ever "treat" yourself with food? If so, when?

_____

What sources of information about nutrition have you found most helpful?

_____

☐ Yes ☐ No   Has someone ever encouraged you to eat something that is not in your best interest? If yes, did you do it? Why?

_____

Your Attitude Toward Exercise: What's the Point of All of This, Anyway?

You need to create a clear, tangible image in your mind of the benefits of staying on your fitness program. It must be vivid and powerful enough to sustain you through difficult times when you feel your self-discipline and motivation slipping. This exercise will help you create that image.

Complete this sentence: "Doing three cardiovascular exercise sessions and two to three resistance training sessions per week will . . ."

	Not likely				Very likely	
Improve my appearance	1	2	3	4	5	6
Allow me to cope with stress better	1	2	3	4	5	6
Help me avoid getting sick	1	2	3	4	5	6
Give me a powerful sense of personal achievement	1	2	3	4	5	6
Increase my self-esteem	1	2	3	4	5	6
Improve my physical strength	1	2	3	4	5	6
Make me more independent	1	2	3	4	5	6
Improve my ability to concentrate	1	2	3	4	5	6
Take up too much time	1	2	3	4	5	6
Cause pain, soreness, and discomfort	1	2	3	4	5	6
Make me very tired	1	2	3	4	5	6
Cause me to get injured	1	2	3	4	5	6

Please rewrite this sentence and complete it in your own words.

Doing three cardiovascular sessions and two to three resistance training sessions per week will . . .

_____

_____

Do you need support from others (friends, family, etc.) to stay consistent with your exercise and nutrition program? ☐ Yes ☐ No Do you have this type of support? ☐ Yes ☐ No

On a scale of 1 to 10 (with 10 being the ultimate nurturing, supportive group), how would you rate your support from others? _____

Are there people in your life who either intentionally or unintentionally discourage you or interfere with your staying consistent in your exercise and/or nutrition program? ☐ Yes ☐ No If yes, how do they interfere? How do you deal with it?

_____

_____

Has someone else ever interfered with your choice to exercise? ☐ Yes ☐ No If yes, what happened?

_____

If you answered yes to questions 3 or 4, how have you dealt with these situations in the past? What are your thoughts about how to improve these responses in the future?

_____

_____

_____

	Not likely				Very likely	
I think it is very likely that I will exercise five times a week.	1	2	3	4	5	6
I think exercise is a waste of time for me.	1	2	3	4	5	6
I know that I will be consistent with my fitness and nutrition program for six months.	1	2	3	4	5	6
When I exercise, I look like a dork.	1	2	3	4	5	6
When I exercise, I always feel beat up afterward.	1	2	3	4	5	6

Staff Performance Evaluation Form

This evaluation will provide a documented history of the employee's development and progress. The purpose is to serve as a personal inventory to pinpoint strengths and weaknesses/areas needing improvement; and to outline and agree upon practical improvement, if needed.

Supervisors should read the performance evaluation procedures and instructions carefully before proceeding and consider performance only during the period reviewed.

Employee: Valerie Kindle   Title: Personal Trainer

Supervisor: Kylie Jackson

Date of Hire: 07/7/2010   Department: Personal Training

Date of last evaluation: 09/01/2010   Current Date: 02/07/2011

Evaluation Type: __X__ Semi-Annual ___ Annual

I. Description Data

	Outstanding	Above Average	Average	Below Average	Unsatis-factory
Quality of Work - thoroughness, accuracy, and neatness of assignments.			X		

Comments: Work thoroughness is of average quality, accuracy needs to be polished up, and continue to improve upon neatness and overall aesthetic view of paperwork (workouts, charts, graphs, etc.).

	Outstanding	Above Average	Average	Below Average	Unsatis-factory
Volume of Work – ability to produce quality and quantity work under normal conditions. Also, consider completion schedules and ability to meet deadlines when necessary.				X	

Comments: Needs improvement on the quantity of work. Average job of handling tasks or projects. Continue to delegate tasks appropriately and to work with other trainers to even the workload.

	Outstanding	Above Average	Average	Below Average	Unsatis-factory
Attendance and Punctuality – being at work when scheduled or needed. Reports to work on time. Completes assigned work shift.		X			

Comments: Great job! Goes above and beyond!

	Outstanding	Above Average	Average	Below Average	Unsatis-factory
Personal Relations – attitude and ability to work effectively and harmoniously with associates and the public.				X	

Comments: The ability to work effectively and harmoniously with associates and the public is not exhibited and needs to be portrayed more profoundly. For improvement in this area, continue to correspond with staff and faculty in both written and oral communications in a proficient and professional manner.

	Outstanding	Above Average	Average	Below Average	Unsatis-factory
Initiative – origination and development of vital job procedures.				X	

Comments: A much needed area of improvement is going beyond what is vital to the position and the company and originating work that allows for increased member retention and participation in programs. Continue to originate sound ideas that benefit both club and the client's experience.

	Outstanding	Above Average	Average	Below Average	Unsatis-factory
Job Knowledge – understanding all phases of work and job related factors. Includes knowledge of internal policies and regulations. Applies the knowledge in practical job situations.		X			

Comments: Great job in seeking increased job related knowledge. Creation of numerous internal/external policies and procedures is excellent. Application of practical knowledge is exceptional. Continue to seek more education and expand on already solid attributes.

	Outstanding	Above Average	Average	Below Average	Unsatis-factory
Supervision – control and leadership over assigned employees (if applicable).			X		

Comments: Although you do not supervise anyone, I encourage the continued practice of providing positive leader and role model attributes for those who you work with.

II. Overall Performance Evaluation

Check appropriate box:

Outstanding in all areas	Above average expectations and achievement	Average – performs satisfactorily	Below average but making improvement and progress	Unsatisfactory
			X	

III. Identify employee strengths: Organized, dedicated, trustworthy, hard working, competent, neatness, accuracy, and thoroughness. Practical skills are exceptional.

IV. Identify weakness and/or areas where employee needs to improve: Improvement on being proactive, accountable, dependable, competent, showing initiative. Writing, implementing, upholding sound operational practices.

V. General comments by supervisor:

Valerie has been a good employee and has done a great job for Extreme Fitness. Her role has developed into a critical role to the company's profitability. Her expert knowledge of training applications is in depth and very much considered professional and her operational skills are above par. Valerie's communication with the client and trainers of Extreme could use some improvement. Overall Valerie has done a good job in her position and has some minor things to work on to achieve average or above average recommendations.

VI. Employee progress made in establishing goals and objectives since the last evaluation period:

Valerie has been proactive on the education side and has pursued higher education by completing several certifications in the personal training field. She has made strides to work closer with some of the senior trainers and to develop her role into a supervisory role.

VII. Future goals, expectations, and objectives employee has agreed to accomplish (if any):

Continue to seek positional training. Continue to be a prominent leader for staff and trainers. Delegate tasks appropriately and direct staff in the appropriate fashion while showing self-initiative. Maintain unbiased view and continue to keep Extreme Fitness's best interest in hand.

VIII. Evaluator: I certify that this evaluation represents my overall judgment and has been discussed with the employee.

_____   _____
Evaluator   Date

IX. Employee: I certify that my supervisor/evaluator has discussed this evaluation with me, and I have agreed to the goals and/or objectives as outlined in Section VII above.

_____   _____
Employee   Date

Please forward the completed evaluation form (and any attachments) to the human resources department for inclusion in the employee's personnel file.

ADA Americans with Disabilities Act.

angel investor Investors who provide funding to early-stage, start-up companies that have used up their initial financial support from other sources.

asset-based lending A loan provided for the purchase of a necessary asset for the business.

asset lease A form of lease tied to a particular asset used by a business to conserve cash and maintain the latest versions of whatever equipment is available.

asset valuation A method of business valuation that simply totals all of the hard assets of the organization and adds in a goodwill value.

at-will employment A common-law rule that an employment contract of indefinite duration can be terminated by the employer or the employee at any time for any reason.

benchmarking Working with and learning from a company outside of your industry that has a particular skill that is potentially critical to your operation.

bonus Similar to profit sharing, a reward offered to the employees based on their performance. Typically, bonus systems are not as well defined as profit sharing; instead, the level of reward is left to the discretion of the small business owner.

bootstrap marketing Marketing efforts that require little capital.

bounded rationality Rational decision making that is constrained by the background and history of the person making the decision.

brainstorming A creative process in which a group of individuals is brought together and asked to generate ideas with little or no effort made to evaluate the potential for each idea.

break-even analysis Tool for the estimation of when a business's income exceeds its expenses.

break-even point The time when a new business has reached a level at which revenue coming into the firm is sufficient to cover expenses.

budget Statement that projects all the costs that will be incurred by the organization over a period of time and allocates those expenses evenly over the relevant time period.

business angels High-net-worth individuals that invest in businesses not as a business, but as an individual.

business brokers Businesses that specialize in selling businesses.

capabilities Resources that combine to allow a firm to do things better than its competitors.

capitalization of earnings valuation A method of valuation achieved by taking the earnings (net profit) of the organization; subtracting or adding any unusual items that the lender/investor feels are not customary, normal, or usual items; and dividing that figure by a capitalization rate.

cash flow Actual cash that flows into the facility, minus the cash that goes out of the firm.

commission Payment by the small business owner of some percentage of sales, typically associated with the compensation of trainers.

competitive advantage The edge a business has over competing businesses, made up of those things that the business does better than anyone else in the industry.

competitive map An analytical tool used to organize information about direct competitors on all points of competition.

contract An agreement between two parties to perform certain activities for some consideration.

cost-plus pricing Pricing in which the small business owner initially determines her cost structure and then determines what profit margin she desires and adds that to the cost.

credit card Card entitling one to revolving credit that is not tied to any particular asset, does not have a set repayment schedule, and is usually tied to a much higher interest rate than that of a bank loan.

debt A generic term to describe any type of nonequity funding tied to the business.

debt instruments Written promises to repay debts.

depreciate To lose value.

deviation analysis Analysis of the differences between the predicted and the actual performance.

discrimination In the workplace, hiring, dismissal, level of pay, or promotions based on race, color, gender, religious beliefs, or national origin of the employee. Such actions are prohibited by federal and state laws.

draw A distribution of funds from the business. It is usually in the form of a cash dispersion in advance of salary, bonus, expected year-end distribution, etc.

economic rents Financial gains garnered from an asset or capability that are in excess of the ordinary returns in that particular industry.

economies of scale A condition that allows the long-run average cost to continue downward as production increases. It leads (in its most extreme case) to a condition where a single firm making 100 percent of the product is the most efficient. In reality this condition is moderated by the ability of management to control the size.

elasticity of demand Consumers' response to price changes. For example, as the price of luxury items increases, the demand usually declines as these goods are not essential and their purchase can be delayed. This would be called elastic demand. However, items such as cancer drugs typically have inelastic demand, as you will not stop using them as price increases.

equity Investment in a small business by the owners of the facility.

equity investment Funds received by a business in exchange for a percentage ownership of the business.

equity theory The theory that we all judge how we are treated relative to how we see others being treated.

exit barrier A barrier, such as investment in capital assets, that keeps a firm from leaving an industry.

Fair Labor Standards Act (FLSA) The act that established a minimum wage for workers.

first mover advantage The benefit of gaining customer loyalty by being the first firm to the market.

fixed costs Costs that must be paid no matter how many goods are sold, such as rent for the building.

float The difference between when the money goes out and when it comes in. For example, if you deposit a check today in payment for some good, you typically do not receive cash when you deposit it. Instead there is a period of float before it is credited to your account.

followers Firms that enter a market after the first mover.

Fortune 500 The list published annually by *Fortune* magazine of the 500 largest corporations (by sales) in the United States.

fragmented markets Markets in which no one competitor has a substantial share of the market and the means of competition varies widely within the same market space.

franchise agreement The basic contract generated by the franchisor for all franchisees; it usually contains clauses requiring the purchase of supplies, the displaying of marketing material, and the payment of fees that are based upon the sales of the branch operation.

franchisee The entrepreneur who buys the franchise from the franchisor.

franchisor The firm that originates the idea for the business and develops the operational methods, then sells them to franchisees.

gap analysis A relatively simple process of systematically examining the difference, or gap, between what is expected and what occurs. One type of gap analysis, called opportunity analysis, examines opportunities in the marketplace side-by-side with the individual's ability to address those gaps.

general partner In an LLP, the individual considered the manager of the business, who, as such, has unlimited liability for any debts or judgments against the business.

grants Special funds, neither equity nor debt, that do not require repayment and are designed to aid businesses in specific areas.

harvest plan A plan to exit a small business. Typically, the owners plan to sell the business to another firm or take it to an initial public offering (IPO).

hourly wage The amount paid per hour for work performed.

human resources As defined in economics, the quantity and quality of human effort directed toward producing goods and services.

hybrid compensation system A compensation system that includes a salary along with commission.

income statement Revenue of the firm minus expenses.

independent contractor An individual who performs services for another person or business but is not an employee.

industry Those direct competitors selling similar products/ services within a specified geographic radius that is consistent with a customer's willingness to travel to purchase those products/services.

initial public offering (IPO) The initial listing of a firm as a public entity in the public equities market.

intangible assets Things that are not physical but are just as critical to success, such as a relationship with a key supplier.

job description Document that describes the job that is to be filled.

legitimacy The acceptance by key stakeholders such as customers and suppliers that you are a genuine business that will still be in operation next year.

LLC A limited liability corporation.

LLP A limited liability partnership.

loan Contractual agreement whereby the business receives some amount of money that must be repaid over a specified period of time at a specified interest rate.

loss leader A product or service that is sold at a nonoperating loss (that is, the price only accounts for the actual cost of the product) to simply get customers in the store.

market estimation A method of business valuation that involves taking the earnings of the small business and multiplying that figure by the market premium of companies in its industry.

marketing plan The plan developed by the small business to specify who the customers are and how they will be attracted to the company.

measurable goal An objective for which success or failure can be judged by an objective standard or measurement.

metric A measure to evaluate whether a person or firm is meeting stated goals.

mission statement A brief statement that summarizes the goals of a business, and how and where it will compete.

mixed-model promotions Promotions that cost something but also have an element of community support.

noncompete clause An enforceable agreement that prohibits an employee from working for a competing company.

organizational slack Excess resources in an organization, typical of large organizations but not of small businesses.

orthodox Describing those areas of a business that are simply standard practice in the industry and are necessary for the business to be a player.

OSHA The Occupational Safety and Health Administration, which is charged with protecting the health of workers.

partnership A type of business formed between individuals directly. It includes both general and limited varieties.

performance review Review by the small business owner of the employee's goals and outcomes on those goals over some given period.

perquisites Benefits paid for by the company. Examples include vacations, vehicles, loans, gifts, financial contributions to retirement plans, etc.

price/earnings (P/E) ratio A value derived from public companies that divides the current earnings per share into the price per share.

pricing floor The break-even point; the lowest amount that can be charged for a product or service while still making a minimal profit.

probation A formal way of starting the process of firing an employee—or of providing a process for correcting performance issues.

profit and loss statement (P&L statement) A financial statement that summarizes the revenues, costs, and expenses incurred during a specific period of time.

profit sharing An example of a hybrid compensation system. The company may set some relatively low level of salary but offer to share a percentage of the profits at the end of the year or some other period of time with the employees.

promotion The means by which a small business advances its product or service.

pure promotions Promotions that are strictly financial arrangements in which a business pays for some outputs, such as radio advertisements.

resource-based analysis A theoretical approach and methodology that examines the functioning of a business in terms of whether a product/service simultaneously meets the criteria of being rare, durable, nonsubstitutable, and valuable.

salary A set amount of compensation for a given time period.

sales management The individuals who build and maintain relationships with customers and their methods for doing so.

scope of practice The appropriate extent to which personal trainers assess, motivate, educate, and train clients.

sensitivity analysis An examination of the best- and worst-case cash flow scenarios.

shrinkage The difference between what is sold and what was brought into the business.

Small Business Assistance Centers Centers funded by the Small Business Administration that advise individuals wishing to start new businesses.

sole proprietorship The simplest form of business organization, characterized by the fact that the person who owns the business and the business itself are treated as the same entity.

standard of care Care that a reasonably prudent, professional, and responsible trainer would provide in a given situation. This includes the standards of practice that are developed and published by professional organizations.

strategy The broad approaches a small business will use to accomplish its mission.

Subchapter C corporation An organizational form that treats the business as a unique entity responsible for its own taxes. There are no limitations to shareholder participation and the "owners" are protected beyond their equity investment.

Subchapter S corporation An organizational form that treats the business as an entity separate from the individuals. This allows the owner(s) to treat the income as they would if the business were a sole proprietorship or a partnership. It has limitations in the number and type of shareholders.

substitute A product that performs a similar function or achieves the same result but is not a precise imitation.

supplier credit A form of nonequity funding in which suppliers provide credit on physical assets and supplies.

sustainable competitive advantage An advantage that others cannot immediately copy.

tangible assets Hard assets such as equipment or a location.

threats to operational financing Specific threats to the new venture in financing its growth, including high development costs, rapid expansion plans, high inventory needs, and/or an entrepreneurial team with a low asset base.

threats to profit margin The threat to the success of a new venture related to its ability to establish and maintain a high-margin product or service.

threats to sales generation schemes The threat to a new venture regarding its opportunity to sell to many customers and to obtain repeat business.

time value of money The value of money over time at a given rate of inflation or other type of return. Calculated as the value of your investment in time and money if you did not do the proposed venture.

turnaround The effort to reverse the decline of a business.

unemployment compensation Financial assistance for some period of time to those people who lose their jobs through no fault of their own; provided in every state by law.

Uniform Franchise Offering Circular (UFOC) The principal governing mechanism of the franchisor/franchisee.

United States Small Business Administration (SBA) The agency officially organized as a part of the Small Business Act of July 30, 1953, to "aid, counsel, assist and protect, insofar as is possible, the interests of small business concerns." It provides a wealth of information and assistance at all levels of organizational development and management. See www.sba.gov.

unorthodox Describing those areas of a business that are unique or unusual when compared to the standard practices of the industry, and that provide the opportunity for the business to gain value over and above the ordinary returns in the industry.

variable costs Costs that vary according to how many goods are produced.

venture capital fund A fund that is organized to make significant equity investments in high-growth new ventures.

virtually free promotions Promotions that have very limited financial cost but have time commitment requirements from individuals in the firm.

workers' compensation Laws designed so that employees who are disabled or injured while on the job are provided with some type of compensation.

endnotes

Chapter 1

1. http://web.sba.gov/faqs/faqindex.cfm?areaid=24
2. Ibid.
3. CHI Research, "Small Firms and Technology: Acquisitions, Inventor Movements, and Technology Transfer," *Small Business Research Summary*, 2004. www.sba.gov/advo/research/rs233.pdf
4. R. Makaodok, "Interfirm Differences in Scale Economies and the Evolution of Market Share," *Strategic Management Journal* 20 (1999), pp. 935–52.
5. C. E. Bamford, T. J. Dean, and P. P. McDougall, "An Examination of the Impact of Initial Founding Conditions and Decisions upon the Performance of New Bank Start-Ups," *Journal of Business Venturing* 15, no. 3 (2000), pp. 253–77.
6. G. Rodriguez, "7 Methods in Choosing a Business," PowerHomeBiz.com, 2004. www.powerhomebiz.com/vol72/methods.htm
7. M. G. Blackford, *A History of Small Business in America* (New York: Twayne Publishers, 1991).
8. www.cdc.gov/nchs/data/nehis/t1B3.pdf

Chapter 2

1. C. B. Schoonhoven and K. M. Eisenhardt, "Speeding Products to Market: Waiting Time to First Product Introduction in New Firms," *Administrative Science Quarterly* 35 (1990), pp. 177–208.
2. J. E. Grable and R. H. Lytton, "The Development of a Risk Assessment Instrument: A Follow Up Study," *Financial Services Review* 12 (2003), pp. 257–75.
3. C. Penttila, "Risky Business," *Entrepreneur* 36, no. 11 (2008), pp. 17–18.
4. J. Hopkins, "More Moms, Fewer Pops," *USA Today,* October 20, 2003, p. 3b.
5. R. D. Atkinson, "The Impact of the Defense Build-Down on State and Local Economies," *Economic Development Review* 10, no. 4 (Fall 1992), pp. 55–59.
6. H. M. Neck, G. D. Meyer, B. Cohen, and A. C. Corbett,

"An Entrepreneurial System View of New Venture Creation," *Journal of Small Business Management* 42 (2004), pp. 190–209.
7. K. Jones and R. Tullous, "Behaviors of Pre-Venture Entrepreneurs and Perceptions of Their Financial Needs," *Journal of Small Business Management* 40 (2002), pp. 233–49.

Chapter 3

1. M. Maddock and R. Vitn, "Innovating during a Recession," *BusinessWeek Online,* November 5, 2008, p. 13.
2. K. H. Vesper, *New Venture Strategies.* (Englewood Cliffs, NJ: Prentice-Hall, 1990).
3. P. P. McDougall, J. G. Covin, R. B. Robinson, and L. Herron, "The Effects of Industry Growth and Strategic Breadth on New Venture Performance and Strategy Content," *Strategic Management Journal* 15 (1994), pp. 537–54; E. Romanelli, "Environments and Strategies of Organization Start-up: Effects on Early Survival," *Administrative Science Quarterly* 34 (1989), pp. 369–87.
4. A. C. Cooper and F. J. Gimeno-Gascon, "Entrepreneurs, Processes of Founding, and New Firm Performance," in *The State of the Art of Entrepreneurship,* ed. D. L. Sexton and J. D. Kasarda (Boston, MA: PWS Kent, 1992), pp. 301–40; K. M. Eisenhardt and C. B. Schoonhoven, "Organizational Growth: Linking Founding Team, Strategy, Environment, and Growth among U.S. Semiconductor Ventures, 1978–1988," *Administrative Science Quarterly* 35 (1990), pp. 504–29.

Chapter 4

1. A. Ardichvili, R. Cardozo, and R. Sourav, "A Theory of Entrepreneurial Opportunity Identification and Development," *Journal of Business Venturing* 18, no. 1 (2003), pp. 104–24.
2. F. Delmar, P. Davidson, and W. Gartner, "Arriving at the High-Growth Firm," *Journal of Business Venturing* 18, no. 2 (2003), pp. 189–217.

3. N. Kumar, "The CEO's Marketing Manifesto," *Marketing Management* 17, no. 6 (2008), pp. 24–29.
4. C. Comaford-Lynch, "The Power of Positioning," *BusinessWeek Online,* June 3, 2008, p. 13.
5. G. Dess, "Consensus on Strategy Formulation and Organizational Performance: Competitors in a Fragmented Market," *Strategic Management Journal* 8, no. 3 (1987), pp. 259–79.
6. W. Bogner, H. Thomas, and J. McGee, "A Longitudinal Study of the Competitive Positions and Entry Paths of European Firms in the U.S. Pharmaceutical Market," *Strategic Management Journal* 17, no. 2 (1996), pp. 85–108.
7. M. Peteraf and M. Bergen, "Scanning Dynamic Competitive Landscapes: A Market-Based and Resource-Based Framework," *Strategic Management Journal* 24, no. 10 (2003), pp. 1027–42.
8. D. Teece, G. Pisano, and A. Shuen, "Dynamic Capabilities and Strategic Management," *Strategic Management Journal* 18, no. 7 (1997), pp. 509–30.
9. M. Porter, *Competitive Advantage* (New York: Free Press, 1985).
10. J. C. Spender and R. Grant, "Knowledge and the Firm: Overview," *Strategic Management Journal* 17 (Winter 1966), pp. 5–10.
11. S. A. Alvarez and L. W. Busenitz, "The Entrepreneurship of Resource-Based Theory," *Journal of Management* 27, no. 6 (2001), pp. 755–75; J. B. Barney, "Firm Resources and Sustained Competitive Advantage," *Journal of Management* 17, no. 1 (1991), pp. 99–120; R. M. Grant, "The Resource-Based Theory of Competitive Advantage: Implications for Strategy Formulation," *California Management Review* 33 (1991), pp. 114–35; E. T. Penrose, *The Theory of the Growth of the Firm* (New York: John Wiley & Sons, 1959); M. A. Peteraf, "The Cornerstones of Competitive Advantage: A Resource-Based View," *Strategic Management Journal* 14 (1993), pp. 179–91.

Chapter 5

1. http://circuitcity.com
2. K. M. Eisenhardt and D. M. Sull, "Strategy as Simple Rules," *Harvard Business Review* (January 2001), pp. 107–16.
3. B. Bartkus and M. Glassman, "Do Firms Practice What They Preach? The Relationship Between Mission Statements and Stakeholder Management," *Journal of Business Ethics* 83, no. 2 (2008), pp. 207–16.
4. R. Lussier, "A Nonfinancial Business Success versus Failure Prediction Model for Your Firms," *Journal of Small Business Management* 33, no. 1 (1995), pp. 8–21.
5. T. Man, T. Lau, and K. Chan, "The Competitiveness of Small and Medium Enterprises: A Conceptualization with Focus on Entrepreneurial Competencies," *Journal of Business Venturing* 17, no. 2 (2002), pp. 123–43.
6. T. Powell, "Organizational Alignment as Competitive Advantage," *Strategic Management Journal* 13, no. 2 (1992), pp. 119–35.
7. A. Davis and E. Olson, "Critical Competitive Strategy Issues Every Entrepreneur Should Consider Before Going into Business," *Business Horizons* 51, no. 3 (2008), pp. 211–21.
8. R. McNaughton, P. Osborne, and B. Imrie, "Market-Oriented Value Creation in Service Firms," *European Journal of Marketing* 36, nos. 9/10 (2002), pp. 990–1013.
9. I. Chaston, B. Badger, T. Mangles, and E. Sadler-Smith, "Relationship Marketing, Knowledge Management Systems and E-Commerce Operations in Small UK Accountancy Practices," *Journal of Marketing Management* 19, nos. 1/2 (2003), pp. 109–31.
10. R. Hall, "A Framework Linking Intangible Resources and Capabilities to Sustainable Competitive Advantage," *Strategic Management Journal* 14, no. 8 (1993), pp. 607–19.
11. M. Lieberman and D. Montgomery, "First-Mover (Dis)advantages: Retrospective and Link with the Resource-Based View," *Strategic Management Journal* 19, no. 12 (1998), pp. 1111–26.
12. D. Miller, "An Asymmetry-Based View of Advantage: Toward an Attainable Sustainability," *Strategic Management Journal* 24, no. 10 (2003), pp. 961–76.
13. M. Porter, *Competitive Advantage: Creating and Sustaining Superior Performance* (New York, NY: Free Press, 1985).
14. C. Christensen, "The Past and Future of Competitive Advantage," *MIT Sloan Management Review* 42, no. 2 (2001), pp. 105–10.

Chapter 6

1. J. Kelly and J. O'Connor, "Is Profit More Important Than Cashflow?" *Management Accounting* 75, no. 6 (1997), pp. 28–30.
2. D. Worrell, "Keeping Tabs on Cash Flow," *Entrepreneur* 37, no. 1 (2009), p. 32.
3. C. E. Chastain, S. Cianciolo, and A. Thomas, "Strategies in Cash Flow Management," *Business Horizons* 29, no. 3 (1986), pp. 65–74.
4. R. Monk, "Why Small Businesses Fail," *CMA Management* 74, no. 6 (2000), pp. 12–14; L. R. Gaskill and H. E. Van Auken, "A Factor Analytic Study of the Perceived Causes of Small Business Failure," *Journal of Small Business Management* 31, no. 4 (1993), pp. 18–32.
5. K. Klein, "How Small Business Owners Can Cope with the Crisis," *BusinessWeek Online,* October 13, 2008, p. 14.
6. R. B. Lorance and R. V. Wendling, "Basic Techniques for Analyzing and Presentation of Cost Risk Analysis," *Cost Engineering* 43, no. 6 (2001), pp. 25–32.
7. J. M. Davis, "Project Feasibility Using Breakeven Point Analysis," *Appraisal Journal* 65, no. 1 (1998), pp. 41–47.
8. R. R. Crabb, "Cash Flow: A Quick and Easy Way to Learn Personal Finance," *Financial Services Review* 8, no. 4 (1999), pp. 269–83.

Chapter 7

1. W. R. Scott, *Institutions and Organizations* (Thousand Oaks, CA: Sage Publications, 1995).
2. Q. Huang, R. M. Davidson, and J. Gu, "Impact of Personal and Cultural Factors on Knowledge Sharing in China," *Asia Pacific Journal of Management* 25 (2008), pp. 451–71.
3. C. S. Galbraith, "Divorce and the Financial Performance of Small Family Businesses: An Exploratory Study," *Journal of Small Business Management* 41 (2003), pp. 296–310.
4. R. Lewis, "Why Incorporate a Small Business?" *National Public Accountant* 39, no. 11 (1994), p. 14.
5. L. Hodder, M. L. McAnally, and C. D. Weaver, "The Influence of Tax and Nontax Factors on Bank's Choice of Organizational Form," *Accounting Review* 78 (2003), pp. 297–326.
6. J. Freedman, "Limited Liability: Large Company Theory and Small Firms," *Modern Law Review* 63 (2000), pp. 317–55.
7. J. G. Bonnice & A. L. Liuzzo, *Essentials of Business Law* (Woodland Hills, CA: Glencoe McGraw-Hill).
8. Ibid.
9. Ibid.
10. M. Bates, *Health Fitness Management* (Champaign, IL: Human Kinetics Publishers).
11. Ibid.

Chapter 8

1. K. Jensen and G. Pompelli, "Manufacturing Site Location Preference of Small Agribusiness Firms," *Journal of Small Business Management* 40 (2002), pp. 204–19.
2. D. A. Shepard and A. Zacharakis, "A New Venture's Cognitive Legitimacy: An Assessment by Customers," *Journal of Small Business Management* 41 (2003), pp. 148–68.
3. K. D. Brouther and G. Nakos, "SME Entry Mode Choice and Performance: A Transaction Cost Perspective," *Entrepreneurship Theory & Practice* 28 (2004), pp. 229–48; J. Liao and W. Gartner, "The Effects of Pre-Venture Plan Timing and Perceived Environmental Uncertainty on the Persistence of Emerging Firms," *Small Business Economics* 27 (2006), pp. 23–40.
4. S. R. Covey, A. R. Merrill, and R. R. Merrill, *First Things First* (New York: Simon & Schuster, 1994).

Chapter 9

1. R. A. Cole, L. G. Goldberg, and L. J. White, "Cookie Cutter vs. Character: The Micro Structure of Small Business Lending by Large and Small Banks," *Journal of Financial & Qualitative Analysis* 39 (2004), pp. 227–52.
2. N. Wilson and B. Summers, "Trade Credit Terms Offered by Small Firms: Survey Evidence and Empirical Analysis," *Journal of Small Business Finance & Accounting* 29 (2002), pp. 317–52.
3. R. McGrath, "A Real Options Logic for Initiating Technology Positioning Investments," *Academy of Management Review* 22, no. 4 (1997), pp. 974–96.
4. D. De Clercq, V. H. Fried, O. Lehtonen, and H. J. Sapienza, "An Entrepreneur's Guide to the Venture Capital Galaxy," *Academy of Management Perspectives* 20, no. 3 (2006), pp. 90–112.

5. S. Prowse. "Angel Investors and the Market for Angel Investments," *Journal of Banking & Finance* 22 (1998), pp. 785–83.

Chapter 10

1. J. C. Hayton, "Strategic Human Capital Management in SMEs: An Empirical Study of Entrepreneurial Performance," *Human Resource Management* 42 (203), pp. 375–92.
2. M. Carroll and M. Marchington, "Recruitment in Small Firms," *Employee Relations* 21 (1999), pp. 236–51.
3. R. Carlson, "The Small Firm Exemption and Single Employer Doctrine in Employment Discrimination Law," *St. John's Law Review* 80 (2006), pp. 1197–1273.
4. E. A. War, "Employee Drug Testing: Aalberts and Walker Revisited," *Journal of Small Business Management* 29 (1991), pp. 77–84.
5. S. H. Appelbaum and R. Kamal, "An Analysis of the Utilization and Effectiveness of Non-financial Incentives in Small Business," *Journal of Management Development* 19 (2000), pp. 733–64.
6. www.bls.gov/news.release/ecec.nr0.htm
7. www.towersperrin.com/tp/showdctmdoc.jsp?url=Master_Brand_2/USA/Press_Releases/2008/20080924/2008_09_24b.htm&country=global
8. Appelbaum and Kamal, "An Analysis of the Utilization and Effectiveness."

9. S. W. King and G. T. Solomon, "Issues in Growing a Family Business: A Strategic Human Resources Model," *Journal of Small Business Management* 39 (2001), pp. 3–14.

Chapter 11

1. R. Grewal, R. Mehta, and F. R. Kardes, "The Timing of Repeat Purchases of Consumer Durable Goods," *Journal of Marketing Research* 41 (2004), pp. 101–16.
2. M. Gruber, "Research on Marketing in Emerging Firms: Key Issues and Open Questions," *Journal of Technology Management* 26 (2003), pp. 600–21.
3. T. McCollum, "High Tech Marketing Hits the Target," *Nation's Business* 85, no. 6 (1997), pp. 39–42.
4. T. Nagle and R. Holden, *The Strategy and Tactics of Pricing* (New York: Prentice Hall, 1995).
5. J. F. Tanner, "Leveling the Playing Field: Factors Influencing Trade Show Success for Small Firms," *Industrial Marketing Management* 31 (2002), pp. 229–40.
6. J. Gregan-Paxton, J. D. Hibbard, F. F. Brunel, and P. Azar, "So That Is What That Is: Examining the Impact of Analogy on Consumers' Knowledge Development for Really New Products," *Psychology & Marketing* 19 (2002), pp. 533–51.

Chapter 12

1. R. Quinn, *Deep Change: Discovering the Leader Within* (San Francisco, CA: Jossey-Bass Publishers, 1996).

2. R. A. Anderson, I. Fox, and D. P. Twomey, *Business Law: Principles, Cases, Legal Environment* (Cincinnati, OH: South-Western Publishing, 1999).

Chapter 13

1. R. P. Dant and P. J. Kaufmann, "Structural and Strategic Dynamics in Franchising," *Journal of Retailing* 79 (2003), pp. 63–76.
2. M. Grunhagen and M. J. Dorsch, "Does the Franchisor Provide Value to the Franchisee? Past, Current, and Future Value Assessments of Two Franchisee Types," *Journal of Small Business Management* 41 (2003), pp. 366–85.
3. J. G. Combs and D. J. Ketchen Jr., "Why Do Firms Use Franchising as an Entrepreneurial Strategy? A Meta Analysis," *Journal of Management* 29 (2003), pp. 443–66.
4. J. E. L. Bercovitz, "The Option to Expand: The Use of Multi-Unit Opportunities to Support Self Enforcing Agreements in Franchise Relationships," *Academy of Management Proceedings* (2002), pp. Y1–Y7.
5. S. B. Kaufman, "Before You Buy, Be Careful," *Nation's Business* 84, no. 3 (1996), pp. 46–48.
6. R. D. Doyle and H. B. Desai, "Turnaround Strategies for Small Firms," *Journal of Small Business Management* 29, no. 3 (1991), pp. 33–43.

photo credits

About the Authors

Page **xii** (top): © Charles M. Ware, (bottom): Courtesy of Charles E. Bamford; **xiii:** Courtesy of Garry Bruton.

Preface

Page **xv:** © Dimitri Vervitsiotis/Getty Images RF.

Chapter 1

Page **2:** © altrendo images/Getty Images; **4-8:** © Royalty-Free/CORBIS; **11:** © Getty Images; **12:** © Mike Powell/Getty Images RF.

Chapter 2

Page **14:** © Paul Bradbury/Getty Images; **16:** © Brand X Pictures/PunchStock RF; **17:** © Brand X Pictures/Jupiterimages RF; **18:** © Comstock Images/Alamy RF; **19:** © liquidlibrary/PictureQuest RF; **20:** © ITstock/Jupiterimages RF; **22:** © Photodisc/Getty Images RF; **23:** © Judia&Jackie/Getty Images RF; **24:** © Corbis/PunchStock RF; **27:** © Keith Brofsky/Getty Images RF; **28:** © PunchStock/Creatas RF.

Chapter 3

Page **32:** © image100/Corbis RF; **35:** © Royalty-Free/CORBIS; **37:** © Jupiterimages/Comstock Premium/Alamy RF; **38:** © Brand X Pictures/Superstock RF; **39:** © Charles M. Ware, Professional Fitness Institute®; **40:** © Jack Hollingsworth/Getty Images RF; **45:** © The McGraw-Hill Companies, Inc./John Flournoy, photographer.

Chapter 4

Page **50:** © amana productions inc./Getty Images RF; **52:** © Ingram Publishing/Alamy RF; **53:** © Assembly/Getty Images RF; **55:** © Ryan McVay/Getty Images RF; **56:** © Charles M. Ware, Professional Fitness Institute®; **57:** © Photographer's Choice/Getty Images RF; **60:** © Ingram Publishing/AGE Fotostock RF; **64:** © Corbis/PunchStock RF.

Chapter 5

Page **66:** © JGI/Jamie Grill/Getty Images RF; **68:** © Comstock Images/Jupiterimages RF; **72:** © Burke/Triolo/Brand X Pictures/Jupiterimages RF; **74:** © Charles M. Ware, Professional Fitness Institute®; **76:** © Ryan McVay/Getty Images RF; **77:** © DAJ/Getty Images RF.

Chapter 6

Page **84:** © Mikael Damkier/Shutterstock; **87:** © Stockbyte/Getty Images RF; **88:** © Getty Images/Digital Vision RF; **98:** © Ingram Publishing/Alamy RF.

Chapter 7

Page **104:** © Dimitri Vervitsiotis/Getty Images RF; **106:** © Burke/Triolo/Brand X Pictures/Jupiterimages RF; **110:** © Corbis RF; **113:** © Brand X Pictures/PunchStock RF; **115:** © Charles M. Ware, Professional Fitness Institute®; **116:** © Lucky Business/Shutterstock; **117:** © The McGraw-Hill Companies, Inc./Andrew Resek, photographer; **119:** © Royalty-Free/CORBIS; **120:** © Dynamic Graphics/Jupiterimages RF; **121:** © Radius Images/Getty Images RF; **123:** © Royalty-Free/CORBIS.

Chapter 8

Page **126:** © Erik Isakson/Getty Images RF; **128:** © Getty Images; **130:** © Imagesource/Jupiterimages RF; **133:** © Ryan McVay/Getty Images RF; **134:** © The McGraw-Hill Companies, Inc./John Flournoy, photographer; **135:** © Comstock Images RF; **138:** © Jupiterimages/Getty Images RF; **139:** © The McGraw-Hill Companies, Inc./Rick Brady, photographer; **140:** © Steve Cole/Getty Images RF.

Chapter 9

Page **144:** © Matt Gray/Getty Images; **148:** © Comstock Images/PictureQuest RF; **149:** © Comstock Images RF; **151:** © Digital Vision/Getty Images RF; **153:** © Royalty-Free/CORBIS; **155:** © Daisuke Morita/Getty Images RF.

Chapter 10

Page **164:** © Image Source/Getty Images RF; **167:** © BananaStock/PictureQuest RF; **169:** © Jack Star/PhotoLink/Getty Images RF; **171:** © Paul Burns/Blend Images/Getty Images RF; **173:** © Digital Vision RF; **174:** © Getty Images/Comstock Images RF; **175:** © Charles M. Ware, Professional Fitness Institute®; **176:** © PM Images/Getty Images; **177:** © Royalty-Free/CORBIS; **178:** © BananaStock/PictureQuest RF; **180:** © Charles M. Ware, Professional Fitness Institute®; **183:** © Blend Images/Getty Images RF.

Chapter 11

Page **186:** © C. Lyttle/Corbis; **188:** © ALESSANDRO DELLA BELLA/Keystone/Corbis; **190:** © Olive/age fotostock RF; **192:** © Getty Images RF; **193:** © Shelley Gazin/CORBIS; **196:** © BananaStock/Alamy RF; **198:** © Blend Images/Getty Images RF; **199:** © Serge Kozak/Corbis; **200:** © Comstock Images/PictureQuest RF; **202:** © Ingram Publishing RF; **203:** © Sven Hagolani/fstop/Corbis RF; **205:** © Ian Lishman/Juice Images/Corbis RF.

Chapter 12

Page **210:** © Andersen Ross/Getty Images; **212:** © S. Solum/PhotoLink/Getty Images RF; **214:** © Charles M. Ware, Professional Fitness Institute®; **216:** © Brand X Pictures/PunchStock RF; **219:** © DreamPictures/Getty Images RF; **220:** © Royalty-Free/CORBIS; **221:** © Stockbyte/PunchStock RF; **223:** © Eric Audras/Photoalto/PictureQuest RF; **226:** © Imagestate Media (John Foxx) RF.

Chapter 13

Page **230:** © Yellow Dog Productions/Getty Images RF; **232:** © AAGAMIA/Getty Images; **233:** © Yellow Dog Productions/Getty Images RF; **235:** © The McGraw-Hill Companies, Inc./John Flournoy, photographer; **237:** © Corbis RF; **239:** © The McGraw-Hill Companies, Inc./Andrew Resek, photographer; **241:** © tim scott/Getty Images; **243:** © Ryan McVay/Getty Images RF.